Divining with Animal Guides

Answers from the World at Hand

Divining with Animal Guides

Answers from the World at Hand

Hearth Moon Rising

MOON
BOOKS

Winchester, UK
Washington, USA

First published by Moon Books, 2018
Moon Books is an imprint of John Hunt Publishing Ltd., Laurel House, Station Approach,
Alresford, Hants, SO24 9JH, UK
office1@jhpbooks.net
www.johnhuntpublishing.com
www.moon-books.net

For distributor details and how to order please visit the 'Ordering' section on our website.

Text copyright: Hearth Moon Rising 2016

ISBN: 978 1 78535 597 4
978 1 78535 598 1 (ebook)
Library of Congress Control Number: 2016962871

A CIP catalogue record for this book is available from the British Library.

Design: Stuart Davies

Printed and bound by CPI Group (UK) Ltd, Croydon, CR0 4YY, UK

We operate a distinctive and ethical publishing philosophy in all
areas of our business, from our global network of authors to
production and worldwide distribution.

CONTENTS

Chapter 8: Into the Mist

Chapter 9: Avian Wisdom

Also by Hearth Moon Rising:

Invoking Animal Magic: A Guide for the Pagan Priestess

Dedicated to:
The Goddess Ishtar
Queen of Heaven and Earth
The One with the
Beautiful Voice

Chapter 1

The World at Hand

Cat Tales

I saw some lions and grew afraid,
I lifted my head to the moon in prayer,
to the lamp of the gods, went my supplications...
—The Epic of Gilgamesh[1]

Figure 1: Mountain Lion, also known as Cougar, Catamount, and American Panther. Smaller than a female African Lion and closer in size to the African Leopard. Photo: K. Fink/US National Park Service.

The scream came the instant I closed the circle. It was a loud piercing scream that seemed to come from all directions. ""A banshee!"" I thought. ""I've heard a banshee."" I had never heard a banshee before; I wasn't sure what a banshee was. That was the only word I had for a sound that fed terror into every muscle. The cry summoned a desire to run—run far away fast in any direction, just run and run and run.

The blood-curdling scream rose again.

"Perhaps it's not a banshee," was my second thought. It could be an outer space alien screeching as it prowled the earth. It could be a space alien abductor. Or it could be some kind of monster...

Whatever it was, I was not moving. "You have cast a circle of protection," I admonished myself. "If you are serious about your magic, you must stay within it." I took a breath and stayed planted where I was.

I was actually in a fairly ordinary place: a campground at a state park along the California coast. I was only a six-mile hike from the car and I hadn't bothered with a flashlight, since the terrain was level and easy. I was feeling good as I arrived at the campsite and dumped my backpack on the ground. I was a little thirsty, but I decided to skip the drink at the faucet and jump into my ritual, not bothering to scout the place since there could be no other campers. No cars had been parked at the trailhead, and it was the middle of the week in the off-season.

Casting a circle of protection when I camped alone was standard procedure. I turned to the direction of the east, my hands raised, and prayed to the guardians of that direction, to the element of air and to the winged ones. In this direction I asked for grace.

I walked a few feet away and raised my hands in the direction of the south, where the dragons and the fiery ones dwell. I prayed for power.

In the west I raised my hands to the creatures of the watery depths, the mermaids, and I prayed for peace.

Walking to the north to complete the circle, I invoked the guardians of the earth and the unicorn. I asked for wisdom. This was when I heard the scream.

The worst thing about that scream was that it wouldn't stop to let my ears recover. A second scream came upon the tail of the first, and after the second scream came a third.

Then a fourth scream came, far away. It reverberated across the landscape and died into a faint echo. The screamer nearby responded and then another cry came from the distance.

"It's an *animal*," I realized. My calves relaxed and the tension poured out of my body. It was just an animal. A very large animal by the noise it was making, undoubtedly with teeth and claws, but only an animal. A known entity, more or less, with four legs and a home on earth. I took a deep breath and commenced my ceremony.

The next morning when I awoke, still inside the circle of protection, there were no animals of any size around me—only sunshine, forest, birds and campground clearing. I walked over to the faucet for that long savored drink and found big ol' cat paws in the fresh mud. I had been listening to the song of a mountain lion last night. The pipe was dripping and the lion had been lapping up the trickle like a domestic kitty drinking from a bathroom faucet.

I have since heard recordings of catamounts caterwauling and they sound similar to what I heard in that darkness, but to get the full effect those shrieks have to be right up close, not echoing over a distance. Perhaps it sounds odd that I could be alone at night in the wilderness and not attribute a wild cry to a wild animal, but being spooked by a cougar is an otherworldly experience.

I did not remain in the circle during those terrible moments to test my faith. I'm not sure I believe in faith, or at any rate I do not believe that faith is a quality that humans are obligated to pursue and cultivate. Faith is not a virtue but a gift, and if we humans are to have faith it is incumbent on the gods to earn our trust. I stayed in the circle because it made no sense to build a sphere of safety and then run off panicked through the countryside. To do so would have invalidated my magic. To do so would have invalidated all I had studied, all I had achieved, all that lay ahead of me. What had been put to the test was not my faith but my commitment.

The ancient Egyptians had a saying that went something like, *Sekhmet yesterday; Bast today.*[2] It means that Sekhmet, the wild lion goddess, gives way to Bast, the domestic cat goddess. Fierceness alternating with gentleness. Hardship alternating with reward. So it was fitting that my encounter with the feline kingdom a few weeks later would be sweet and playful.

I was hiking back to the car an hour after sunrise, having spent another night solo backpacking. Rising above a crest I found below me a mountain lion playing in the open field: pouncing, flipping around, chasing herself, leaping in the air. I had never heard that the mean cats played, but there was no other explanation for what I witnessed over the next five minutes. Eventually I moved toward the cat, since she was directly in my path, and as soon as she became aware of my presence she turned and skedaddled. Evidently mountain lions were also scaredy-cats.

My next wildcat encounter would not be as amusing.

It didn't start out as a cougar hunt; it never does. I decided I would do a vision quest. I would go out on my own, build a fire, and instead of sleeping I would stay up all night and have visions.

I chose the dark moon for my journey. I walked a few miles along a deserted beach, with cliffs along the edge that had small caves and alcoves. When I reached a sheltered place I pulled firewood out of my backpack, gathered kindling along the beach, built a small fire, and in the approaching twilight commenced scrying into the flames. I didn't have any visions.

I sat there a long time, getting up only to add more fuel. It began spitting rain and I became chilled even with the fire. I felt silly, shivering all by myself in a deserted place with a car less than five miles away and a warm bed within a few hours' drive. "This is boring," I said to myself. I gathered my belongings and scattered the fire. As I stamped out the last embers, I had a vision.

A fat Chinese Buddha appeared, so rotund that I could not discern the outline of his body within my psychic frame of reference. I intuitively understood that he appeared to me thus to show that he was bigger than I could envision. The limits of his influence were beyond the scope of my understanding.

The Buddha raised his hand in a gesture of protection and the apparition dissolved. I commenced my journey home.

As I trekked northward, the cliffs at my right and the ocean to my left, I discovered it was not raining at all; the fine droplets were from an unusually rough tide. How had I blotted out the sound of that surf? I realized that I was now in danger of being cut off from dry land; cliffs to one side of me with water butting up against them. Though it was very dark, I put my flashlight in my backpack because I needed both hands to scramble over the slippery rocks. I felt angry with myself for having bumbled into such a dangerous situation.

Finally the cliffs ended and the beach opened up. I had made it. I unloaded my backpack and retrieved my flashlight.

I was now only two miles from the car, two rather slow miles over sand or a short brisk walk via a trail close by. The logical option was to take the trail, but I felt an unexplained reluctance. It was one of those feelings that don't make sense at the time, but you understand later. I was sopping wet from struggling with the surf, and I was rattled, so despite my misgivings, the trail won out.

I practically ran along the narrow path, so I was very close before I saw her. She was huge, the largest carnivorous beast I had confronted in the wild. She appeared confused. She moved a few steps from the beam of my flashlight and stood there, staring at me.

"You're supposed to run away," I said helpfully. The conventional wisdom was that cougars would not attack humans unless cornered, though they might possibly eat children. Many well-publicized deaths from unprovoked mountain lions have occurred since, but this was the prevailing belief at the time. I was not reassured by this while standing face-to-face with my cougar, however, because I am not a large woman. I thought to myself, "I hope this cougar understands that I'm a grown-up and not a child."

"Listen, you're blocking the path," I reasoned. "Turn and follow this other path, or run back the way you came. I have to go in this direction because my car is there."

The mountain lion took a few steps forward, slightly left of my shoulder.

"Okay, I give you the path," I said quickly. "I'll go another way." I took a small step backward and shone my flashlight directly in the animal's eyes. I took another slow step backward, and another, and another. I began shining the flashlight away, then back in her eyes, then away, then back, rationalizing this would interfere with her ability to focus. She remained still.

As I finally turned away, I let out the loudest, most terrifying scream I could muster, just to give her second thoughts about following me. "Take that, you big scream machine," I thought.

My relationship with wilderness changed that night. After my third cougar encounter I still went out by myself, sometimes after dark, but I interacted with my environment in a different way. Hearing an unfamiliar sound I would investigate not only out of curiosity, but also out of concern for safety. I remained vigilant; I became cautious. Magical protection was no longer an abstract concept. Once there was a girl who roamed the wilderness alone at night, aware that there were mountain lions in the woods and completely unafraid. I am no longer that girl.

A few weeks later I encountered another wildcat at night, this one standing in front of my tent. Even at a distance I could tell this was no cougar. "Much too small—maybe a young bobcat," I mused. Still I felt a twist of fear in my heart as she rushed toward me—

And then I realized this was only a domestic yellow cat, gone feral. She had been waiting for me, to say hello. The kitty rubbed against me and purred as I petted her. I praised her fervently. She accepted my tribute with warmth, then turned and bounded back into the brush.

Sekhmet yesterday; Bast today.

Though the ancient Egyptians plumbed the very depths of feline mysteries, modern research on the cat has been remarkably slow in coming. The first scientific exploration of domestic and wild cat behavior was a German treatise by Paul Leyhausen published in 1956.[3] The dearth of information before hidden camera technology is somewhat understandable, as the solitary forest cats are elusive and well camouflaged, while cats such as the Canada Lynx and the Snow Leopard inhabit remote inhospitable geography. Still, the domestic cat is reasonably accessible. Research on the domestic cat has until recently focused on health issues, but in the past twenty years there has been progress in other areas. Behavior studies of both feral and house cats have proven so fascinating, for scientists and for cat owners, that researchers are wondering why the study of cat behavior has remained so long the purview of writers and eccentrics.

Part of the reluctance has to do with the well accepted notion that cats are individualists. *There is no such thing as an ordinary cat*, said a fortune cookie I once received, also a quote attributed to the French author Colette. Scientists like to do things in a standardized way, with all variables accounted for, so how could a methodology be developed for a population so predictably unpredictable? Moreover, how could general conclusions be drawn and how could they be replicated in other studies?

Researchers began, logically enough, by seeing if they could objectively verify what "everybody knows" about cats. Are cats individualists in personality and temperament? (Yes, very much.) Do cats bond better with people when handled as kittens? (Again, yes.) Are cats good at catching mice? (Come on.) Are

Siamese Cats loud and chatty? (Now you're being ridiculous.) Often this kind of research is boring and seems pointless, but occasionally there are surprises. Have you heard that the house cat is maddeningly "independent"? It turns out that our puny domestic cat is more like the big bad lion than other cats in one critical area: she is a highly social animal.

Figure 2: African Wildcat, *Felis sylvestris libyca*. **Photo: Sonelle/Wikimedia Commons.**

Felines in a multi-cat household have no choice but to learn to get along, but studies of feral domestic cats reveal that mother cats choose to raise kittens cooperatively, even nursing kittens who are not their own. This is not because they are like certain species of birds, fooled because they cannot recognize their offspring. Mother cats know their kittens and kittens know their mother. If availability of food permits, daughters and sisters remain with the cat family as adults. Sons will wander off and join another group, but in a large cat family with stable food resources there will be multiple unrelated male members of the group interacting in a hierarchy that has complex rules. The social order within feral domestic cat colonies does not appear to be mere accommodation around a food source. A study from Saudi Arabia compared wild domestic cats with their *Felis silvestris libyca* cousins, the species from whom all modern cats were domesticated. Both species congregated around the food source, but the *Felis silvestris libyca* developed an accommodation strategy while the domestic cats formed a bona fide social group.[4]

Feral cats live in groups only when there is a rich, reliable source of food nearby, such as a fishing dock or garbage dump. When food sources become unreliable or dispersed, meaning cats must rely entirely on hunting small animals, the domestic cat reverts to a more solitary existence. The remarkable adaptivity of the domestic cat may partly explain her "individuality": she adjusts her lifestyle to fit the situation. The range of survival strategies employed by feral domestic cats has caused biologists to reevaluate the role of environment in determining animal behavior. What has been assumed to be evolutionary adaptation through DNA may be precipitated more by spontaneous adjustments to circumstance than has been supposed. Place feral

Figure 3: Painting from Chauvet Cave. France, 30,000 BCE.

kittens from the same litter in wildly differing habitats and their behaviors will be quite different.

Throughout this discussion I've been using the odd term "feral domestic cat," which sounds like a contradiction. I employ this oxymoron because it's the simplest, least confusing way to refer to this species when it returns to the wild. There are indoor domestic house cats, outdoor domestic cats who may never go inside but still rely on humans for food and medical care, feral domestic cats who are basically on their own even though they may take advantage of garbage piles and the occasional handout, and small wildcats who may also eat refuse or the rodents congregating around human habitations. These wildcats are in some cases the stock from which the domestic cat was derived, and their behavior patterns may be influenced by human settlements just like their feral domestic cousins. Hybridization between the two groups further complicates the picture. It's fair to ask whether "wild" small cats are really wild, and certainly many cat owners wonder if their "domestic" cat really is domesticated.

Figure 4: Cat goddess defeating the snake god Apophis. Note the long ears, styled after the native jungle cat, *Felis chaus*, rather than the domestic cat or her predecessor *Felis sylvestris libyca*. Tomb of Inherkha, 1300 BCE.

The oldest evidence of a symbiosis between cats and humans comes from Cyprus, from a grave with human and cat remains dating back to 7000 BCE. What makes this skeleton tantalizing is that were no cats naturally living on Cyprus at this time, so this cat (or an ancestor) would have been captured or even bred somewhere else, suggesting a significant human-cat relationship. The Cyprus cat is of the subspecies *Felis sylvestris lybica*, the African Wildcat, the subspecies from which the domestic cat, *Felis catus*, was derived. The African Wildcat is a desert cat native to North Africa and the Middle East.

Whether the cat was first domesticated in Egypt is uncertain. The African Wildcat is not indigenous to the Nile Valley, and early Egyptian artwork features the *Felis chaus*, the Jungle Cat. Small cats of various species began living among humans as soon as permanent settlements formed, attracted by rodent infestations. An animal is not considered domesticated, however, until she becomes genetically differentiated from her wild ancestor, indisputable evidence of a captive breeding program. By 2000 BCE evidence of a domestic cat does appear in Egypt, and this cat is clearly related to the African Wildcat. This is a full 5,000 years after the earliest record of cat-human graves, which seems suspiciously late, but since the domestic cat readily returns to her wild state the issue of when and where she was domesticated may not be an answerable question. As James Serpell notes, "It is probably more accurate to view *Felis catus* as a species that has drifted unpredictably in and out of various states of domestication, semi-domestication, and feralness according to the particular environmental and cultural conditions prevailing at different times and locations."[5]

Though they may not have been first on the scene, the Egyptians were indubitably the most enthusiastic cat breeders. Cats hunt not only rodents but also snakes, and the Nile Valley was plagued with poisonous snakes that proliferated with mouse irruptions. The brave guardian cat was a valued member of both royal and humble households, and at her death her human family would go into mourning, sometimes even shaving their eyebrows or mummifying kitty remains. Cats had elaborate sarcophagi and were entombed with offering dishes. Cat cemeteries have been uncovered in three cities. Though both men and women owned cats, the cat was more often associated with women, and the

Egyptian word for cat, *Mau,* was a common affectionate nickname for a girl.

The Egyptians bred or tamed a variety of animals for religious as well as practical reasons. Each city had its totem animal deity, often with a temple complex that might house a large number of sacred representatives. Temple cats would have been selected not only for their docility and hunting ability, but also for their willingness to live sociably with other cats.

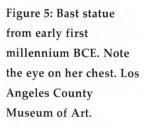

The most important cat temple was dedicated to the goddess Bast in the city of Bubastis. It was a beautiful temple located on a tree-covered island in the Nile. Here favored kitties lounged in comfortable surroundings attended by priestesses who entertained them with music. Some cats were taught to "write" oracles with paws dipped in ink.

Bast was a healing goddess propitiated for safety in childbirth and the wellbeing of children. Bast amulets for health, good fortune, and protection were tremendously popular. Greek observers reported that more than a half million people attended the ecstatic annual

Figure 5: Bast statue from early first millennium BCE. Note the eye on her chest. Los Angeles County Museum of Art.

festival of Bast, which featured music, dancing, and much drinking. Priestesses played flutes and rattled sistrums as Bast's entourage proceeded down the river while celebrants clapped and sang. It was a noisy, happy festival.

Bast was originally not a domestic cat but the lion goddess of Bubastis, one of at least ten Egyptian deities with a lion aspect. The lion was probably the totem for numerous towns and villages along the Nile. Sometimes lion deities retained their feline manifestation as their primary characteristic, as in the case of the goddesses Sekhmet and Pakhet. Other times the lion became a minor aspect of a deity in a more prominent religious cult due to political alliances or military defeats. This is probably how Hathor, usually pictured with cow horns, obtained her lion association. In the case of the brother-sister dyad Shu and Tefnut, other roles were bestowed on the lion deities as priests sought to establish a coherent theological framework from a myriad of animistic beliefs and practices—a framework that would justify patriarchal power structures, legitimize dynasties, and assure the prominence of favored religious cults.

Egyptian lion deities were repositories of sun energy, because lions once frequented the hot, semi-arid regions bordering the Nile Valley. The majority of these deities were female, which makes Egypt different from Greece, Anatolia, and Mesopotamia, where the lion companions of both gods and goddesses are usually pictured with manes. The male lion is more powerfully built than the female, but he uses his strength to discourage other males from entering his territory. The smaller but more agile females do most of the hunting for the tribe.

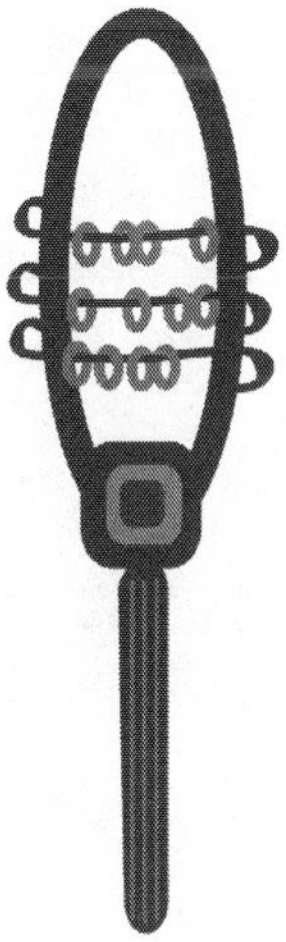

The Egyptian lion goddess is ferocious, blood-thirsty, and relentless. She is active in warfare and the source of contagious fevers. She is also a devoted mother who protects and nourishes her community. She is sexual and highly fertile. She embodies powerful, graceful beauty. She is a goddess you want stay on the right side of, not the wrong.

Figure 6: Sistrum.

The people of Bubastis had a warm relationship with their lion goddess and viewed her more as an ally than an adversary. This may explain why she came to be portrayed as a tame pussycat after the arrival of the domestic cat. Eventually Bast came to represent the gentle side of the feline goddess while Sekhmet became the fierce manifestation of the same goddess. The Egyptians understood that lions, like cats, belong to the feline family. This seems obvious to us today, but the behavior and lifestyle of the lion would lead to a different conclusion. Mesopotamians categorized lions as a type of dog, because like many species in the canine family, and unlike all other wild felines, lions hunt cooperatively and live in large family groups.

Figure 7: Sekhmet from Kom Ombo Temple, second century BCE. Photo: Remih/Wikimedia Commons.

Starting about 1000 BCE Bubastis became a major ruling city in Egypt and would remain so for several centuries. During this time the cult of the domestic cat goddess spread throughout Egypt and the goddess Isis acquired a cat aspect. It was probably at this time that Hathor, who was also developing a cat aspect, lent Bast her sistrum. Cats love the sound of this instrument.

The Greeks associated Bast with their own goddess Artemis, and when they conquered Egypt they attempted to syncretize Artemis with Bast. On the surface there doesn't seem to be much commonality between these two goddesses, but both cults were highly feminine with an emphasis on safe childbirth and healthy children, and both goddesses were unmarried. The Egyptian populace was conservative in religious belief and resistant to influence from foreigners, so Bast ended up changing percep-tions of Artemis more than Artemis changed understanding of Bast.

During the Roman occupation of Egypt the domestic cat, along with some aspects of her cult, became dispersed throughout the Empire. Egyptians had tried to prevent expor-tation of domestic cats for a millennium, even sending agents abroad to discover smuggled kitties and repurchase them. But, despite this high level intrigue, the domestic cat wanted to see the world, and so she made herself indispensable to commerce by hunting rodents that multiplied on increasingly large trade ships. The ubiquity of the ship's cat meant that domestic cats were eventually jumping ship at harbors all over the world, often to the detriment of indigenous fauna.

Perceptions of the domestic cat were influenced both by the Egyptian cults from which she evolved and by the perceptions Europeans had of pre-Christian Egyptians. The cat was associated with women because the cult of Bast was a feminine one. The cat was associated with sorcery because Romans had great respect for Egyptian magical acumen. The cat was associated with ancient wisdom because Egyptian civilization was very old. The cat was mysterious because Romans found Egyptians hard to understand, particularly in their relationship with animals.

The syncretism of Bast with Artemis (who was later syncretized with Diana) may explain how the Germanic goddess Freya got her cat-drawn chariot. Although Freya is more commonly linked with the Roman Venus, she may have also been associated with Diana-Artemis since she has a twin brother, and like Artemis (whose twin is god of light Apollo) Freya's twin has a sun aspect. Freya has characteristics of fertility, generosity, and prophecy in common with Bast, and the image of her in a chariot drawn by cats evokes pictures on Egyptian tombs of lion-drawn chariots.

When Charles Godfrey Leland collected material for *Aradia*[6] in Tuscany at the end of the nineteenth century, a black cat goddess Diana featured prominently in creation stories. This is curious because early Greek and Roman sources do not stress a domestic cat companion or aspect for Artemis-Diana, nor would they be expected to since only a few lucky people outside Egypt owned tame cats. Greek literature does say, however, that Artemis transformed herself into a cat when she went to Egypt. Despite the cat innovation, the Tuscan myth has Greek antecedents, with Lucifer-Apollo a mouse god and a god of light as well as a brother to Diana. The preference Diana shows for women and children is also familiar. Diana could be a black cat in the creation myth to balance the light of her brother, but she could also have been viewed as black because many of the Bast statues exported from Egypt were black. The original Egyptian *mau* had tan tabby coloration, but black was an early color mutation. Black was a sacred color to Egyptians because it symbolized the rich delta soil that appeared after the annual floods. Europeans considered black, white, and red to be the sacred trinity of colors, at least before Christianity.

Figure 8: Lions line the procession to the Gate of Ishtar. Babylon, sixth century BCE. Photo: Miia Ranta.

The Roman Catholic Church and later Protestant churches distrusted and persecuted the cat, but she was still considered lucky in countries influenced by the Oriental and Eastern Orthodox churches (and within Islam). While Christianity succeeded in rupturing an Egyptian animal-worshiping tradition thousands of years old, it is unlikely that Egyptian Christians would have countenanced a campaign of tyranny against cats. Rome's antipathy toward cats was probably influenced by prejudice toward Egypt: prejudice fueled by ideological differences with other Christians, the rise of Islam, and the belief that Egypt remained a repository of pre-Christian magic. Christian leaders also looked at the cat suspiciously due to her association with women, and the stubborn persistence of various cults of Diana was probably the deciding factor. Mass burnings and torture of cats, along with arrests and executions of women who owned cats, did not occur until the Renaissance, but the foundations for this distrust were laid over many centuries. Western Europe has a long history of uneasiness about cats that persists today in various superstitions about unlucky cats.

Given the part that all-black cats play in witch-hunt scenarios, it is interesting that cats are not necessarily pure black in folklore of pagan origin. The Scottish *Cat Sith* is a black-and-white fairy cat who haunts the bedside of the nearly departed, waiting to snatch the spirit as it leaves the body. The *Cat Sith* is black on her head, limbs, and body, but has a white patch on her chest. She is big as a dog, which is impressive until you consider that her dog counterpart, the *Cu Sith*, is as big as a calf. During the time between death and burial, when the soul is hovering around the corpse, mourners would attempt to thwart the *Cat Sith* by distracting her away from the room containing the body. In this other room they would build a warm fire, scatter catnip, wrestle with one another, and tell riddles.

Another otherworldly cat is the Grimmalkin, whose name seems to be an amalgamation of gray + mawkin (a Scottish word for cat or hare). The word "Grimmalkin" first appears in print in the 1561 English story *Beware the Cat*, by William Baldwin.[7] Grimmalkin is a cat queen slain in Ireland who provokes her minions to seek revenge. In Shakespeare's *Macbeth* one of the witches addresses her feline familiar as "Greymalkin."

Perhaps the diabolical nature of the *Cat Sith* and the Grimmalkin is derived from Christian sources, but where the popular depiction departs from the script—Devil as pure black animal corresponding to Christian conceptions of sin—it is reasonable to ask if elements of the story reflect earlier folk belief. Could the Grimmalkin reflect Iron Age Celtic ideas about the hare or be rooted in magic surrounding the indigenous European wildcat? The antics of mourners trying to distract the *Cat Sith* correlate with feline inclinations: the love of play, warmth, and catnip. The riddles may allude to the Sphinx, who blocks the path of the Greek hero Oedipus and other wayfarers with the command to answer her riddle or be devoured. As for the association of the *Cat Sith* with death, the link between a departing soul and an animal, especially a nocturnal animal, is an integral part of shamanism around the world.

The connection between cats and death may explain the ubiquity of cat images at Halloween. In folklore of Britain and Ireland a fairy cat visited each house on this night and would bless the family who left her a saucer of milk (or curse the cows if the family was stingy). Of course the Halloween connection could be related to the knowledge that cats are witches' familiars: a witch was believed to be able to shapeshift into a cat nine times, but on the ninth transformation she had to remain a cat. (My spirit guides assure me that this is not true; you can change into a cat as many times as you like.) Another link between witches and cats has to do with weather. Witches are famous for being able to invoke storms, but there is a belief that cats can also bring a terrible storm through vigorous face washing. This is one half of the saying "raining cats and dogs." I discuss the dog portion in my previous book, *Invoking Animal Magic*.

Historians say that cats were persecuted during the sixteenth and seventeenth centuries due to their association with witches, but cats were already considered diabolical creatures in their own right for their origin in Egypt. Today this guilt by association is extended to the "crazy cat lady," who endures social stigma for her devotion to her cats. Every town has at least one cat lady. We had one in our neighborhood when I was young, and we kids used to spy on her and invent pretexts for knocking on her door. Our parents would discuss her at the dinner table and at neighborhood klatches. She kept to herself, or rather to her cats, and everyone admitted she was clean. Unfortunately the neighborhood became a lot less interesting when The Cat Lady's landlord discovered she had twenty-four cats in her one-bedroom apartment. She was told she could only have twenty, so she decided to move.

Figure 9: Louis Wain postcard, 1916.

There's a lot of finger pointing toward the cat as a source of schiz-ophrenia due to the ability of domestic felines to harbor the toxoplasmosis parasite. The case for toxoplasmosis as the culprit in schizophrenia has a lot of holes, although there probably is an infectious agent involved in the disease. Toxoplasmosis is a potentially serious infection, particularly if contracted in utero or by HIV-infected individuals, but a sizable percentage of the world population has been infected without any psychiatric symptoms. Even if toxoplasmosis does turn out to be implicated in some cases of schizophrenia, most people are not infected through cats. Undercooked meat, unwashed vegetables, and dirty water are the most common culprits. Cats contract toxoplas-mosis themselves by eating infected rodents, and they are only contagious for a few weeks, so if you keep your cat indoors and you are diligent about cleaning the litter box, your chance of being infected through your cat is very small. Still the drumbeats continue for finding a link between cats and insanity. Some researchers are even trying to link bipolar disorder with cat ownership, although the association of bipolar disorder with genes, trauma, and substance abuse is better established. As I demonstrated in *Invoking Animal Magic*, belief that an animal causes disease follows rather than creates cultural hysteria around that animal.

The cat insanity hypothesis has been used to explain the mental illness of cat illustrator Louis Wain. This artist and cat

Figure 10: Dutch painter Henriette Ronner-Knip (1821–1909) was a forerunner of Louis Wain who painted many cats and had a significant influence on Wain and other painters.

lover did more than any other person to rehabilitate the image of the domestic cat in the Western world. He drew thousands of tremendously popular pictures of cats for books, magazines, and postcards, starting out with clothed anthropomorphic cats, moving on to whimsical cats, and ultimately exploring abstract cats with geometric designs. You are familiar with Wain's cat pictures even if his name is unfamiliar to you. Wain had some kind of degenerative psychotic disorder, exhibiting prodromal signs in adolescence before beginning his career as an artist. His illness progressed slowly, and it's possible that his interest in cat welfare improved his mental state rather than causing his insanity. But of course most people blame the cats.

Figure 11: John Tenniel's drawing of the Cheshire Cat disappearing tail first from *Alice's Adventures in Wonderland*, 1865.

The subject of cats seems to come up when we are trying fervently to understand something but cannot. The cat's name is invoked to describe one of the most disturbing conundrums in our current perception of the world, one involving the behavior of small particles. In physics it is impossible to predict the exact position of a discrete subatomic particle, like an individual electron or photon. Physicists make calculations in their formulas based on percentages, saying for example that a particle has 25 percent chance of being one place and 75 percent chance of being in another place—unless they actually measure the position of the particle, in which case they naturally use the position they find it in. So far, so good. But many physicists argue that this is not just a matter of fudging data to make the equations balance, and that a particle actually exists everywhere and nowhere within its calculated range *until the position of that particle is measured*. What's more, some sophisticated experiments appear to support this belief.

To illustrate how bizarre and counterintuitive this idea is, a man named Erwin Schrodinger came up with a "thought experiment" that has become known as Schrodinger's Cat. Hypothetically, a bottle of poison gas is placed in a box with a timing mechanism that has a 50 percent chance of releasing poison after one hour. To make this more interesting, the mechanism is triggered by radioactive decay, so that the 50 percent threshold is dependent on the behavior of subatomic particles. A cat is placed in the box with the poison gas and the erratic release mechanism and the box is closed. (Again, this is just an imagined scenario.) After one hour, is the cat living or dead? Common sense says that the cat has a 50 percent chance of being alive and a 50 percent chance of being dead. But according to the logic applied to subatomic particles, the cat is both living and dead until you "measure" the situation by opening the box and looking inside.

In reality, is the cat alive before you look inside the box, or is it both living and dead until you've checked? Of course the cat has a 50/50 chance of being alive whether or not you open the box. Yet in the world of subatomic particles when something can't be measured physicists operate—indeed it appears that they must operate—on the supposition that all possibilities exist at once. This seems to mean that the world of the small and the large operate under different laws, yet if the behavior of small particles determines whether the poison is released, how can these worlds be separate?

I am not going to reveal the answer to these questions here today. (I both know and don't know the answer until I tell you.)

Figure 12: Gold lion from eastern Black Sea. 3000 BCE. Photo: Mischvalente/CC license.

Instead I am going to propose a question I don't believe anyone has thought to ask: why did Schrodinger choose a cat to illustrate his point? He could have chosen a rat—scientists usually work with rats, don't they? He could have chosen a canary, since poison gas evokes the idea of the "canary in the coal mine." I believe Schrodinger chose the cat reflexively, without thinking, because cats have been indelibly imprinted on the Western mind as unfathomable mysteries, as the embodiment of paradoxes that cannot be explained. Perhaps long after Schrodinger's paradox is explained, the cat will remain an unresolvable puzzle in the popular imagination.

How the Pussy Willow Got Her Name
This is reportedly an old Polish legend.[8]

Early one morning early one spring, a lovely gray cat gave birth to half a dozen lovely gray kittens. The ungrateful farmer, discovering these adorable creatures, cursed them and tied the poor babies in a burlap bag. He stalked down to the river, with the mother crying piteously at his side, and he threw the bag of kittens into the water. Then he strode callously back to his barn.

(He was an awful man.)

The mother mewed anxiously and the kittens mewed horribly and the willows on the riverbank, who know so much about sadness, mewed sympathetically with them. The agitated river cried so hard that the bag unraveled, and the pathetic kittens swam toward the mewing branches of the willow. Each creature clung fervently to a branch, refusing to let go, and each one changed into a little gray catkin.

The willow who took pity on the kittens now gives birth to a litter of catkins every spring. That is why this willow is called the Pussy Willow.

Tefnut and Her Feud with Ra

In many Egyptian myths, the gods communicate with one another in writing, utilizing the god Thoth or the goddess Seshat for this purpose. There are several versions of the following myth, some of them fragmentary, written in a number of scripts. The common thread through all of them is a lion goddess who wreaks havoc on the earth and is eventually appeased. Though a letter is not mentioned in any of the versions I am aware of, I chose to write this story in the epistolary style because the scribe Thoth is an intermediary here. One legend says Thoth pleaded with Tefnut 1,077 times, but we don't have time to read that many letters.

Letter from the Illustrious Scribe Thoth, also known as Lord of the Moon, Sacred Ibis, Beloved Eye of Ra:

To the Magnificent Goddess Tefnut, also known as Mistress of the Red Land, Lady of the Dew, Mother of All Creatures, Goddess of Eternal Life, Beloved Eye of Ra

My Dearest Queen,

I am writing this letter on behalf of Lord Ra, God of the Sun, who is saddened and distraught by your behavior. The channels of the Nile are bereft of water but they trickle with blood from your carnage. Why do you wander in the desert devouring humans and beasts? What has the world done to earn your displeasure? Remember it is life that you brought forth from your Eye and life that you suckled at your breast. Now fire issues from your nostrils and the reverberations of your roar are heard at all corners of the earth. Turn away from evil and make amends to Ra, who is anxious to welcome you back.

I am sending this letter through your brother, The Great Lion Shu, because everyone else is afraid to come close to you now.

I beseech you, Beautiful Lady, Great Goddess, Merciful Queen, to consider my plea, which is sent in all devotion and sincerity.

Your dedicated servant,
Thoth

Letter from Queen Tefnut to Ra, Shu, and Thoth:

Stop bothering me! I'll kill everybody if I want to.

Letter from the Illustrious Scribe Thoth, Keeper of Knowledge, Lord of the Nile:

To the Beautiful Lion Goddess Tefnut, Mother of Life, Mistress of the Water

Dearest Most Lovely Lady,

I neglected to tell you in my last letter that, should you decide to leave the high desert and desist in the atrocities, which we will not mention further, the people of the Nile Valley are prepared to build you a magnificent temple, the most spectacular that has yet been built. Please forgive this omission; I don't know how I could have forgotten to mention it last time. At your new temple there will be much singing and dancing. The finest musical instruments will be crafted to delight your ears. Laughter and celebration will fill your new home. And, of course, an abundance of meat will be prepared for you by the finest chefs, so that you need not hunt for your dinner ever again.

Please consider this offer and let me know if it is agreeable to you. I am also sending you papyrus, reed pens, and ink, so that you do not need to scratch your answer in blood on the haunch of Shu.

Your servant,
Lord Thoth

Letter from Queen Tefnut:

To the kind people of the Nile Valley, via my good brother Shu and the faithful scribe Thoth

I have always wanted a magnificent temple, and so I will be leaving my desert abode soon to direct you in its completion and to teach you my favorite songs. I will come in the form of a small cat instead of a lioness so that you will not be frightened of me. In consideration of your offer of abundant meat, I will restore the Nile to its former generous level, and I will give you lasting wealth. I will also give you healthy children and protect you from all your enemies.

I look forward to a long and mutually beneficial friendship.

Your Goddess,
Tefnut-Mau

Cat Review

Magical Qualities: beautiful, intelligent, nocturnal, clean, preter-naturally aware of environment, moves silently, lives commu-nally (domestic cat, lion), benefits humans through rodent control.

Magical Applications: divination, healing (especially infertility, fevers, insomnia), protection (especially involving children and childbirth), rainmaking

Other Associations: sun, desert, fire, women, sexuality, motherhood, eccentricity, unbridled destruction, paradox, mysteries of all kinds

Divining in the Natural World

It's sunrise, and you are walking a deserted path. You notice a Black Bear peering at you from behind thick brush. An alarm sounds. You shake yourself awake to the raucous call of Blue Jays.

Over breakfast you notice that a Gray Squirrel is pilfering the birdfeeder. You finish your food and it is time for work. Walking to your car you pull a medium-size sycamore branch out of the driveway, and driving to the office you brake to avoid a calico cat. You notice that today there are three pigeons perched at the entrance to the parking garage.

These and other incidents can be dismissed as accidental or recognized as the voice of nature, speaking directly to you. Inner and outer worlds are teeming with information that can guide you on your life journey.

Tools of divination like the tarot are popular and serve a purpose, but they also have their limitations. The answer to a burning question may not be important in the scheme of things, and sorely needed information may not coincide with questions being asked. Staying attuned to the surrounding world keeps you aware of what is unfolding while preparing you for the road ahead. The caw of a crow or the growl of a dog can provide a needed warning to change course, or a cabal of chickadees can convince you that time is ripe for risking a new enterprise.

Experienced psychics are leery of providing data about death, the course of a pregnancy, and many other things, but you and your environment will reach a subconscious agreement on the kinds of information you are able to accept. Signs can be misinterpreted, but ideas you are unwilling to contemplate cannot be foreshadowed. Often it is worry or confusion that provokes a visit to a card reader, but divination in the natural world can be quirky, humorous, or insightful, an ambush of delightful surprises. It is an ongoing conversation with the Goddess.

This book is designed to help you recognize and interpret signs in nature. It will help you make better use of information in your surroundings, whether you live in an urban or rural area, and add depth to your understanding of dreams and visions. It will improve your knowledge base while challenging you to notice details that you might never have considered. Context is everything when interpreting a sign, so there is no attempt in this book to catalog the "meaning" of different animals. Every sign for every individual in every circumstance is unique. Still, a loose framework can help make sense of things within that context.

The system I am presenting draws on pagan beliefs originating in Europe and the Middle East. This focused approach aids with clarity and cohesion of the material, as the integrity of any shamanic framework is compromised by jumbling disparate elements outside cultural context. As you become more adept in this type of divination, you will be able to integrate other material into this system.

It may be necessary for you to reassess and question beliefs you have unconsciously absorbed. Christian ideas about a hostile wilderness, man's dominion over the nature, the inferiority of animals, and the evilness of things associated with women do not facilitate divination within the natural world. Some have objected to my criticism of Christianity on this basis by pointing out that the other Abrahamic religions, Judaism and Islam, can be faulted for the same things. I am aware that denigration of the physical world can be found in these religions, as well as in Hinduism and Buddhism. For that matter, antecedents for these views can be found in ancient Egyptian, Mesopotamian, and Greek paganism. At the same time, it is a Christian acculturation that people in the

West still experience to a great degree, even if they are not nominally Christian.

Re-examination of beliefs must go deeper than religious programming, however. There is a tendency for fears about the world, especially fears about ominous signs and portents, to be handed down mother to child. We absorb the fears of our mothers because they are motivated by a desire to protect us, yet fears of threatening portents often arose in circumstances different from today, for murky or unintelligible reasons. I invite you to reassess ideas about things like broken mirrors, spilled salt, a "murder" of crows, blood on the moon, and bad things coming in threes. Maybe you will decide to keep these beliefs after giving them a hard look, but ideas about bad luck should not be perpetuated without reflection.

This book deals mostly but not exclusively with animals. I am more interested in the subject of divination through signs than in the specific vehicles. Signs in nature are quite often carried through animals, however, and so each chapter begins with a study of a particular animal. I have tried to be representative in my selections, including denizens of the forest, field, desert, water, and sky. Animals that migrate and hibernate are included, and there are three domesticated species. Predators, scavengers, insectivores, and herbivores are explored in depth. Some species live in communities and others remain solitary outside repro- ductive roles. There are two arthropods, two ungulates, one reptile, four carnivores, and three birds. Birds are emphasized because augury is the oldest and most universal of the divinatory sciences as well as the most expressive. This is a text, not an encyclopedia, and concrete examples are presented with the aim of generalizing the material.

Myths and folktales accompany each chapter, and sections on general topics will help you understand the significance of details you might have glossed over. Stories and art are the primary ways that pagan knowledge has been conserved over the millennia, surviving even conquests and monotheism. Some of these stories you will be familiar with. I encourage you to indulge yourself and me by enjoying once again the stories you have "already read." A good folktale doesn't share all its secrets in the first or even the tenth reading, because absorbing mythology is a right-brain activity. Repetition is a key ingredient.

I have included a set of questions and activities for further reflection at the end of each chapter. These questions are not a list of afterthoughts or opportunities for classroom tests: they represent material I chose to present in an interactive rather than didactic manner. Do the activities or don't do them, write down your answers or don't write them, but you will find it worth your time to at least read and think about these sections. In the back of the book are three glossaries: a brief description of deities, a short explanation of ethnicities and geography referred to in the text, and an explanation of basic mathematical terms. I don't mean to insult anyone's intelligence, but I am aware that witches and other pagans tend to have either an acute interest in math or a studied avoidance of the topic, so if you're one of the avoiders, review these easy terms so you can follow the discussion.

In the next chapter we are going into the swamp, which is a metaphor for the disorienting landscape of nature divination, where fleeting objects lurk in the murky depths. In this chapter we will meet the crocodile.

In Chapter 3, you will find a foundation for understanding the significance of numbers. This chapter will convince you that numbers are not only important, but absolutely fascinating.

Since our physical world is three-dimensional, the form and shape of what we encounter is also significant. Geese fly in formation and bees construct hexagonal honeycombs. Chapter 4 brings you a geometry they didn't teach in high school.

In Chapter 5 we will delve into the numbers seven, eight, and nine. It will be like turning over a rock and watching the scorpions scatter. Only for the intrepid.

Ravens are considered ominous oracular birds, so why do witches treat them as friends? In Chapter 6 ravens will introduce the topic of vision.

Humans are highly visual creatures, yet wild animals are more likely to be heard than seen. Chapter 7 will encourage you to pay more attention to your auditory world. The flamboyant woodpecker pounds the point home.

Animals that are neither seen nor heard leave riddles for us to ponder. In Chapter 8 we will be tracking the signs. We will begin by spotting the deer as she disappears into the mist.

Divination is a passive activity, but it often provokes action. It was through patient observation that our distant ancestors were able to formulate laws of nature, laws that allowed them to manipulate the world directly and magically. In the final chapter, signs will point the way to laws and spells, as we examine the avian roots of symbology. Honing powers of observation will make your spells more effective—and, more importantly, provide you with the discernment for deciding where to apply your magic.

After finishing this book, you may not need to "look up" the meaning of an animal or seek clarification of a sign from the *I Ching*, though you may still decide to do this. You will definitely scrutinize the animal encounter more closely and notice signs you would have overlooked before.

Mistresses of Prophecy

The Thriae (pronounced THREE-eye) are from the Aegean islands or possibly Anatolia. They have bee bodies and women's heads, and they are covered in pollen. An artifact depicting a Thriae is in Chapter 4.

The sun knew nothing but the time of day, until on a certain island, along a certain mountain slope, beside a certain pond, three powerful sisters emerged. These were the Thriae, the bee maidens, who could read the future in the shapes of clouds, the flight of birds, and the patterns on the water. They could hear the voices of tiny stones. They could read the history of mountains, understand the stories of trees, and decipher the music of insects. By consulting the three sisters the sun could not only measure time but also understand what it contained.

For a long time this remained proprietary knowledge, because it is the nature of the sun to witness but not to speak. But the observant crow, who can steal anything and keeps no one's secrets, learned about the bee maidens from watching the sun and told anyone who would listen. All the people of the island could now ask the three maidens anything, knowing they would have the answer.

The bee sisters became capricious in response to the crow's treachery. They told correct answers, wrong answers, conflicting answers. They gave one response in the morning and reversed themselves in the afternoon.

So as with any miffed and temperamental creatures, the Thriae must be approached in the right way, lest they respond in the wrong way. They must be sweetened with presents and kind words, and still they will not favor everyone. The maidens who wallow in the pollen know everything, however, so it is worth your while to coax them into truthful prophecy, if you can.

Questioning the World

1) What positive message could be contained in the "black cat crossing your path"?

2) My mother used to say "It's going to be a clear day tomorrow" when every scrap of food she put on the table was devoured. Clear plates were a portent of clear skies. Make a list of your mother's sayings for various situations.

3) Consider this exchange between Alice and the Cheshire Cat:

"Come, it's pleased so far," thought Alice, and she went on, "Would you tell me, please, which way I ought to go from here?"

> *"That depends a good deal on where you want to get to,"* said
> the Cat.
> *"I don't much care where —"* said Alice.
> *"Then it doesn't matter which way you go,"* said the Cat.[9]

Do signs matter if you don't care where you go?

4) There has been a lot of research on the various methods for handling kittens, with the aim of understanding how the cat-human bond is established. These studies have shown, for example, that the presence of cat mothers during kitten interactions with humans facilitates kitten trust, and that attachments form more readily when kittens are handled between two and seven weeks of age. This is called the "sensitive" or "critical" feline attachment period. What if a study examined the possibility of a "sensitive attachment period" in child development for successful human bonding with animals? Is there such a period? Can you think of benefits of behavioral training in humans to make them more sensitive and responsive to the needs of cats?

5) Be on the lookout for lions. Notice lion statues, streets with leonine names, lion door knockers, pictures of lions, casual speech that uses a lion metaphor. Lion encounters, even symbolic ones, contain messages.

6) Some psychics keep their cat or dog in the room with them when they work. Does having your pet close by help with your divination?

7) Many famous writers were solidly devoted to their cats, even writing stories and poems about them. Yet cats seem decidedly anti-literary, sitting on top of books while their owner is reading, tearing up papers, and stealing pencils. How do you account for the lionization of cats?

8) Think of words and phrases that refer to cats like catnap, cat burglar, copycat, pussycat, catwalk, pussyfoot, cat's meow.

Do any of your chance encounters with a cat point to one of these words?

9) If you can't throw runes with your cat in the room because she interferes with the process, put the pieces in a pile and ask her to arrange them for you.

Chapter 2

Into the Swamp

Alligator Owlyout

The crocodile who gives no sound is feared most of all.
—Instruction of Amenemope

Figure 13: Nile Crocodile. Photo: Stuart Burns.

My grandmother used to spend her day off from the hospital in the company of alligators. She would ask what we should do with the free day, and the two of us would look at each other and say, "Corkscrew!"

Corkscrew Nature Sanctuary is a swampland in southern Florida with miles of boardwalk allowing people to experience the Everglades in an intimate way. I suppose my grandmother was seeking communion with nature in a rich vegetal environment. I was looking for alligators. I began counting as soon as we reached the murky water, and there were hundreds. They stayed mostly submerged with only eyes and snouts showing, craftily blending with their surroundings. I was too sharp to be deceived. Like most children I believed the ultimate in unadulterated evil was the eating of children, and alligators were high on the chain of depraved killers. I chuckled as I moved across the raised boardwalk, knowing I was, for the moment, beyond the reach of the sordid plots hatching in their diabolical minds. Still, it was a breathtaking risk. One false step and I could land in the drink, and bloody mayhem would ensue as they tore me limb by limb, with even my grandmother's CPR powerless to save me.

Looking back from a more mature perspective, I admit it's pretty hard to fall off a boardwalk unless you're trying. In the unlikely event that I plopped into the water, the alligators would probably have scurried away, as most vertebrates will do when startled by unexpected movement. My grandmother would have reached down and pulled me out, and I would have been wet and maybe a little slimy.

I am going to conflate alligators, caimans and crocodiles a bit in this chapter. The three are pretty similar. They are from the order *Crocodylia* and are the living reptiles most closely related to dinosaurs. Because their hearts have four chambers instead of three, some link them more with birds than with other reptiles. In my opinion the American Alligator, with her broad rounded snout, is the winner of the crocodilian beauty contest, but some prefer the South American Dwarf Caiman, and the Nile Crocodile has posed for the most cherished pieces of museum artwork. The species differ most in their ability to tolerate salt water and cool temperatures. The alligator has a low tolerance for salinity but is able to withstand cooler temperatures and can even become dormant in cold weather by digging what is called a "gator hole." Caimans need fresh water and warm temperatures, and they are smaller than alligators. Crocodiles thrive in both fresh and saltwater, but are limited to very warm climates. Most alligators live in the brackish and freshwater swamps of the American

South, but there are a few survivors along the Yangtze River, giving the United States and China a special bond.

Figure 14: Sobek. Photo: Guillaume Blanchard.

Crocodiles are unquestionably more dangerous to humans. In deep water they snap their victims' backs with their huge muscular tails. They drown their prey as they pin bodies under rocks or logs in order to dismember them. The ancient Egyptians feared crocodiles more than any other animal, because what frightened them most was not death but the disappearance of the body. Without the proper funeral procedures the spirit along with the body could drift back into the waters of eternity and be forgotten.

From the earliest predynastic gravesites to the last monuments of the pharaohs, religious animal symbology in ancient Egypt is ubiquitous. Dedication to animal gods must have been especially enduring among the lower classes, because during periods when central authority became weak, or a foreign ruler courted popular support, evidence of animal cults becomes more prominent. It is important to remember that ancient Egyptian religious belief was shaped by an animal environment that is typical of east-central Africa today, not one for the eastern and northern Mediterranean at any time in history.

Most books on Egypt treat animal worship as peripheral or even seem dismissive and embarrassed by it. Egyptologists give most attention and credence to the burial practices of royalty and to rites designed to deify the Pharaoh. This is unfortunate, because what is exciting about Egyptian religion is that remembrance of animal deities continued even as society became complex and technologically advanced. Thus there is much more data about animal gods and goddesses.

Wading into Egyptian religion is made more difficult by the absence of any thorough textual analysis discerning where and how religious beliefs developed to accommodate male and class dominance, similar to what Robert Graves did with the Greek myths.[10] I do not fault religious beliefs simply because they are practiced by the wealthy and well-connected, nor do I find the presence of male deities and male-centered myths objectionable, but like most people of sincere religious belief I consider myths and symbols designed to consolidate male and class dominance to be invalid examples of religious sentiment. Modern texts on ancient Egypt do not attempt to hide the hierarchical nature of the society or the subordination of women, but they also make no attempt to understand how the religion relates to this hierarchy. Juxtaposing religious beliefs that may have developed organically, through observation of nature, with myths that smack of cynical attempts to control the masses is not neutral or unbiased. Rather, it betrays a sympathy with social hierarchy or a belief in the illegitimacy of religious faith.

Some of the challenges in exploring ancient Egypt lie with the Egyptians themselves and what they recorded, or rather didn't record. Considering the amount of writing, there is surprisingly little written mythology, and many of the Egyptian myths we have were recorded by Greek travelers. Scenes etched on temples or painted in tombs were designed to invoke stories that would have been familiar to the observer, but we do not have access to them. Sometimes there are slightly more detailed references to stories that are outlined but not well developed. The mythology of ancient Egypt must have been rich and immense, but people generally do not write down things that "everyone knows."

When stories are detailed there is the fragility of things written on papyrus, as opposed to clay, to contend with. There is a charming story we call "The Tale of the Doomed Prince," believed to go back to about 1500 BCE or earlier, which has only been partially recovered on degraded papyrus. The story follows an infant prince, a late gift to his long-suffering parents, who is given a prophecy at birth by the Seven Hathors that he will be killed by either a dog, a snake, or a crocodile. The king seeks to protect his son by keeping dogs away from him and severely limiting his movements. The prince cajoles his father into giving him a dog, then convinces his father to allow him his freedom, arguing that his fate is inevitable, since the Hathors have decreed it, and he might as well enjoy what life he has. The boy and his dog venture outside Egypt, where he wins the hand of a coveted princess by climbing into the window of the tower where her overprotective father has imprisoned her. The couple born in captivity, who have now found each other, return to Egypt, and the solicitous wife thwarts a poisonous snake who threatens the prince. The first omen has been vanquished. Later the prince sallies forth with his dog, has some kind of argument with the dog that is unclear from the fragmented papyrus, and ends up at a riverbank, where a crocodile menaces him. Here the papyrus becomes too degenerated to indicate the outcome, although speculations from scholars and amateurs abound. How does the prince overcome the crocodile to vanquish over the fate given to him by the Seven Hathors? Perhaps the dog saves the prince? Perhaps the prince kills a monster molesting the crocodile, and the crocodile spares the man's life through some crocodile code of honor?

Actually, I can tell you exactly what happens in the end: the crocodile gets him, and he can't return home to finish writing the story.

Here's how the last scene probably went:

Crocodile: I'm going to eat you now.

Prince: No, you can't! I've been recording this story for posterity and if you kill me now no one will know how it ends.

Crocodile: They'll be able to figure it out.

Prince: No, they won't! My life so far conforms to the "changing of luck or fate" folklore motif, along with the motifs of "princess in tower," "birth of long awaited child," and "hero seeking fortune abroad." All of these motifs require a happy ending.

Crocodile: I think having you for dinner is a happy ending.

Prince: No! You are the helpful talking animal, otherwise fierce but through the machinations of benevolent spirits disposed to aid the deserving son.

Crocodile: I never heard of anything so ridiculous. Come to mama! *Crunch*!!!!

The crocodile is not an enemy but a helpful friend in a funerary papyrus known as the Amduat. A crocodile appears to retrieve the pieces after the sun god Ra, passing through the underworld, has been thoroughly dismembered and flung into the amorphous waters. The crocodile is a representative of the goddess Neith and her son Sobek or analogous crocodilian deities. Neith is the goddess of the inundation of the Nile: self-created, birthing herself from herself out of the limitless primordial waters. Her worship was particularly strong at the start of the Old Kingdom, with more than a third of women's names derived from hers. Her cult continued into the time of the Roman conquest, and stretched from the southern part of the country to the Mediterranean. Her name is often translated as "terrifying one," and she may be depicted as two crossed arrows, in keeping with the fierceness of the crocodile. Before the Nile was dominated by agriculture she may have been a hunting goddess. There were probably many crocodile deities who became syncretized with Neith and Sobek as the country became unified, since numerous communities adopted the crocodile goddess and son as their patron.

During early days of the kingdom Neith was often depicted as a Click Beetle. This insect, prevalent along the Nile, makes a clicking sound as it leaps away in an impressive somersault. In the last years of the kingdom Neith was more commonly a cow with the sun between her horns, rebirthing herself annually from the Nile. She could also be pictured as a bee, and she had many other associations, such as the acacia tree and the Nile Perch. Syncretism of deities was an ongoing process in Egypt. The crocodile connection is the most enduring for Neith, however, with even a late image showing her as a woman with a crocodile head nursing twin crocodile babies.

Figure 15: Horus standing on crocodiles and holding snakes, scorpions, a lion, and an oryx. Above him is the head of the god Bes, flanked by goddesses holding scorpions with scorpion hats. Fourth century BCE. Walters Art Museum.

All the major Egyptian goddesses are mother goddesses, but Neith stands out as a mother of mothers. While most Egyptian origin stories relate how male deities created the world or humanity, Neith is an exception. Her stories place her at the very beginning, birthing herself and all the major gods—including the sun god Ra. Though the gods often usurp her role, they remember who their mother is when they are in a jam, such as when the protracted battle between the gods Horus and Seth gets out of hand, and the gods appeal to Neith for judgment as oldest deity. They also appeal for her intervention in a dispute between Osiris and Seth, under the same auspices as the eldest deity. Unlike most goddesses, Neith is never given a consort; she remains a virgin mother.

The crocodile is an appropriate mother deity not only for her position as apex predator (and thus ruler) of the Nile, but also for her maternal instincts. Crocodiles are more like their bird cousins than other reptiles in taking responsibility for their young. Mothers do not feed while they are nesting, and they guard their eggs continually except for brief periods when temperatures rise so high that they must enter the water to cool off. Nile crocodiles prefer colonial nesting, although predation by humans discourages this behavior. Eggs are buried in sand, and babies squeak as they are hatching. As soon as the mother hears the squeaks, she uncovers the eggs and carries the babies in her

Figure 16: Crocodile mummies. Photo: Olaf Tausch.

mouth to the water. During their first months of life, juveniles seek out and receive protection from adults, usually but not necessarily the mother.

Crocodilians have a reputation for being smart. A significant facet of their intelligence is their ability to learn through observation. Crocodiles take a keen interest in the habits of wildlife along the river and plan their predation strategy accordingly. They seem to anticipate daily schedules and migration patterns. Sometimes they hunt cooperatively, using combined strength to drown a large animal or pull it apart. They may form two separate groups and herd fish into an ambush. They remain still and hidden for long periods of time, then move with lightning speed when it's time to strike. They are long-lived animals, which might be another reason Neith is considered the oldest deity.

Wealthy Egyptians liked to keep crocodiles as pets. A household crocodile was a pampered creature, given a courtyard pond for lounging and freedom to explore the house. Having the croc around brought the family fertility, wealth, protection and general good luck.

The temple crocodile was treated as the living representation of the crocodile god, usually but not always Neith's son Sobek. As with any deity, the crocodile god lived in lush surroundings, entertained by temple musicians, and wore bracelets and body piercings of the most exquisite workmanship. When a divine crocodile died, he would be mummified like any great leader and given a funeral. Pet crocodiles were also mummified, according to the family's means. During the last millennium BCE, some temples kept a stock of crocodiles to be sold as sacrifices to Sobek, and these crocodiles were also mummified, occasionally with their babies, although not with the same precision as a divine crocodile or a pet croc. From this temple stock, a new living deity would be chosen and given the same name as the crocodile now making his journey to eternal life. There are many questions about this process that the Egyptians left unanswered. Questions like, how do you tell the difference between a divine crocodile and an ordinary one? Outside culinary donations, how do you know when a live crocodile approves of your offering, since they appear to have only one facial expression? And, most importantly, who takes a job as a crocodile body piercer?

Figure 17: Weighing of the heart in the hall of Maat. Crocodile headed monster Ammut is at right. 1300 BCE.

Perhaps it is the funerary role of the crocodile that makes Neith the goddess of the mummy cloth. Actually, Neith is the goddess of all weaving, but Egyptians wore more clothing in death than they ever wore in life. Most families steadily saved pieces of cloth for eventually wrapping dead bodies, a kind of pre-paid burial plan. Weaving goddesses are almost invariably sun, snake, or spider deities. Neith does not necessarily fit this pattern, though she's linked with the cobra at times in what seems to be later syncretism. Neith may be a weaving goddess as mother of the sun, with the sun god Ra ineligible for that position as a male. There could also be some underlying logic governing reptile weaving deities. The crocodile, like the snake, is a patterned animal, and crocodile-inspired weaving motifs are popular around the world in places where crocodiles are plentiful. Egyptians generally wore plain white cloth, but weavers displayed a more artistic side of their craft through intricately designed girdles and capes.

According to some underworld schemes, the sun enters the crocodile Penwenti's mouth at dusk, travels under the earth through the gullet during the night, and is reborn at the tail each dawn. Some underworld crocodiles are scary. A particularly feisty bunch is the group of eight that seeks to swamp the ferry of the deceased and must be fended off with magic. By far the most feared is the hybrid Ammut in the Hall of the Double Maat. This is where the gods weigh sins, receive defensive testimony, and

Figure 18: Sobek at Kom Ombo Temple. Second century BCE. Photo: Hedwig Storch.

record judgment. Ammut waits with his snout gaping. He has the head of a crocodile, the claws of a lion, and the bulky rear end of a hippopotamus. He is hoping to gobble the heart of the deceased should the petition for admission to the afterlife be rejected.

Sometimes the crocodile is linked to the god Seth, reflecting the ambivalence Egyptians had toward both Seth and the crocodile. Seth is the god of chaos and disorder, the foil of the vegetation god Osiris, a necessary catalyst for the cycle of birth and death. He is associated with the desert, black boar, Nile Carp, hippopotamus, and donkey. *The Book of the Dead* and other funerary literature relates the struggle between these two from the point of view of Osiris, and therefore Seth is cast as the enemy. He is a more complex deity than this literature suggests. Seth had his own cult, which became distorted through political disputes and efforts to create a cohesive theological structure.

**Figure 19: Crocodile amulet with a sun disk under the snout.
Inscribed to Amen-Ra. Tenth century BCE. Walters Art Museum.**

Reverence for the crocodile was not universal. Some areas in the Nile Delta forbade the hunting of crocodiles for religious reasons, while political leaders in other regions would organize eradication efforts. The crocodile god Khenty Khety might be cast as the protector of the child god Horus, or Horus might be petitioned to destroy crocodiles. In the afterlife anyone could say a spell to turn themselves into a crocodile, but magicians of Thoth impressed (or alarmed) onlookers in this world by transforming pieces of wax into live crocodiles. Spells designed to protect herd animals or humans were plentiful, but other spells promised to sic crocodiles on unfaithful spouses or romantic rivals.

Although crocodiles could be dangerous to people, they helped in Egypt's defense. Egyptian rulers liked to compare themselves to crocodiles and they propitiated the crocodile god Sobek to establish themselves as fierce warriors. Crocodile amulets protected the soldier and made him more lethal to his opponents. The legendary crocodile in the moat was an Egyptian military strategy recorded by the Greek historian Diodorus Siculus in the second century BCE.[11] Crocodile cults and the crocodile herself made a deep impression on Greek and Roman travelers, and it was through their writings that the crocodile entered the European imagination.

Figure 20: Crocodile chained to a palm tree. Gaul, first century. Photo: CNG Coins.

If Egyptian crocodile symbolism reflected ambivalence acquired through varied experience, the European crocodile was more fanciful and less equivocal, an allegoric staple fed by fantasy and divorced from observation. The fabled crocodile invariably swallowed whole the humans he came in contact with, yet he shed tears doing so, crying for his victim and his own evil nature. In the words of Bartholomeus Anglicus, "If the crocodile findeth a man by the brim of the water, or by the cliff, he slayeth him if he may, and then he weepeth upon him, and swalloweth him at the last."[12] This crocodilian concept developed alongside Christianity, and there is something of Judas Iscariot in the weeping crocodile: fated to betray man, sorrowful of his deed, possessing an inescapable wickedness to be pitied. There is only a grain of truth to the crying crocodile myth. The crocodile does have a gland that produces fluid around the eyes, and this gland appears to be active while the crocodile is feeding. Other reptiles, mammals, and birds possess this gland, but it is not the same gland that produces tears in humans.

The weeping crocodile morphed into a more sinister figure: the duplicitous felon feigning sorrow for calculated gain. A man succumbing to treacherous insincerity is characterized in Shakespeare's *Henry VI* as, "Too full of foolish pity, and Gloucester's show beguiles him as the mournful crocodile with sorrow snares relenting passengers." Today people who indulge in "crocodile tears" are merely insincere and hypocritical, not necessarily predatory, but the crocodile retains a reputation for perfidy in some quarters.

Figure 21: Section of a larger Roman mosaic dedicated to the god Neptune in a wealthy merchant's home. Italica, Spain, first century.

In other places crocodilians are more welcome. Along the Yangtze the emergence of the alligator from winter dormancy is a sign of spring. The alligator shares some emblematic traits with the benevolent water dragon. Drums made from alligator hides and bones have been found in Neolithic archeological sites in China.

Along the Ganges River, the Hindu goddess Ganga rides her

crocodile from the Himalayas to the Bay of Bengal. Ganga washes away sins, which is why millions make the pilgrimage annually to bathe in her holy place.

In northwest Australia there is again some ambivalence about the crocodile, as the saltwater crocodile is the most dangerous in the world. The crocodile is prevalent in the art and mythology of the region. Among the Yirritja moiety there is a tale about the crocodile ancestor Baru, who caught fire and dragged flames into the ocean, where they remain beneath the water. The burn marks Baru suffered during this incident gave the crocodile his characteristic pattern.

The American Alligator is cherished because we almost lost her. In the twentieth century the country was horrified to learn she had been driven nearly to extinction by unregulated hunting, but after decades of conservation this key swamp predator is no longer endangered. Continued conservation efforts focus on habitat preservation rather than hunting, which is now better controlled. The alligator hunting traditions of the Seminole Indians inspired the American sport of alligator wrestling. The moves originated in techniques for capturing large alligators, which would then be penned until ready to grill.

You may think crocodilian symbology has no relevance to you

if you cannot reasonably expect to encounter an alligator in a parking lot or on a golf course, but if you cultivate a gator mind you will observe that this creature is all around you. It is common in advertising. You may have a tiny crocodile emblem on your shirts, and you may wear Crocs on your feet. Words

Figure 22: Baba Yaga riding a pig (right) fighting a crocodile (left). Russian early eighteenth century.

referring to the crocodilian family arise frequently in conversation, and noticing this, and other animal signs around you, is the starting place for animal divination.

Crocodile Goddess Creates the World

There are many Egyptian creation myths, a fact that did not seem to trouble the Egyptians intellectually or politically. This account, which cannot be found in any specific text, is pulled from several fragments and reflects some core Egyptian understanding of cosmology.

The place where the world begins is a place that is no place and every place... No landmarks—no land!—no sensation of heat or of cold. Nothing above or below or on any side but the constant fullness that admits no space. If you can imagine a place of infinite weight and complete buoyancy...you are there, in the waters of birth, in the waters before creation.

When the first vibration emerges you cannot know, for it is slight, so slight its awareness of itself is only gradual. The vibration grows into an undulation, then a ripple, then a wave, then a torrent, then a magnificent roar that fills the endless watery void. Out of this roar the mother crocodile creates herself.

The crocodile mother swims freely in the infinite waters, for there are no boundaries yet. In a warble of excitement she circles and twirls and swirls to make the boundaries of the first world.

She yelps in her thrashing body, separating the world into two parts: sky above and water below. She raises her snout above the water and coughs, forcing air between water and sky.

The crocodile mother splashes down, writhing her tail, churning the water until specks of silt coalesce. Eventually she tires and yawns, a gaping groaning yawn. She floats along the surface while silt settles to the bottom of the waters, forming the ocean floor.

When the crocodile mother awakes the first hillock is poking above the water. She drags her body onto this mound, where she drops her eggs. The first egg hisses as it matures and breaks into the first light. This light is brilliant and diffuse, everywhere at once, but the crocodile rattles her throat and the light scatters to form the sun, the moon, and the twin star Sothis. Still there is no night and day until her squawk sets the lights in motion in their path across sky and under earth. Now the measure of time can begin as the planets wander: the sun measuring the day, the moon the month, and Sothis the year.

The second egg chirps. A creature emerges that is an image of his mother: beautiful green eyes, big smile, heavy muscular tail. The mother teaches her crocodile son the sounds she made when creating the world: the warble, the yelp, the cough, the yawn, the rattle, the squawk. Then she takes him to the edge of the world, where the gates hold back the primordial waters. Here she teaches him the sound she made at her birth, the gathering roar. He is only to make this sound yearly, when the Twins peak over the eastern horizon. At this time the gates open and the waters flow into the Nile from beyond the world. There is a cascade of movement and a churning of black silt and a roar that is insistent and permeating and all-encompassing and inexorable, like the beginning of the world.

Sherit's Bid for Power

The journey of magician and apprentice to the cave is a ruse for presenting bare-bones accounts of Egyptian wizardry. To my knowledge the spells used by Thoth magicians to enliven their pieces of wax have not been written down and translated, though I have no doubt that even today there are people claiming to have the authentic Egyptian incantation, for a price.

One would think that the last thing on Sendjehuti's mind as his sandals crunched over the desert floor was attack by crocodile. He was far from any body of water and he was headed west, away from the river. Still, crocodiles were in his thoughts. He was not afraid of any beast, but he had to be sensitive to the fears of others.

At the top of the hill he waited for the child, who was scrambling to keep up with him. Further back, her panting nurse paused and forced air into her stout body. "Are you certain you are prepared to proceed with this, Sherit?" he asked, giving her a final opportunity to turn around. The girl had been named for him, but they called her Sherit.

"Of course I am prepared!" the girl replied, indignant. "I have been repeating those words in my mind for days. I have memorized my lesson. How could you think I would be thoughtless about something you have told me to do?"

"No, I did not think you would be disobedient," he soothed. "But perhaps you are frightened. What we are doing today is extraordinary. Many adults would decline this opportunity without hesitation, and you still wear a child's hairstyle. There is no dishonor in retreating."

"I am not frightened," replied Sherit, now more incredulous than angry. "I am with you."

"You must think of me, as well as yourself. What if you lose your nerve and this becomes a disaster? People will say it was my fault for leading you into this. They will say I am a poor father and do not deserve any children."

The child laughed. "If anyone finds the nerve to criticize you, they had better watch out. You will send a pair of leopards to tear off their heads. You will point their severed heads toward their bodies and make their mouths tell their hearts how foolish they are."

Sendjehuti snorted as he walked on. Yet he knew the nurse Khenty-Nebet, breathing heavily behind them, had an opinion of his capabilities not much less fantastic than his daughter's.

"After today, people will call me Sobek-Sherit, instead of Sherit," the child continued.

"You will never get a husband with that name," he teased.

She appeared to consider this. "It will be a secret name, and you and Seti will call me that."

Wer-Seti was Sendjehuti's nephew and the reason for this expedition. A very bright boy with more persuasiveness than diligence, Wer-Seti had instigated a campaign to get pulled from his school so he could be tutored by his famous uncle. Finding the boy filled with more abstract curiosity than true commitment, Sendjehuti had brought his daughter into the lessons to spur Wer-Seti into making an effort. Now Sendjehuti suspected his nephew of pretending to be slow in order to prolong the agreeable companionship of his cousin.

"Hurry up Nebet!" Sherit squealed behind him. "We're going to be late for the crocodiles." Khenty-Nebet groaned.

Eventually they reached the mouth of the small cave. He was surprised to see a lamp burning, although no one appeared to be around. He had brought materials for starting a fire, but this would make things easier. Sendjehuti reached in the pouch around his waist for a vial of olive oil and a flax wick, which he placed in a second vessel.

"Do they leave these pretty lamps here for anyone to steal?" asked Sherit.

Sendjehuti chuckled. Several magicians in his coterie used this cave. Outsiders who knew about this place would sooner raid the Pharaoh's tomb than dare to trespass here. He lit the second lamp and examined the outer room, which fortunately was free of debris.

Khenty-Nebet had arrived and her breathing had returned to normal. "I will wait here while the two of you go inside," she said.

Sendjehuti said nothing for several seconds. "If that is your choice," he replied coldly. He would make sure to tell his wife of the nurse's dereliction of duty. The girl was safe with him, but still.

Khenty-Nebet appeared to deliberate over whether she was

more frightened of the crocodiles or of him. "I will stay here while you are inside," she repeated.

"Wait with Khenty-Nebet," he told Sherit, then made a more thorough inspection of the cave. In the second room a large animal scurried away in a furry blur. He had no idea what it was, and it escaped into a crevice too tight for him to squeeze through. He returned to the outer room and motioned for Sherit to follow him.

At the second entrance she hesitated. "Father, what if I don't say the words right?"

He looked back at her. "You know the words. You told me earlier, remember?"

"Yes, but what if I don't say them right? What if the crocodile says, 'You are only a small girl; I don't have to listen to you'?"

"Come in here and sit down," he said. The room was small, dominated by a pool of water the diameter of a large snake. Writing covered the walls and the girl examined the dedications with interest, even through her fear. She could read almost as well as Wer-Seti. This lesson had been planned for the boy's benefit, but he had begged off this morning with a stomachache.

"Nefert-Satendjehuti," he addressed her, using her real name. "You are growing up and growing older, and before long you will be grown. You will untie that braid and wear your hair like a woman and you will have a woman's duties. Eventually you will die. You will make that terrifying journey that no one escapes. At the gate to the world below the Great Ibis will be standing, and he will ask you to justify your bid for a second life.

"If you are allowed to pass there will be dangerous animals for you to confront: snakes, demon wildcats, and crocodiles. There is a snake down there so huge he has swallowed a donkey. There is a big-headed cat with putrid flesh dripping from her teeth and breath that will make your eyes water. There are menacing crocodiles, eight of them, surrounding you from every direction. They will flap their tails and try to capsize your boat, so they can tear your body in pieces.

"And what will you say? Will you say the words to make them slink away or will you say, 'I am just a small girl'? Will you command them to leave you alone or will you say, 'I don't know how to say the words'? The crocodiles will laugh at you. They will yell, 'Where is your braid, little girl?' They will yell, 'Let us say the words.' They will take your arms, your legs, your head, and your heart far underwater to dissolve into oblivion. Is that what you are waiting for? Is that what is going to happen to you?"

A chastened Nefert-Satendjehuti put her fingers on her eyes. "No, I will not let that happen to me."

Sendjehuti took a piece of dyed wax from his pouch and massaged it in his palm to make it pliable. He gave the beast he was molding a long fat tail and pronounced spines, not neglecting the teeth and claws. The eyes he made larger than a typical crocodile, but they rested on top of the head in a realistic fashion. He turned toward the pool and in the old language pronounced loudly:

Out of the waters of Nun, hear your name Bulging Blinker
Out of the waters of Nun, turn your head to my voice
Out of the waters of Nun, roll your body and recognize yourself
Out of the waters of Nun, come to this place now
You must obey me, because I created you
You must obey me, because I bestowed your name
You must obey me, because I call you now

He plunked the figure into the water. As the droplets splashed upward they erupted into an enormous creature, far larger than the pool. He had not anticipated making the crocodile this huge. The child emitted a high-pitched scream. The crocodile raised his head, opened his mouth, and let loose a long bellowing roar.

As the sound died away, he heard the thin, wavering voice of

Nefert-Satendjehuti:

Back in the waters of Nun, Bulging Blinker
Back in the waters of Nun, you cannot molest me
As she spoke her voice gained volume.
Back in the waters of Nun, return to your abyss
Back in the waters of Nun, I command you to go
Back to the waters of Nun, I thrust a spear to your head
Back to the waters of Nun, retreat from my attack
You must obey me, because I am the one who commands you
You must obey me, because that is the way of Maat
You must obey me, because Thoth has written it so

The crocodile sighed and disappeared. There was a soft plop like a drop of water. Nefert-Satendjehuti put her arms around her father tight.

He held her a long while. The girl had performed surprisingly well; he had been sure when he saw the crocodile's size that he would have to take over.

Eventually they heard a muffled sound outside the cave. Khenty-Nebet. "Go and tell her you're all right," he whispered. The child scampered off and he followed, more slowly. At the exit from the inner chamber he raised his lamp to make sure he hadn't left anything. From behind the dark crevice two eyes shone back at him.

Outside the nurse looked as though she had tussled with a crocodile herself. "Oh how great is the protection of the Two Ladies," she wailed. "I thought that child had been eaten alive."

"Nebet, I was fine the whole time," Sherit protested.

Sendjehuti did not speak but began trekking quickly back to the village, leaving the two scrambling to catch up with him. He heard Sherit tell her nurse, "Nebet when we come here next time you will *have* to go inside. There is beautiful writing all over the walls." He sighed with resignation. The girl had gotten a taste of power, and there was no possibility that the lessons were going to stop now, even if he succeeded in sending that lazy Wer-Seti back to school. He felt like he had been tricked into making his daughter his apprentice. He wondered if his nephew had masterminded the whole scenario, then wondered if he was giving the boy too much credit for guile.

He stopped and gave his daughter time to catch up. "Sherit, I think you know that you recited your spell today in an exemplary manner. Your speech was flawless. You did well."

The girl responded with a grin. "I was not certain of that until you said so."

He teased her gently. "I think you should make your mouth tell your heart how foolish you were, when you hesitated before the cave."

She was silent for several seconds, then decided to acknowledge his point. "My heart, you must always remember that you have the ability to overcome the evil crocodiles. They can never harm you now."

Crocodile Review

Magical Qualities: fierce, long-lived, ancient lineage back to dinosaurs, inhabits water and land, startles prey, maternal behavior (rare in reptiles), keen observer

Magical Applications: protection, fertility, healing (especially mental illness), wealth

Other Associations: weaving, water, sun, motherhood, negative judgment, insincerity, death, mummies

Noticing the Signs

A coyote on his daily stroll is reading a story about the recent past and assessing impending twists to the plot. He identifies other animals in his territory: friends, competitors, potential mates, interlopers, prey, possible threats, and others who cannot be classified but are duly noted. He is interested not only in who they are but also in what they have been doing. He makes good use of his senses: his sharp hearing, his incomparable sense of smell, his ability to recognize patterns. He is alert and curious. He takes notice of changes around him, treating his environment as if it held messages intricately tied to his self-interest.

Engaging with the natural world means letting go of the idea that the world can only be seen as a reflection of our own mindset. The world must contain fresh information if we are to recognize and interpret signs. Fresh information carries with it the possibility of a change in viewpoint; divination in nature is not for those who have no room for questioning their beliefs.

There are those who contend that personal belief is the essence of self. According to this view, if core beliefs are challenged, a person is erased. Yet on serious reflection most people can remember changing their mind about a deeply held belief and maintaining a sense of self. We are not our beliefs, not any of them. They are nothing but a basket of polished stones that we carry: big lies, little truths, pretty ideas, ugly opinions. Throw them back in the river and we exist as much after as before. Our identity is not predicated upon belief.

There are those who contend that anything outside individual conviction is unimportant, since we must view the world through a prism of personal experience and limitation. Pure objectivity cannot be achieved, assuming it even exists, so any opinion is equally valid. Reality becomes not something you perceive but something you choose.

The coyote who follows this belief system is not going to live long. Selecting an agreeable territory and defending that territory requires data, not conviction. The coyote has his own perspective, his own needs, his own experience—but he does not get to choose his own world. He can pick his own way through the forest, but the forest itself must be contended with.

In practice, people who subscribe to the idea that "everything is subjective" are highly selective in how they apply this idea.

They will insist that only personal self-concept is valid when asserting a position that, logically, cannot be defended *(I'm a coyote; respect my identity)*, but revert to collective agreement when it suits them *(I'm a coyote; therefore, I approach rules and regulations as a trickster and should not be expected to respect them)*. The cult of subjectivity is especially critical of the tools society has constructed in order to understand the world. Language and mathematics are "social constructs" and therefore things to be rejected, or better yet subjectively redefined.

If you are not willing to be disabused of at least some of your beliefs, individual and personal though they may be, there is no point in doing divination. In that case, it would be better to put this book down, get on the internet (where you can certainly find validation for "your truth"), and utilize your walks in nature as a backdrop for self-reflection. If you are going to engage in natural divination you will need to observe nature, and that means acknowledging that there is a something *to* observe.

It is not just members of the cult of subjectivity who impose their own template onto events. We all do this to some extent, and it may even be adaptive to a degree. For one thing, we have to filter information coming through our senses, because there's so darn much of it, and yet even before this filtering we don't necessarily have all the variables to the equation. This is why it was believed for so long that the sun revolved around the earth. The heliocentric theory was actually proposed in Classical Greece, but it did not fit with the available fund of information. With the invention of the telescope, new observations provided data that contradicted the idea of all the planets revolving around earth, and counterintuitive as heliocentrism might be, astronomers had to find a way to make it fit.

Even having all the data doesn't provide answers when an assumption is too tightly held. Physicists at the turn of the last century were grappling with a significant conflict between observation and belief and ascribed it, reasonably enough, to a limited fund of information. The problem involved the behavior of light, which seemed in increasingly sophisticated experiments to always be moving at the same speed. The speed of light. But that made no sense, because it meant starlight would always reach the earth at the same time, dependent only on distance, no matter how fast or in what direction the earth and star were moving. Physicists decided that light waves must be traveling through a medium, analogous to the way sound waves travel through the medium of air, and that the behavior of this unknown medium was producing unexpected results...in a consistent manner. Albert Einstein provided the way out of this dilemma, by positing that what was being observed was actually what was happening. The speed of light was absolute, and other factors in the equation were variable. Since speed is distance multiplied by time, time itself must be changeable.

And time doesn't even change in the way you would expect it to. You might think that time never moves so slowly as when you're sitting at a desk, but it's actually moving a teensy tiny bit faster there than when you're walking in the woods. Einstein's Theory of Relativity changed the way we think about time and challenged our subjective view by highlighting the limitations of our lived experience.

Inspired in a superficial way by Einstein's breakthrough, there is an enthusiasm at the moment for ideas that collapse boundaries and refute prior understandings, a rapture with the outré for its own sake. It might be linked in part to our position on the cusp of the Aquarian Age, a time when our survival requires profound changes in how we view the world. Regardless of the motivation, spinning outrageous theories without bothering to study, build on, and critique prior knowledge does not advance the occult sciences or even make good science fiction. A theory that has useful prediction makes sense of observation: it resolves conundrums and provides clarity even as it raises more questions.

The Theory of Relativity is rather conservative, in that it accepts a great deal of prior knowledge. It does not say, as disciples of the cult of subjectivity maintain, that everything is relative; it challenges assumptions about the inflexibility of time. Rather than supplanting all of the physics that came before, it requires attention to an additional variable in certain circumstances. I do not anticipate needing to account for the elasticity of time in any situation that I will run across in daily life, though people who work in high tech areas do have to take this into account. The theory reaffirms one of the basic tenets of physics and of alchemy: that there is not a unique set of laws governing earth. The Theory of Relativity holds here as it does everywhere else, even though we live at such a slow pace that we are usually unaware of this. In the words attributed to the alchemist Hermes Trismegistus, as translated by Isaac Newton: "That which is below is like that which is above and that which is above is like yet which is below..."[13]

Divination in nature is scientific in the sense that it is based on observation. We observe reality and use a framework to organize information. A theory is used to explain reality, while a framework is constructed to approach and understand a situation, making no claim to reality in and of itself. The taxonomies used by zoologists to classify animals into classes, orders, families, and species would be an example of a framework. I am trained as a psychotherapist, and in this field frameworks are used to solve problems such as insomnia or anxiety. The diagnostic manual (DSM-V) does not describe disorders that exist in themselves; it categorizes symptoms in such a way that professionals can address and study problems.

Tarot cards, tea leaves, cowrie shells, and runes are divinatory frameworks. The cards are nothing but cardboard pictures in themselves but they facilitate understanding of the real world. The framework in this book, which is looser than formal systems of divination, draws mainly on interactions with animals, since in this type of divination probabilities are an essential consideration. When you walk down your street, the maple that was on the corner yesterday is almost certain to be there today, and it tells you nothing new about your world. The Blue Jays in that tree screaming at you, however, do have something to say. In statistics we say that something that is certain to occur has a probability of one and something that could not possibly happen has a probability of zero. We will be concentrating on encounters with probabilities between zero and one, with probabilities closer to zero usually having more significance. (Probabilities of less than zero occur only in the dream realm.) You do not have to do any math here, by the way; your own approximation of an event's probability will be good enough.

In compiling data for divination, it is important to recognize what to look for. How many Blue Jays are in that tree? Were they in the tree when you first noticed them, or did you watch them fly into the tree, and what direction did they come from? Did they fly straight to the tree or circle it, and was the circle clockwise or counter-clockwise?

The place you are in time and space may be relevant. If there is a major event occurring in your life, such as a job possibility or an impending breakup, you will naturally tie the signs to that event, but there are more subtle situations to take into account. Are you in your own neighborhood or far from home? Visiting your parents? On a pilgrimage? In a town named Jay? In your tradition, do you give a name to the particular moon cycle you are in? Where are you in your own moon (menstrual) cycle? What sign of the zodiac is the sun in?

The meaning of a sign is usually a personal one. Though the sun may be the center of the solar system, there is no center to the universe that we know of, so we might as well place ourselves at this center. An exception would be when the signs are shown to a group that is closely bonded. In that case, the sign is meant for the group, even if not everyone saw the sign, and it should be interpreted from a shared perspective.

Cultural constructs are important when interpreting a sign. For example, the butterfly is a symbol of transformation and rebirth by virtue of its period of dormancy followed by its metamorphosis. For Christians, the butterfly is linked with the resurrection of Christ. Within lesbian culture, the butterfly is associated with the labrys, a symbol of lesbian power. Within gay male culture, the Spanish word for butterfly, *mariposa*, signifies a gay man, especially an effeminate gay man.

You may not have been aware of some of this butterfly information, even though it may be pertinent, which is why it is a good idea to discuss an omen with other people, especially if it strikes you as significant. The downside of this is that you may be tempted to disregard your intuition, which is why some teachers will emphasize the importance of *not* discussing this information with others. Also, you release the energy around an event if you talk about it too much. Occult secrets are used not just to withhold knowledge but also to contain energy. Yet an animal that comes into your orbit may be saying, "Learn more about me so I can be a teacher." Using a natural encounter as an impetus in your studies will increase your knowledge tremendously. It's okay at this stage to look outside your culture and to do research; in fact I recommend it. The only caveat is to consider the first two steps before going to animal sign compilations outside your frame of reference. Integrate outside information; don't apply it without reflection. It is unfair to your experience and your journey to give away your power in this way.

Don't be too quick to decide the meaning of a sign. Some portents will be immediate and unmistakable, but others will take time to digest, and in some cases the meanings will change over time. A sighting of extreme rarity may have information that reaches far into the future.

At the Trowe Ring

The following is based on legends of the Ring of Brodgar, a standing stone circle on Mainland in the Orkney Islands. I had to give the main character a name, so that's my invention. Otherwise I've reported the story straight.

Man Claims 70-Year Hijack By Trowes

A *Real True World News* Exclusive!

Orkney Islands, Scotland (RTWN) — An indigent Stenness man says he joined a group of trowes for a few hours' revelry and landed many decades in the future.

Figure 23: Salt Knowe from the Ring of Brodgar.
Photo: Paddy Patterson.

Irving Quholm showed up at the local constabulary on Sunday morning complaining there were strangers occupying his house who refused to vacate. The family in question was discovered to be lawfully inhabiting the lodging. Quholm, who was carrying a violin but had no identification, admitted he had been drinking the night before but insisted he knew who he was and where he was. He seemed unclear about time, however, identifying the year as alternately fifty or seventy years in the past.

Quholm, who spoke through an interpreter because he apparently only uses or understands an archaic form of Orcadian, says he had been attending a gathering with friends in a nearby town and was walking home past the Ring of Brodgar sometime after midnight, when he heard music and went to investigate. At the Salt Knowe barrow he found a small group of trowes dancing and playing instruments.

A trowe is alleged to be an ancestral spirit indigenous to the islands, analogous to a fairy or troll.

Quholm claims he danced and fiddled with the troop for a few hours at most, then continued home at daybreak to find his village much changed and all familiar people vanished.

Constable spokesman James Farrer said there were no plans to commit Quholm, as he has been evaluated by professionals and appears to be otherwise sane. Farrer added, "Still, anybody who would explore noises at a knowe after dark has to be off their head."

Questioning the Signs

1) If the fiddler experienced a two-hour interval of time while his village sped through seventy years, how fast were he and the trowes dancing?

2) If you were walking past a circle of standing stones at midnight, would you: a) Investigate the music coming from the enchanted place? b) Walk on and take the musical sounds as a sign? c) Try to convince yourself you didn't hear the music?

3) The "Curse of King Tut" has met with a lot of skepticism, but there often were curses on tombs directed at intruders. How would you interpret this line on the tomb of a fourth dynasty courtier named Meni? "Let the crocodile be against him in the water, the snake against him on land. I have never done anything against him and it is the god who will judge him for it."[14]

4) What would be the characteristics of a "gator mind"?

5) Direction can be important when interpreting a sign. How well-oriented are you to direction? Take compass readings of your residence and place of work.

6) The alligator has become prominent in advertising, usually wearing sunglasses and sipping a cocktail with a tiny umbrella. Next time you come across a picture of an alligator in a chaise lounge chair soaking up rays on the beach ask yourself if this could be a sign.

7) You are at a bus stop listening to music, when a bird lands close by and faces you, obviously squawking about something. You take out your earbuds and listen, but unfortunately you don't understand birdspeak. What might the little bird be saying in this context?

8) Take note over the next day or so of unexpected sightings of animals, either in corporeal or symbolic form. Notice the setting in which these encounters occur. Don't try to force a divinatory interpretation for now.

9) Your mother includes a new pair of Crocs in your birthday package, something you most definitely did not ask for. What wonderful powers might this gift herald?

Chapter 3

By the Numbers

Count Your Horses

Night rides before with the horse named Frosty-Mane, and on each morning he bedews the earth with the foam from his bit. The horse that Day has is called Sheen-Mane, and he illumines all the air and the earth from his mane.
—The Prose Edda[15]

Figure 24: Pre-domesticated horses were short and stocky, with a rounded belly. Photo: Chinneeb/Wikimedia Commons.

I started riding ponies before I started school, but I am not by any stretch of the imagination a horsewoman. The animals I rode growing up were the kind parents felt okay with children riding unsupervised. As an adult my riding experiences have been years apart, usually with a friend from the city who has ridden once or never and is thrilled at the idea of getting on a horse. It is these experiences with humoring friends that have taught me that every stable has in it one naughty horse, reserved for Hearth.

On the day I met my nemesis I had long ago learned to understate my experience, but my friend was eager to brag about me. As the stable owner left to grab "Apache" for me, I had a sinking premonition. I suspected a pony with that name was not going to embrace the White Man's rules.

The ride went pretty well at first. Apache was a spirited animal who wanted to break out on his own, but I managed to hold him back and enjoy the afternoon. When we returned to the barn and the owner disappeared for a moment, though, Apache decided to make an all-out bid for the upper hand. This involved dropping his head down, rearing on two legs, making dumb noises, and other tricks I'd never seen before.

Fortunately I'm a tricky lass myself, and I managed to regain control. The group watching was badly frightened and had no judgment of me, but I felt embarrassed by the episode. I made a vow (at the time of this writing, still unfulfilled) that I was going to take a few lessons.

Several years later I was chatting with a man who had horses and Apache's name came up. My friend gave me an earful about what a dangerous animal Apache was. Two people had landed in the hospital seriously injured, and no one would ride him anymore. I was sorry to hear that people had been hurt, but I did feel slightly better about my own interaction.

"A rose by any other name" and all that, but the name you give an animal partially determines the energy in your relationship. If you want a feisty horse, give her a feisty name. At the time of this writing the names Slowpoke, Goldbricker, and Naptime are all available on the Jockey Club Registry. Highly recommended. But most pagans will give their horse, or the horse they'd like to own someday, a name like Equirria, Macha's Prophecy, or Loki's Romance, all of which are ill-advised.

Figure 25: The fluidity of this Epona statue from France reflects a Roman influence. Photo: Siannan/Wikimedia Commons.

To jog your memory a bit: Equirria sounds like one of those Roman festivals everyone feels like they should remember but can't, and that's exactly what it is. It was celebrated in mid-March and dedicated to the god Mars. Horses were groomed and purified, and a sacrificial horse was offered to the goddess Vesta. Chariot races were a centerpiece of the program, although it is speculated that these were originally horseback races or exhibitions. Mars was the focus of these displays as the god of war. It was the use of horses in warfare, even more than bronze weapons, that shifted the balance of power in Old Europe and established patriarchy there.

The goddess Macha is considered an equine warrior deity. In general I disagree with the concept of warrior deities, because people who engage in warfare have characteristically taken their protective deity with them into battle, leading to conflation of that deity with warfare by those with an incomplete understanding of that culture. Even Mars, whose war associations are well documented, had a more benign beginning as a woodpecker and agricultural god. Still, even I admit that there is a historical rationale for considering horse goddesses like Macha "warrior goddesses," at least in part, as horses were an important part of Irish warfare. But warrior goddesses can also thwart battle plans. Those familiar with my previous book, *Invoking Animal Magic*, will recall that Macha cursed the Men of Ulster, decreeing that they would be incapacitated by phantom labor pains when they needed to fight.

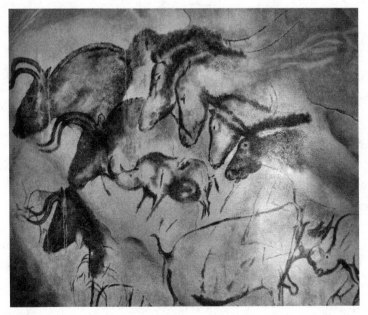

Figure 26: Replica of horses, bison, and rhinos from Chauvet Cave. The lowest horse has horns to signify that he is male. 30,000 BCE. Photo: Thomas T.

Another Celtic mare deity, Epona, developed a following throughout much of the Roman Empire during the conquest of Gaul. Though Epona's battle associations are unambiguous, even here it is important to recognize that she is usually depicted as an unarmed woman seated on or beside a horse, sometimes holding a sheaf of grain or a basket of apples. Often she is portrayed with a foal, underscoring not only her maternity but also her role as bringer of wealth, which was once measured in number of horses.

The feminine portrayal of Celtic horse deities in Iron Age iconography led to a curious school of cave art interpretation: the horse as a Paleolithic metaphor for woman. The next most frequent animal in southern European cave art, the bison, was correspondingly proposed as a metaphor for man. This explanation grew out of unsatisfactory attempts to fit cave art into men's hunting societies or scenarios that imposed an "art for art's sake" mentality onto prehistoric man. With more discoveries and deeper analysis, this horse = woman, bison = man conjecture fell apart. For one thing, many bison—as well as other animals with horns—appear to be female. Cave artists painted male and female animals, and it is difficult to sex the male without a female present. Females, on the other hand, can be shown pregnant or with young. Sex is usually not readily apparent; perhaps it was not quite the obsession for Paleolithic humans that it is under modern male domination. Archeologists no longer believe European cave art can be classified under one narrative, but the magic hunting theory has come back in vogue, with a twist: the magic may have been employed to increase the numbers of animals, not their capture. This fits with analysis of hand stencils in the caves suggesting a higher proportion of women artists. As givers of life, women would be better positioned to increase fertility of the herds.

Horses are represented in about 30 percent of European cave art, more than any other animal, despite being less commonly consumed than deer. Perhaps they were a preferred food item. It doesn't look like they were ridden during this era. Horses died out in Western Europe at the end of the last Ice Age, a combined casualty of changing weather patterns and overhunting. Not until the arrival of Indo-European conquerors would horses again become a part of the landscape. Utilized for trade, livestock management, agriculture, hunting, and warfare, the horse would then become too valuable to be eaten.

**Figure 27: Detail from North Cross with horses, riders, dog and bird.
Aheny, Ireland. Note the eight spokes on the chariot wheel.**

Indo-European tribes saw the horse as a vehicle for journeys to otherworldly realms. The horse moves like a sea wave, at times slow and at other times furious, which is why the Greek ocean god Poseidon rides in a chariot across water. In Irish legend, ocean horses come out of the water at night to graze or damage crops. The Germanic god Odin rides his magic horse Sleipnir into the underworld realm of Hel and across the sky as chief of the Wild Hunt. Sleipnir's conveyance of the god to the underworld illuminates the link between horses and mice. While horses transport humans on their backs, making them a logical means of travel between worlds, mice dominate the world below. The spirit of the old-time shamanic traveler would often emerge through the mouth in the form of a mouse to journey below. This is why in the fairytale Cinderella the godmother can transform six white mice into carriage horses. The horse is the alternate form of that subterranean denizen, the mouse.

Sleipnir is described as a gray or black horse who races swift as a cloud on a windy day. He can travel with inordinate speed because he has eight legs. This eight-legged attribute could be explained in these ways:

1. Sleipnir's divine parentage, from the god Loki and the giant stallion Svadifari, could only have produced an extraordinary horse, one that needed twice as many legs to travel twice as fast.

2. The stories of Odin's legendary steed were recorded on a rock carving for posterity, and the horse was pictured with extra legs to convey the impression of speed. Such depictions of running animals are occasionally found in rock art, the most famous being the Running Bison of Chauvet Cave. The eight legs in this earlier Sleipnir image may have been an artistic convention that moved into oral literature.

3. Odin's horse took over some functions of the spider, perhaps from cultures of Old Europe, and references to eight legs originated in this folklore.

4. The number eight refers to arcane numeric symbolism and philosophy, perhaps related to interlacing geometric images such as the double square or the octagon.

5. The eight-legged "steed" represents the legs of four men carrying a casket. This explanation appeals to the idea of the soul on its way to the underworld in a final journey. Dead bodies are heavy, and the funerals that I recall have had six or eight pallbearers, creating a steed of twelve or sixteen legs, but perhaps men *were* more hale and hearty in the days of yore.

6. The eight legs belonged to a large costume horse used for ceremonial purposes, like a hobby horse covering four people.

7. The hero Odin was a historical figure whose horse had an extra toe attached to each leg. Horses with this mutation were considered special, and both Alexander of Macedon and Julius Caesar had such mounts. An extra toe might have been useful for navigating the ice on the trail to Hel's land and might explain Sleipnir's name, which means slippery.

8. The divine horse as carrier of the sun is related to the eight-spoked sun wheel. The traditional Norse sun wheel has four spokes rather than eight, corresponding to the solstices and equinoxes, but many witches today use an eight-spoked wheel combining the Celtic and Germanic (and pre-Celtic) quarterly reference points.

Figure 28: 'Neptune's Horses,' by Walter Crane, 1892.

It may seem like a contradiction for the horse to be associated with both the sun, bringer of light, and the underworld, a place of darkness. It was once a common belief, however, that the sun traveled through the underworld at night in a journey parallel to her trek across the sky. An alternative belief was that the sun traveled through the water, which brings us back to the idea of the horse as a water traveler. The salient point seems to be that the horse is comfortable in many worlds, which is why the horse is a friend of the priestess, the shaman, and the adventurer.

As the sun horse travels around the world, the domestic horse has traveled through both the Eastern and the Western hemispheres. Ancestors to the modern horse originated in North America, and members of the species moved between the continents across the Bering Strait during the Ice Age. It was once believed that the horse died out in North America before the arrival of the first Americans. Today we know that human habitation of the continent began much earlier, possibly as early as 30,000 years ago, and it looks like horses died out in North America for the same reason they disappeared in Western Europe: climactic changes at the end of the Ice Age stressed the population, which was subsequently overhunted. Some theorize that the horse would have become extinct altogether at this point if she had not already been domesticated in Central Asia.

Figure 29: Tjangvide Picture Stone showing Odin riding Seipnir. Pre-Christian. Gotland, Sweden. Photo: Berig/Wikimedia Commons.

The return of horses on Spanish ships changed life in the Americas immediately and irrevocably, so much so that some tribes divide their history into before and after the horse. Hunting big game became easier and less dangerous, and some tribes gave up farming and followed the buffalo. Trade became possible over longer distances. Wealth began to be measured, at least on the Plains, in number of horses.

The arrival of the horse also shifted the balance of power among tribes. Raiding became easier and more lucrative, and tensions flared between the settled agricultural tribes such as the Pueblos and Tohono O'odham and semi-nomadic tribes such as the Comanche and Apache. As the Spanish missions were established, labor and resources became diverted to support the churches, leaving settled Southwestern tribes with less surplus for barter and exacerbating the need of hunter-gatherers to raid for survival. Mexican settlements, with their wheat, horses, and manufactured goods, were a particularly tempting target. The American conquest of northern Mexican territories in the mid-nineteenth century met with less resistance than might be expected, because many Mexicans and Indians believed the American government would solve the problem of raiding.

And solve the problem they did, with forced relocation, internment, and even massacre. The government understood the role horses played in Indian power, and confiscated or destroyed the horses of conquered tribes. Fleet Appaloosas, the jewel of the American West, were no longer allowed to be owned by the people who had bred them. The horse had again shifted the balance of power, to the benefit of the large, well-equipped American Cavalry.

Horses remain a source of conflict in the American West, though the battle today is less bloody, if no less intense. At issue is whether mustang herds should be drastically reduced or elimi-

Figure 30: First century Gaulic coin of a horse with the sun. Photo: cgb numismatic.

nated altogether. Feral horses and donkeys undoubtedly have an effect on plant composition, yet many wonder if a population that was probably wiped out by humans to begin with can be called an "invasive species." The American public, while viewing the wild horse as an indelible part of national identity, tends to be unresponsive to the challenges of land management officials in managing herds. Ranchers, who have the clearest economic stake in the issue, are the loudest voices decrying the erosive impact of mustangs, yet this politically well-connected group has undercut their credibility by their lack of concern about the ecological impacts of cattle grazing. Complicated cultural issues make it difficult for objective facts to emerge, due to shifting alliances between major players—government officials, ranchers, scientists, traditional Indians, animal rights activists, and libertarians—all of whom have a history of mutual distrust. Will the horse forever be at the heart of human conflict?

We have a unique opportunity when evaluating the meaning of the horse within divinatory systems, because this animal was wiped out in two places and then reintroduced. Both times the

Figure 31: Greek horse god Pegasus. Bronze handle, sixth century BCE. Photo: Mari-Lan Nguyen/Wikimedia Commons.

horse brought radical change. Intense warfare was the most pronounced change, but there were others, including enhanced trade, social alliances, and cultural exchange.

The prominence of horses in the cave paintings of southern France and Spain indicate that this animal was highly valued even before domestication. After domestication, the number and quality of horses became an indicator of wealth. Even today, when the horse is rarely used for physical labor in developed countries, horseback riding is more commonly a part of childhood for those in the privileged classes, and some highly moneyed subcultures revolve around equine competitions.

Feral horses, like feral cats, have helped us better understand their pampered cousins. Mustangs are descendants of domesticated horses, however untamed, and by studying feral herd behavior much has been learned about equine instincts and proclivities. Again like the cat, the question has been raised whether we can talk about domestication of the horse on a timeline or whether this animal has simply moved back and forth between captive and wild state many times. It would explain why the ability to survive in the wild has not been bred out of this animal. Regardless of how this came about, the horse is an animal of extreme adaptability, able to move in many worlds.

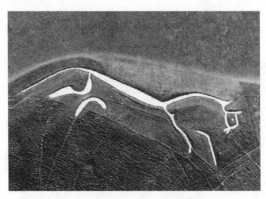

Figure 32: Horse image in white chalk. Uffington, UK, 800 BCE.
Photo: NASA.

More than anything else, the horse is about power. We even talk about the power of an engine in terms of numbers of horses: horsepower. The power of the horse has manifested often in war, conflict, and competition, but this power has also been harnessed for benign purposes like trade or adventure. How you interpret the sign of the horse depends on context.

The Fairy Seminary

This story was adapted from "The Boy Who Served the Fairies," in Lewis Spence's Legends and Romances of Brittany.[16]

Poulain groaned, moaned, sighed, whimpered, and ran his fingers through his mane. The lone candle threw dark shadows across his dank cell and he reminded himself that he was "here on scholarship." Troll taxes and devil paste, he wished he was back at home. He thumbed backwards through his exercise book, trying to draw courage from challenges already met.

Here was a memorable one:

Chop all the trees in a 33 *dragon-pieds* radius and stack in neat cords using a lead ax, a paper saw, and an oak-leaf wheelbarrow.

He had borrowed Blanche's wand for that one, and even she had enlisted her friends Violette and Cinderella to assist them in getting the forest back in shape. *Monsieur le Sorcier* had reviewed his work and reluctantly given him a satisfactory mark, implying he suspected Poulain of getting help. If he only knew.

Here was another good one:

Using this glass mattock and clay shovel, plant a garden with flowering pear trees, swans, and a lily pond.

He had cried when his tools broke, and Blanche had laughed, but she had loaned him her wand again.

He had met Blanche the first day of the semester, as he was trudging up the hill to the pretentious sounding *Le Feie Seminaire*. She and her friends were sneaking out to go bathing in the river, and they warned him that the food contained goblin livers and dragon toenails. Blanche was dressed in white gauzy material, Violette wore clothing in the indigo spectrum, and Cinderella seemed to prefer gray (or "ash tones" as she snottily corrected him). He guessed these two were also relying on Blanche's skill, but he couldn't expect to keep a girl like Blanche to himself.

This exercise had nearly cost him his friendship with the white maiden:

Climb the tower of polished marble, catch the turtle dove that roosts under the eaves, and bring her down safely.

Monsieur had sent Blanche into the village on some errand that day, thinking to foil any attempt on her part to aid him, but Violette had gone instead, disguising herself in Blanche's filmy chiffon. This particular task could not be accomplished with only a wand, so Blanche had told him to drag a huge cauldron over to the tower, cut her into pieces, and toss her into it. Poulain had argued with her a long time, but she insisted that as long as he collected every part of her she would be safe. As he spoke the magic words over the girl in the cauldron he felt himself flying to the top of the tower. All he had to do was subdue the turtle dove. Thunder spit and demon's eyebrows, but that dove had been hard to catch! Finally he buttoned her in his pocket and brought her down. When he touched Blanche's wand to the side of the cauldron she jumped back out, and then the real trouble started. He had missed throwing part of her left little toe in the pot, and she was not pleased. Eventually she had forgiven him, and that missing toe had proved invaluable (to him anyway) when he had to pick a magical sciences laboratory partner from behind a curtain. The professor had erroneously given him a high mark for psychic ability, proving the Monsieur himself was not as psychic as he thought.

Now here was tonight's assignment:

Go to sleep on a bed suspended over a dungeon a hundred thousand *dragon-pieds* deep. After the ropes are cut use pillows to soften your fall. Find a way back to the surface by knotting the bedsheets.

Monster burps and gremlin vacillations! He cautiously poked his head outside his door and then slid down the hallway, tapping at Blanche's room.

"If you can get me out of a dungeon at the bottom of the earth, you can get me out of this school," he whispered.

"Go to the stable and get the horse they call Little Wind," she whispered back. "Ride him under my window and I'll jump down."

As they were riding away they heard the Monsieur yelling in the background.

"Centipede hexes and millinery millipedes!" Blanche exclaimed.

"We do swear a lot at *Le Feie*," he observed.

"Poulain, you still don't understand what you did, do you?"

"What are you talking about?"

"You took the horse called Great Wind, not Little Wind."

"Is that going to be a problem?"

She said nothing and in a moment they were surrounded on all sides by flames. They were riding through fire. Suddenly the landscape changed and the horse became a garden, Blanche became a pear tree, and he was dressed in gardener's clothes. The headmaster and his wife ran into the garden.

"Did a boy and a girl on a large horse ride through here? The girl was wearing white and the horse—"

"For three pears I will take a peacock," said the gardener.

"That's not what I said. I asked if—"

"Okay, two pears for a turtle dove, but I will not go lower than that."

Madame tugged at the sleeve of Monsieur and they continued on. Blanche turned them back into girl, boy, and horse, and they soon passed the couple. Poulain wondered if all this time he had been matching wits with Madame and not the male sorcerer. That would explain a lot of things.

As Great Wind whistled faster and faster, they were again enveloped in flames. Blanche struck her wand three times and the horse changed into a church, the girl changed into the altar, and Poulain found himself in priest's robes. The headmaster and mistress were not far behind.

"Did a boy and a girl on a large horse ride past?" said the master. "The girl was wearing white and the horse—"

"*Dominus vobiscum,*" intoned the priest, making the sign of the cross.

"No! You don't understand—"

"*Pater, ignosce illis, non enim sciunt quod faciunt.*"

Madame interjected, "Come, we will get nowhere with this imbecile."

"*Amen,*" said the priest.

Soon Blanche and Poulain were riding past the couple and into the flames. Blanche tapped her wand three times and said, "I change this horse into a river, myself into a boat, and this boy into a ferryman." They waited at the dock until the headmaster and his wife appeared.

"Did a boy and a girl on a large horse ride past? The girl was wearing—"

"Do you have the fare?" the ferryman asked.

"No, I was just asking—"

"You do not have the fare?"

"Yes, but what I want to know—"

"If you have the fare, give it to me please."

Madame produced two coins. "We will travel by boat to find them," she told her husband. "I sense they are close by."

They now had the couple in a vulnerable position, and as the ferry headed downstream Poulain clenched the ropes tightly. Sure enough, as they reached the center of the river the boat rocked unexpectedly, though it was a calm day. *Les Professeurs Sorciers* were swept overboard and disappeared into the current.

The ferry guided itself back to the bank. Blanche changed back into herself, she changed Poulain to himself, and she changed—

Poulain grabbed her arm. "Wait. Let them get a very long way away first."

Blanche giggled wickedly. The two of them held hands as they traipsed back to the castle. This might not be such a bad term, after all.

The Blessing

This diary is adapted from the popular Russian folktale "Vassilissa the Beautiful."

She gives me too much work to do, but I don't care. She makes me tend the gardens, carry water, feed the stove. She has two daughters who are as ugly as she is, pinched thin from spite though they eat more than I. When she yells at me and beats me I can't help but think of my lovely real mother, and this comforts me.

I have something else that soothes me, a blessing my mother gave me when she died. She said to me, "Vassilissa, this is your blessing." It's a doll, a small one I can fit in my pocket. I only take it out when I am alone because that woman, that seducer of my father, must never know of my blessing. She has said I cannot marry until the other two, the not-my-sisters, have wed. No chance of that ever happening, I will always live in this house.

My father has gone away and we have moved to another house. Now it is even further to the stream for water, but what do they care? They make me do all the work. They don't know this, but I don't do the work either. I give my Dolly a choice morsel from my supper—or as choice as that miser will allow me—and she does all the work. My Dolly talks to me and says things to comfort me in this awful place. Still, I am afraid to go in those woods. They say Baba Yaga lives there in a hut made of dead men. She catches people and eats them like they were chickens.

We have to work at night now, as well as in the day. That cruel woman says we must. After she goes to bed tonight not-my-sisters and I are to finish our textile work or risk her displeasure. The stingy grouch will only allow us one candle. I have learned more about Baba Yaga. She flies above the trees in a grinding mortar and she uses the pestle to steer. I am afraid I will meet her in the woods while I do my chores but my Dolly tells me how to avoid her.

So much has happened! I have never been so terrified, and none of this is my fault. I would think I was pursuing my own death if my Dolly did not reassure me constantly. I am going to Baba Yaga's hut. I am trying to find her! I stumbled through the forest the whole night with Dolly directing me. As the hours passed my legs began to tremble so much I could hardly continue, and I was almost ready to cry, when I became distracted by the oddest sight. A white horseman galloped past me. He was dressed in bleached linen and his hair was the lightest blond and his horse was as pale as his face. As he passed me the sky lightened and it was daybreak. I sat down to reflect on this and saw from the same direction another horseman approaching. His was a bay horse, and he had ginger hair and his face was ruddy and he wore a red cape. When he galloped past the sun was on my face. I have rested now and my Dolly says we must continue, for we still have far to go. We will travel in the direction of the two horsemen.

I am in Baba Yaga's hut now. Yes, I am here! And I am still alive, at least for the time being. Baba Yaga says she will eat me tomorrow. She is a hideous old crone. Her bulbous nose curls downward and almost meets her jutting chin, and she has prickly hairs popping out of her face. She has a thick frame and waddles when she walks, but her legs are thin and bony underneath her short dress. Right now she is snoring, because it is night and I have served her a huge dinner. She barely left me anything to eat, and I fed most of it to my doll, but I have no appetite anyway. There is death all around this house. I mean literally, death encloses everything. The fencing is made of bones and a human skull hangs on every pike. The doorposts are made of human legs and the lock is a mouth with teeth. Disembodied hands bolt the door. The eyes in the skulls gleam into the night making it so bright that I wonder how Baba Yaga can sleep. For myself, I have traveled so long and so far that I think I could slumber through my own execution.

When I awoke today it was not yet light, and the eyes in the skulls were fading. Baba Yaga was rustling around doing her evil witch crone thing, when the white horseman flashed by the window and daylight arrived. She ran whistling outside, and her mortar, pestle, and broom materialized. She uses the broom to sweep away her sky tracks, and it raises an awful wind. While she is gone I am to clean the hut, sweep the yard, wash the linen, prepare the dinner, and separate a bushel of wheat kernels from chaff. Otherwise Baba Yaga will cook me when she returns. I don't think even my Dolly can complete this much work. I don't know where to start.

My Dolly insists that she can do most of the work and that I am to rest. If she can perform this miracle I will have at least another day's respite and may complete my account of this journey. Yesterday I arrived at the glade where the hut stands—and I do mean stands, because it has chicken legs and walks around the tiny yard—and I stood for a while in the fading light, unable to muster the courage to go inside. Suddenly a horseman appeared from the direction I had come. He wore dusky clothes and cap, his face and hands were dark, and his mount was coal black. He rode swiftly by me, like the others taking no heed of my presence, and as he passed the day became night. Though it was too dark to see, I had a sense of him disappearing into Baba Yaga's hut, without opening the door. I did not stand long in the shadows, because the eyes in the skulls slowly began to glow, growing brighter and brighter until the glade was as light as day. Then she came.

I awoke from my nap a few hours ago and discovered that Dolly had finished most of the work. I have now prepared the supper and I am anxiously anticipating the return of Baba Yaga. When she arrived last evening in the black horse's wake, the trees crackled and the leaves swirled from the motion of her broom. She stopped at the gate and twitched her nose exclaiming, "Fie, fie, I smell the Russian smell." I was almost petrified from fear, but I bowed respectfully and told her that my stepsisters had sent me for light. It did not seem like the time for long explanations. She told me she knew my stepsisters, but she did not seem to hold this against me as she told me she would give me light to take back if I lived here for a time and worked for her. She told me if I did not accept this arrangement, she would make me into her supper.

The black horse has come again, and now it is night. Baba Yaga is highly displeased. She had expected me to fail at my tasks and is annoyed that she could not find fault in any of the work. She accepted the wheat, however, then did a strange thing. She called for her "faithful servants" to grind the wheat for her, and there was no one in the room but she and I and my hidden doll. Yet three pairs of disembodied hands appeared out of nowhere, ground the wheat, and put it away. She obviously has no need of me and is only keeping me around for amusement until she boils my unhappy skin. Tomorrow I am to wipe the dust off a bin of poppy seeds. Each seed must shine, Baba Yaga says. Dolly will help me of course, yet I wonder how long this will continue, with Baba Yaga dreaming up impossible chores for me and throwing tantrums when her orders are fulfilled.

Baba Yaga has left the premises, in the wake of the red horse. As I mentioned before, I gave her the short version of why I showed up at her ghoulish fence. It seems my diabolical maternal imposter instructed my eldest non-sister to tamp out that single candle while we were plying our textile skills at that wholly inappropriate time. I should have guessed some craftiness was afoot. She said, "Oh, I accidentally snuffed the candle. But I guess it doesn't matter. The reflection of my knitting needles will give me light." My other non-sister chimed in that the light from her pins was sufficient for tatting, but that I would be unable to complete my spinning without light. The two then ordered me, as my older supposed-sisters, to go to Baba Yaga and get a light from her. The whole thing was ridiculous, and I had no intention of playing along, but rather than intervening for me my doll said that I should take off for Baba Yaga's and trust that things would work out. So far she has been right, but I fear that with too many more days of Baba Yaga's predictable displeasure I will not mind joining the skulls on the picket fence.

Baba Yaga is really the most amazing mistress. I could not have predicted how the last evening went. I am free again, on my way back to my former prison with the requisitioned light. I did not steal this light from Baba Yaga. She gave it to me. She did not berate me for accomplishing the task she had set for me. She followed the black horse home, and when she saw that the poppy seeds shone, she only called for her "faithful servants," those three pairs of hands, to grind the oil out of the seeds. She ate her dinner in silence. At last she told me to stop being silent and say something. I asked permission to ask a question. "You should not ask too many questions," she replied. "Questions make you grow too old too soon." Then she told me to proceed with my question.

The white horse has come and gone, and the red horse will soon be on his heels. The light in the skull I carry is fading, and I am not nearly home. The question I asked Baba Yaga involved these horsemen. Who are they? Baba Yaga said the white horseman is her "bright day," the red her "red sun," and the black her "dark night." She volunteered that these three are her "faithful servants." I thought about the three pairs of hands who do her bidding, whom she also refers to in those words. She prodded me to ask other questions, but I declined. They say that Baba Yaga does not like to answer questions, that she ages a year for every question she answers, and that is why she is so wrinkled. Baba Yaga approved of my reticence. She said she prefers to answer questions about what happens outside of her house, and that queries regarding what goes on inside the hut annoy her. She reminded me that those who annoy her get eaten.

Now the black horse has passed me, on his way to his wizened mistress no doubt, and night has fallen. I can write this because the eyes of the skull, which I carry on a stick, have begun to glow again. I will press on through the night, because I am anxious to leave Baba Yaga's forest. She is very angry with me. Last evening, after she had answered my question, she told me that it was now her turn to ask something of me. In a quiet voice she wondered how I had fulfilled her tasks with the wheat and the poppy seeds. She was calm and conversant, almost gentle, and I forgot how changeable she is as she lulled me into a confidence. I began telling her how my mother at her death had given me this blessing—but Baba Yaga cut me off here. "Blessing?!" she screeched. "How can you stay here with a blessing? Blessings do not belong in this house!" She pushed me out of the hut before I even had time to panic, grabbing a skull from her fence and thrusting it into my hands. "Here is the light you came for," she yelled. "Take it!" I did not have to be told twice. I ran away quickly.

Now I am at the edge of the forest, and I can see my stepmother's house in the distance. By the waxing moonlight I could find my way to her door without the glowing skull, but the skull has told me not to discard it just yet. Yes, this skull talks, and I have chosen not to argue with it. I can't believe the sisters still need a light. I don't believe they ever needed a light. They just wanted to imagine a gruesome death for me. I have always been so afraid of these woods, and in the anxious days of my journey I have prayed for nothing but deliverance, but now that I am back I dread continuing my dreary life. They will greet me with sneers and belittlement while berating me for taking their demand for light from Baba Yaga literally. The house is dark and quiet now, so perhaps I can sneak inside and postpone dealing with their surprise and disappointment until tomorrow. How will I survive this life I struggled to save?

My stepmother and stepsisters were not asleep, and they greeted me with oily smiles and endearments. I was suspicious. Could their feelings for me have changed so markedly in just a few days? There had been no light, they told me, since the evening I had left, and they could not even start a fire from a neighbor's embers. They were grateful I had brought a torch, and I quickly brought the skull into the house. The glowing eyes mesmerized them, until their cheeks burned and they tried to move away. The flame followed them everywhere, however. They could not get away from it. They screeched in pain and screamed for mercy from the light they had sent me for. In the morning my stepmother and stepsisters were three piles of cold cinders.

I keep remembering Baba Yaga's words, "Blessings do not belong in this house." I locked the door to my stepmother's house and buried the skull, then I walked in the direction opposite the dark woods. I am headed I know not where, me and my little doll.

I have met the kindest old woman. I came upon her hut as the day was waning and I was growing hungry. I begged a cup of water and she insisted that I eat, then asked why I was wandering so bedraggled and alone. I explained that I was not alone, that I carried my mother's blessing, and that I was searching for a place where this blessing belongs while I await my father's return. She was not put off by my cryptic reply. She says I can stay with her as long as I like, and she caters to me instead of making me earn my keep. She has no children and I believe she is lonely.

I cannot believe I am writing this, but I have grown tired of laziness. I have had such an abundance of hard work since my mother died that I thought idleness would be the greatest blessing, but I have discovered it does not suit me. I asked my agreeable benefactress to buy me some flax so I may take up spinning again. When the cloth is woven I will give it to her so she will have something in return for her kindness toward me.

My sweet godmother brought me some good flax, and I have woven a quantity of it in strong filaments that are as thin as a strand of my hair. Now my problem is finding a comb that is fine enough for these threads. We have tried several without success. I am pleased to discover that my Dolly is willing to come to my rescue in good fortune as well as bad. She tells me to bring her any old comb and shuttle, along with hair from a horse's mane, and she will make me a decent loom.

I have presented the woven linen to my godmother. It is the finest work I have ever done, so sheer it can be threaded through a needle. She was taken aback and insisted that she had not expected payment for her hospitality, and that she did not have use for cloth of such high quality. "Take the linen and sell it then," I said, "and use the money to buy something you need." She told me only the czar can afford merchandise as special as this, so she is off to the palace.

My godmother has returned laden with luxuries and with a story to tell. She shrewdly refused to show the cloth to anyone but the czar himself, and when she finally received an audience he was so impressed that he asked her to name her price. The czar was impressed with my work! The old lady told him the cloth was priceless and she could only bestow it as a gift. Of course he could not accept something so elaborate from one so poor without remuneration, and he was more generous than she expected. Really, I am more impressed with her cleverness than with the presents of the czar, which are beautiful indeed.

My godmother has been to the palace again and back. She is becoming quite the traveler in that rarefied place. The czar summoned her because the cloth has been cut for shirts, but he can find no one to sew them. None of his tailors know how to work with such fine material. I can't say I'm surprised. No one could ever work with the products of my loom besides me, and this is the most delicate fabric I have woven. The czar insisted that the old woman must sew his shirts herself, and when she confessed that she was neither the spinster nor the weaver he ordered her to return home with the linen so that I can stitch his shirts. My godmother and I are giddy, expecting that another large gift will be forthcoming.

My father has returned. I was afraid he would not know where to find me, since I have moved so many times, but news of my wedding has traveled far. I have married the man for whom I sewed the dozen fine shirts. He sent for me as soon as he saw them. I had already combed my hair and put on my best clothes, expecting that he would insist on thanking me at the palace. The czar told me he had never seen shirts of such high quality, and he believed I was the finest seamstress in the kingdom. He then asked me to be his wife. The old woman who has been so kind to me has come to live with us, and now my father is here too. I have not forgotten that I have my little doll, my mother's blessing, to thank for all my good fortune. I carry her in my pocket and will cherish her the rest of my life.

Horse Review

Magical Qualities: swift, strong, follows herd instinct, tolerates harness, highly sensitive to environment, unique personality, adaptable

Magical Applications: power (particularly related to control and conflict), money spells, enhancing psychic ability, spiritual journeys, weather control, safety in travel

Other Associations: motherhood, wealth, commerce, labor, agriculture, war, ocean, flying, wind

Counting to Three

When I was beginning my study of the occult I was taught to avoid even numbers in favor of the odd. Odd numbers allow for continuity, I was told.

In ceremonies of some Native American tribes I observed that leaders tended to avoid odd numbers and favored the numbers four, six, and twelve. Even numbers provide stability, I was told.

When I began studying feminist witchcraft I was told the

Abrahamic religions (Judaism, Christianity, Islam) were patriarchal because they were dualistic, and therefore inevitably fell into harmful dichotomies of good/evil, heaven/hell, enlightenment/ignorance, etc.

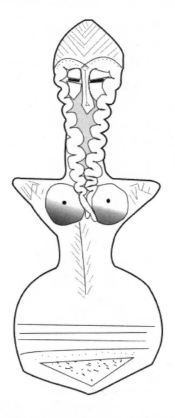

Figure 33: Triangles are prominent in Neolithic art. Anatolia, 2000 BCE.

While exploring Taoist spirituality I learned that the number two was complementary, simultaneously creating the paradoxical qualities of tension and balance, thereby leading to wisdom.

When I looked into Vedic philosophy the number two was out (dualism again) and the number three was exalted because it described the infinity inherent in the cycles of creation, sustenance, and destruction.

Numeric philosophy differs according to ethnicity, and there are obvious pitfalls in naively mixing and matching symbology without respecting the underlying structures. At the same time, what strikes me about the above scenarios is that they do reflect a *common understanding about the nature of numbers,* with the differences more reflective of cultural values than with disagreements about the basic qualities of numbers themselves. This is to be expected, since numbers themselves are real things, not cultural constructs, even if the language of mathematics is constructed. A dozen eggs is a dozen eggs, anywhere in the universe. Stating a preference for odd numbers as agents of "continuity" is professing a value for progress over tradition. Using odd versus even numbers in your shamanic practice depends on whether you view your work as promoting change or maintaining balance.

Western magical traditions are built on number systems with European, Semitic, Sumerian, and Egyptian origins. Semitic cultures revere the number two, European the number three, Egyptian the number four, and Sumerian the number seven, although these systems do not revolve around a single number. If you're thinking this could get complicated, you're right, but we will concentrate on basic qualities of the numbers themselves and avoid getting unduly bogged down in cultural contradictions.

One

This is the number for the all-that-is: Creator, Goddess, or Great Mother. The wholeness of the number one is exemplified in the circle, which has no angles or sides; no beginning or end. The fundamental reality of the number one is easy to grasp intellectually, even if it is harder to understand experientially. This number must be feminine, since it contains everything and gives birth to all other numbers by division of itself. In other words, one is the parthenogenetic number. The majority of numeric systems seem to divide numbers into masculine and feminine, a practice I disagree with, but with the first number the feminine is inescapable. The number one will usually not be relevant in a predictive sense, unless you run across an individual animal that is usually paired or grouped. Then you must ask yourself, why only one?

Two

This is a highly unique number, because it is the only positive whole number that does not exist in the scope of totality. When one splits itself into two parts there are now two entities individually, plus the entities as a whole, making three. This is synthesis, in Taoist terms the resolution of Yin and Yang. Two is the polarity that as a whole becomes a unified field. Two is the number of the couple, yet in marital counseling the therapist views the relationship as an important third element rather than conceptualizing the couple as two individuals. Despite what I said earlier about even numbers being more stable, two is a highly unstable number. Think of a teeter totter or a pendulum: this number seeks balance but is easily pushed into disequilibrium. Two is the number of the twins, who seek both association and individuation. Stories of divine twins abound in mythology around the world. So do stories of divine couples. Before monotheism won out, the Hebrew ruling divinity was a mother-father pair, El and Asherah. The concept of masculine and feminine divinity reasserted itself later in Jewish mysticism with the Kabbalah. Another common pairing in Western mythology is mother-child (Frigga and Baldur; Demeter and Persephone) and same-sex friends (Gilgamesh and Enkidu; Athena and Pallas). With the number two, think attraction, repulsion, resolution, individuation, sameness, opposites, and a lot of contradictory concepts that are hard to wrap your mind around. I said it was an unstable number. It is also the only even prime number; more on the instability of prime numbers in the next chapter.

Although some numbers, such as one, three, and nine, will have strong Goddess associations, I caution against automatically applying a masculine/feminine dichotomy to numbers. The number one as the totality of everything must be female, or there could be no birth; otherwise, there is no fundamental reason for sexing a number.

Three

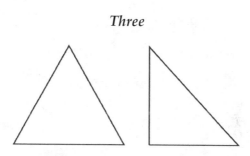

Figure 34: Equilateral triangle (left) and right triangle (right).

Now we get to the critical number for those of European heritage, possible proof that pagan programming endures underneath all that Christianization. Ask a Jehovah's Witness for their thoughts on the word "trinity" and you're bound to get an earful. The Father/Son/Holy-Ghost triad ("God in Three Persons; Blessed Trinity," as we sang in church when I was growing up) has no scriptural basis and was introduced because Europeans simply could not stop thinking in threes. "Why do we always give *three* referrals," a social work colleague of mine mused aloud one day. "Why don't we give two or four or five?" The answer is, because of the three blind mice, and the three little pigs, and the third time's the charm. There, I just gave three answers to a question with three parts; try to stop thinking and talking in threes for three days and you'll understand how pervasive this thought pattern is.

The most basic shape, the triangle, has three sides and three angles. You can draw a line between two angles on any polygon with more than three sides to form a triangle inside that shape, but you cannot reduce a triangle. Understanding the mathematical relationships between the sides of right triangles (the Pythagorean Theorem, $a^2 + b^2 = c^2$) enabled engineers of the earliest temples to build on triangular units.

Figure 35: The Romano-Celtic Matronae (seated) are usually but not always depicted as three women. The convention is for one of the figures to be smaller or without a headdress to signify that she is the youngest. Germany, second century. Photo: Brigid Piron/Wikimedia Commons.

Depending on how it is manipulated, a triangle can focus, amplify, disperse, and balance energy. Creative power is exemplified by a woman's pubic triangle, and the nine legs of pregnancy, divided in three parts, describe the journey from conception to birth. During the first trimester pregnancy is confirmed, and while the nausea most common in these months has a physiological basis, there is the psychological element of having committed oneself, of having, in Sylvia Plath's words, "Boarded the train there's no getting off."[17] The second trimester is a time of planning. The baby begins to show and move, making itself less abstract and more real in the minds of expectant adults. The last trimester is an edgy time. While miscarriage is more common in the earliest months, risks to the mother between this point and birth become greater. New mothers, weary of the physical discomforts of pregnancy, become anxious to see and hold their baby, while experienced mothers, who know how much work is involved in caring for an infant, are content to let the baby hang out in the womb a bit longer.

The association of three with fertility and birth explains why there are so many triple goddesses. Iron Age images of the three Celtic mother goddesses, known to us by their Roman name, the Matronae, were once common in Western Europe, and these goddesses are considered both a triple and a single unit, like a triangle with three angles.

Another triple goddess is Hecate, originally (in my opinion) a goddess of the waterways, incarnate in the water-loving willow tree. Later she became goddess of the three-formed crossroad. Streams tend to converge in a Y and organic paths, as opposed to planned roadways, also tend to fork in a Y. Hecate is sometimes drawn with three faces or sides, but she is usually considered a single figure with three aspects. In life there are three roads and three roads only:

Figure 36: Relief of Hecate as a triple goddess. Photo: Zdenek Kratochvil/ Wikimedia Commons.

the road you take, the road you don't take, and the road you leave behind. The future is the juncture that greets us at every step.

Winning Numbers

Promethean Classifieds

Olympic Sale!

One 3-legged stool; 1 apple (inscribed with gold, cannot be divided); 4 pomegranate seeds; 2 fine tapestries, depicting godly scenes mighty and ignoble; 13 lady armor suits, size large; 3,000 cattle, very clean; 36 hunting dogs (dangerous); 100 peacock feathers; 3 matching spindles (slightly squeaky); 1 finely crafted gold box (small but holds many things).

Ereshkigal's Eternal Restock

"You can take it with you, but it goes in my bargain bin"

7 dancing veils; 7 gate bolts; 7 note musical scale; 7 day week; 7 basic colors; 7 as your lucky number; 7 clay tablets containing names of *the* 7 planets. Note: The 7 demons are not for sale.

Morrigan's Price War

Triple Savings!

3 cows (1 red, 1 white, 1 black); 2 bulls that get along poorly (1 white, 1 brown); 12 white cows with red ears; magic twig that grows 3 apples in 3 days (each apple can be eaten continually for 40 days); 51 beautiful migrating birds, all female; 4 talking and singing swans (900-year lifespan); twin foals of racing champion (1 gray, 1 black); trip for 21 to 34 exciting remote islands.

Jeremiah's God-Fearing Deliveries

12 days only!

Premium lamp oil, lasts 8 times as long; 1 mammoth houseboat (has 40 days' water damage); 2 stone tablets (what, you think we don't have paper?); luxury home of 45 pillars made with Lebanon cedar (15 pillars per row); 5 gold ingots and 5 gold mice (sold as a set).

Exit 42 Rv Park and Happy Hunting Grounds
Plastic Accepted
5 squash blossom necklaces; 3-sisters vegetarian tacos; 2 clan animals arguing over whether ceremony goes clockwise or counterclockwise (currently on loan to Wiccan community); 4th direction of medicine wheel (poison ivy growing in that spot); 6 directions to the powwow (you're welcome).

Sheshat's Catalog of Treasures
Financial Screening Required to Bid
1 funerary deity broken in 15 places (one delicate piece is missing); 7 scorpions, complete with armor; 8 rambunctious crocodiles (scary type); twin brother-sister lions (comes with 7,000 jars of red beer); 1 eye in 6 pieces; 12 sun gates (sold as a set); 4 solar ram heads; 8 singing baboons; 4 unopened canopic jars (contents labeled).

Holy Roman Surplus
"You ain't never gonna see a seven times seventh of what we got"
4 thundering horses, delivery date uncertain; 7 earsplitting trumpets, also awaiting delivery; 27 New Testament Books (moving to Kindle); 3 baby gifts (expensive but impractical); 1 casket, used only 4 days (man decided not to stay dead); 10 drachma coins (currently nonnegotiable). Note: 7 loaves and 3 fishes temporarily out of stock.

Questioning the Odds
1) What name would you give your fantasy horse?
2) A friend unexpectedly gives you a pair of pewter earrings in the shape of little horses. How might you interpret the symbolic meaning if you are:

a. Leaving soon on a shamanic retreat

b. Anticipating a testy meeting at work

c. Trying to conceive

3) You are driving slowly down a lonely dirt road and pass some people on horseback. How might your interpretation of this sign change if there are two horses versus three?

4) Make a circle of stones, any diameter and any number/size stones, and sit inside this circle for a short while. On a different day, make a triangle and do the same thing.

5) The oracular priestess at Delphi prophesied while sitting on a three-legged stool. Why did the stool have three legs?

6) Consider the following riddle: The white rider came at daybreak; the red rider came with the heat. The world clicked to the beat of the hooves and the black rider came at night.

7) What does Baba Yaga mean when she calls these three horsemen her "servants"?

8) Why is Baba Yaga's compound bright as day during the night? Why does she dislike answering questions about her house?

9) Why would you be able to knit or tat in almost total darkness yet not be able to spin?

Chapter 4

In Formation

An Amazonian Kingdom

Hold your peace! The bee-keepers are at hand to open the house of Artemis.
—Aristophanes, *The Frogs*

Figure 37: European Honey Bee, *Apis mellifera*.

While planning a poetry award ceremony, a friend of mine was contacted by the local insurance company that was footing the bill for the reception. What, they wanted to know, did poets like to eat? My friend was nonplussed for a moment. What does anyone like to eat? Then, being a literary wag, she recovered and told them "ambrosia and honey." Sure enough, the refreshment table featured a bowl of honey and that awful fruit salad with coconut and marshmallows they call ambrosia. I made a point of sampling both.

Good poets have drunk deeply from the nectar of the gods, widely believed to be honey. The honeybee is the "Bird of the Muses," granting gifts of honeyed verse. Ambrosia is thought to be another bee product, possibly the honey-based alcoholic drink mead. It was mead that the Germanic shamanic deity Odin stole from the goddess Gunlod, and when he delivered the fermented beverage to the land of the gods, a few drops fell to the earth, granting the rare poet unusual eloquence. To the ancients nourishing food was not an inert nonliving thing, but a container enveloping the life force. In this mode of appreciation, honey, with its sublime taste and healthful qualities, becomes the god of food as well as the food of the gods.

Let's take a look at the qualities of pure, unpasteurized organic honey, a complex food on many levels. Taste wise, honey varies according to the flower it is produced from. I prefer the darker, stronger tasting honeys, unalloyed by milder alfalfa or clover nectars, and I regret that I can no longer find the uncompromising buckwheat honey I enjoyed in Ohio. In Arizona, I grew to appreciate the tangy mesquite honey that overpowers any recipe. Alas, mesquite honey purchased through retail chains has proven to contain only a hint of the Sonora Desert. Clover and alfalfa honeys have their place, but anything truly flavorful requires research.

On an analytical level, honey is also complex, and laboratory findings will differ according to the variety, location, and time of collection. Honey contains a mixture of simple and complex sugars as well as trace amounts of iron, magnesium, potassium, and other nutrients. Honey is high in calories, but it tastes much sweeter than table sugar, and most people are easily sated with small amounts. It should not be heated, either in cooking or pasteurization, because this breaks down the complex sugars, bringing on the dreaded "sugar rush." A teaspoon in a cup of tea is fine, but it's not a sweetener for baking.

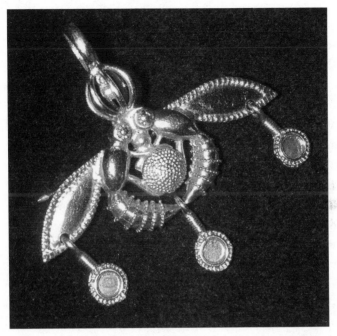

Figure 38: Minoan bee pendant (replica). Crete, 2000 BCE.

Honey has too many medicinal properties to describe extensively here, and whole books have been written on the subject. The most common application is as a cough suppressant, mixed with either whiskey or lemon. Because honey has antibacterial properties, it is used along with other herbs in salves for wounds and sores. Honey can be used as a medium to extract the healing properties of herbs, similar to alcohol, vinegar, or glycerin. In addition to the applications already described, the ancients used honey to improve eyesight, alleviate ear and hearing problems, aid digestion, and promote long life in general.

Honey and beeswax are found in many nature-based cosmetics, lotions, and hair products. Beeswax has historically been a base for artistic as well as cosmetic pigments, though crayons today are made with paraffin. Beeswax does not perform as many waterproofing, lubricating, sealing, and polishing functions as it once did, having been replaced by processed petroleum and vegetable products, but chances are that anything called a "wax" once upon a time began in a beehive. Wax was used to fashion molds for mass production of jewelry and votive offerings going back to the Bronze Age. Wax figurines have been found in Egyptian tombs depicting the deceased and the gods. The Greeks made wax images of deities and decorated them with feathers.

The earliest evidence of beeswax candles comes from Minoan Crete, where bee images appear on jewelry.[18] In Crete the infant god Zeus was nursed by bee-maidens, the Melissae, after the goddess Rhea gave birth to him a cave. Priestesses called Melissae served the earth mother Demeter, who had the title Pure Mother Bee. The Melissae were priestesses of Artemis at Ephesus.

It is not known when humans first became aware of the existence or importance of the queen bee, who can be difficult to spot even when the observer is practiced. Stone Age peoples recognized a mother ancestral spirit for all animal species, and these ancestral mothers came to be referred to as goddesses or queens, so the presence of bee goddesses doesn't necessarily tell us anything. Certainly by the fourth century BCE, and conceivably much

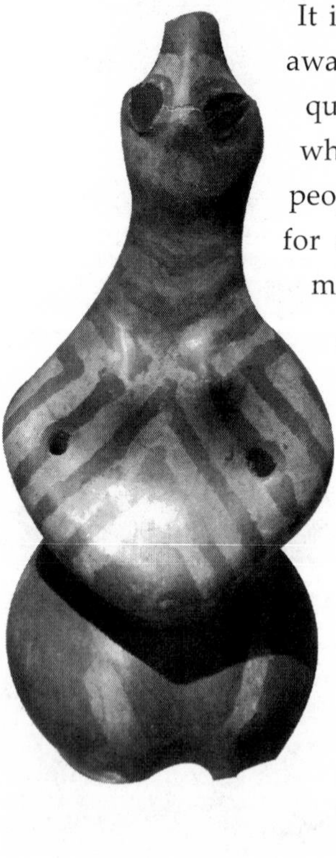

Figure 39: Bee goddess from Anatolia, 5000 BCE. Note the small head with big eyes, stripes, arms bent insect fashion, clearly segmented body. Her hat could be a hive. Photo: sailko/Wikimedia Commons.

sooner, the presence of a Very Important Insect was recognized for every hive, although in these patriarchal times this insect was usually called a king, and he was assumed to govern. In 1586 Spanish apiarist Luiz Mendez de Torres[19] correctly postulated the egg-laying function of the presumed king, and Charles Butler's 1609 *The Feminine Monarchie* argued for recognition of the queen bee, an idea too late for Elizabeth I, but which doubtless flattered other female rulers. Butler said of the bees, "males heere beare no sway at all, this being an Amazonian or feminine kingdom."[20]

Twentieth century apian scientists focused on swarm decision-making and in the process debunked the idea of the queen as leader of the hive. She is important, even central, since she lays the eggs that perpetuate the colony, but she does not govern. Decisions within the hive are made by consensus based on data collected by workers. Bee scientist Thomas Seeley concludes, "So the mother queen is not the workers' boss. Indeed, there is no all-knowing central planner supervising the thousands and thousands of worker bees in a colony. The work of a hive is instead governed collectively by the workers themselves..."[21] Seeley asserts that, "We humans can learn from honeybees about how to structure a decision-making group so that the knowledge and brainpower of its members is effectively marshaled to produce good collective choices."[22]

This interpretation ignores the fact that the worker-managers, as well as the queen, are female. The male drones, despite their worthy purpose, are marginalized as democratic stakeholders. The most obvious conclusion to draw from honeybee behavior is that governance should be left to females. The hive is an Amazonian kingdom, and bee behavior reflects the feminist definition of matriarchy: collective, inclusive decision-making geared toward consensus. This is how many feminist organizations have operated since the 1970s. Scholars within the Goddess Movement theorize that pre-patriarchal societies, including the Amazons, also functioned in this way, though they believe men as well as women had a voice in this consensus.[23] Still, "humans" dismiss feminine decision-making styles, disregard information presented by women, fight women's attempts at limited sovereignty, refuse to entertain ideas proposed by women, and subject women in authority to relentless criticism—while upholding a governing model from nature for other "humans" to emulate without acknowledging that it is entirely female.

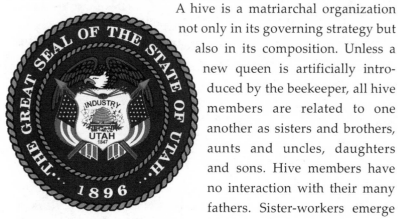

A hive is a matriarchal organization not only in its governing strategy but also in its composition. Unless a new queen is artificially introduced by the beekeeper, all hive members are related to one another as sisters and brothers, aunts and uncles, daughters and sons. Hive members have no interaction with their many fathers. Sister-workers emerge as larvae from the same fertilized eggs as queens, while drones emerge from unfertilized eggs, laid in the same hexagonal wax cells that store honey. The queen will lay as many as 1,500 eggs per day early in the summer, but if her production of fertilized eggs begins to fall short of sustain-

Figure 40: Many seals, flags, coats of arms, industry symbols, and association emblems contain bees or beehives to emphasize the cooperative nature of the organization. This is the seal of the State of Utah, 'The Beehive State,' with hive pictured in center of the emblem.

ability, or if conditions become overcrowded in the hive, new queens will be reared. The larvae designated to become queens will gorge on a nutrient-rich food called royal jelly. There can only be one queen to a hive; a queen emerging earlier than the others will either leave the hive with a sustainable colony, called a swarm, or she will sting her sisters to death in their cells.

Eggs hatch in about three days and the larvae destined to become workers are fed royal jelly, which gradually becomes thinner and mixed with pollen. The larvae will go through five molts in five days, at which time nurse workers will cap the cells with wax while the larvae spin cocoons around their bodies and enter the pupa stage. In twelve days the transformation is complete and the young adult workers chew their way through the wax caps. For the first three weeks workers attend to tasks inside the hive, such as feeding larvae through special glands on their head or producing wax through glands on their abdomen. They will hold nectar in their open mouths to allow it to evaporate, or fan nectar in the cells with their wings to hasten evaporation. Eventually they begin taking on other tasks, such as foraging, scouting, or guarding.

When a guard bee encounters a predator, she releases a scent that alerts other workers in the hive, who fly quickly into defense mode. At first the bees feint or bounce against the attacker. Workers prefer not to sting, as they are unable to retrieve the barbed stinger from their victim and so die in the process. The stinger trapped on the victim works like a hypodermic needle, pushing venom deeper into the skin. A scent released during the stinging encourages other workers near the hive to sting. The bees deliberately select sensitive areas to attack, such as eyes, nostrils, and lips.

Scent is an important part of bee communication. Organs on top of the abdomen release pheromones to indicate when it is time to swarm and to mark desirable home sites. The queen releases pheromones that facilitate hive cohesion, expose stealth robber bees, suppress ovary development in workers, and indicate by their weakness that the aging queen must soon be replaced. Larvae emit a scent to attract nurses. When beekeepers open a hive, they fan a few puffs of smoke inside to cloak the alarm pheromone.

Bees also communicate with sound. The angry buzzing of a

disturbed hive is well known, as is the contented hum of the productive hive. Less proverbial, but of great significance to beekeepers, is the mournful hum of a hive that has lost its queen. Bees produce humming through rapid wing beats, and on a warm summer day chances are they are humming to cool down or to evaporate nectar into honey. A different sound, shorter and higher in pitch, is caused when bees vibrate their thorax either against the comb (emerging queens) or against the body of another bee (workers). This sound, called "piping," heralds the appearance of the new virgin queen, alerts this queen that she has rivals, signals that it is time for a group to leave the home nest, and alerts the swarm that transport to new housing is imminent. A buzz that is less discernible to humans, but probably important to bees, accompanies the "waggle dance" of foraging scouts in the hive.

Dancing is one of the most fascinating traits of bees, and the one that makes them seem most like us. The scouts dance to convey the direction and distance of the nectar or pollen source, along with the quantity available. Scouts researching potential home sites dance to communicate the desirability of a particular site as well as directions that enable other scouts to investigate.

Scouts on a swarm are in the open air, but inside the hive it is very dark. Here workers rely on touch to track dances. When there is an abundance of nectar inside and not enough workers to process it, bees will vibrate to convey to foragers that they are needed at the home base.

Bees are inactive at night, since they rely on sight to navigate and have poor lowlight vision. They rely both on the position of the sun and on landmarks to traverse their territory. Like most diurnal creatures, their color vision is excellent, effective well into the ultraviolet range. This helps them locate their preferred flowers.

The workers give the busy bee its motto, but the drones are famous for doing nothing. Actually, they do have a function. The mature drones leave the nest every morning hoping to mate with a queen from a neighboring hive. There are pickup hotspots for bees where a number of drones hang out hoping a queen will show up. She will be accompanied by an entourage of workers who have led her far from her home so she will not be inseminated by her brothers. The queen mates in flight only for this one period in her life, and she will be inseminated by many drones over the next few weeks until her sperm compartment is full. The drone dies in the process of insemination.

While the drones serve a purpose for *apis mellifera* as a whole, ensuring genetic diversity in the propagation of the species, they don't appear, under our crude gaze, to be contributing to their particular hive. We have to ask ourselves, however, why the workers would make enlarged drone cells, with the queen obligingly laying a haploid unfertilized egg, if the drone provided no benefit to the hive. Tammy Horn says in *Beeconomy* "There is strong evidence that worker bees will become demoralized without the appropriate number of drones in the hive."[24] This rather whimsical way of putting it makes it sound like the drones are amusing their sisters by telling funny stories. If so, then by the end of the nectar flow the jokes are getting stale, because the workers push the few remaining drones outside as the hive prepares to go dormant.

Figure 41: The hieroglyph for the pharaoh was the sedge (a type of grass) representing northern Egypt and the bee representing the south. This is a detail from the tomb of Thutmose II. Photo: Hedwig Storch/Wikimedia Commons.

The image of the idle drone, eating but not producing, expendable when cold weather approaches, has been the rationale for quite a bit of antisocial sentiment among humans. The

Greek poet Hesiod, writing in the eighth century BCE, compared drones to women, writing "...the bees are busy and lay the white combs, while the drones stay at home in the covered hives and reap the toil of others into their own bellies—even so Zeus who thunders on high made women to be an evil to mortal men..."[25] During the Industrial Revolution in England, when scores of dispossessed and jobless country people filled the city, the poor were compared to drones and, using another bee analogy, they were encouraged to "hive off" to America. But in colonial America the officials of the British government were condemned as drones, for taxing the colonies heavily and giving little in return. As industrialization flowered in the United States in the latter nineteenth century, striking workers were disparaged as drones by factory owners who considered their capital investments the only real contribution to the economy. Socialists in turn called the robber barons drones for gaining riches through the labor of workers.

Understanding that drones do play a vital role in the bee world, and that they literally kill themselves trying to fulfill that role, has not changed the negativity associated with them. This may have something to do with our realization that drones are males in an "Amazonian kingdom." They do not dominate, but rather are dominated by the females, and lacking stingers they are weaponless. Unable to produce honey, they are dependent on their sisters. In patriarchal societies the man who does not fight or dominate is seen as insignificant. So the drone image suffers.

A worker bee will live for about six weeks or six months, depending on how close to the dormant season she emerges from her cell. In her short life she will make one teaspoon of honey. This honey will be sought after by ants, wasps, wax moths, other bees, mice, raccoons, skunks, martens, weasels, badgers, bears, and apes, especially chimpanzees and humans. Chimpanzees go after stingless bees, using tools to break open the hive. The calories expended in the operation far exceed what can be obtained from the honey, so honey craving in primates probably serves another purpose. Humans, of course, will endure stings to obtain honey. Gathering wild honey is usually a man's occupation, because climbing and travel distances make it difficult for mothers in hunter-gatherer societies to participate. The Russian and Lithuanian words for beekeeper, which translate literally as "tree climber" or "bee climber" harken back to hunter-gatherer days when honey was stolen from hives in tall trees. The first beekeepers were probably men seeking a less arduous and dangerous way of collecting honey. Once bees were domesticated, other labor divisions began favoring women as beekeepers. Men have always dominated the field, but not overwhelmingly, and worldwide over the past twenty years women have been catching up.

Figure 42: Watercolor of St. Gobnait by Harry Clarke, 1914.

The earliest record of domestic beekeeping comes from an Egyptian temple inscription around 2400 BCE, although beekeeping almost certainly began much earlier than this.[26] The panel shows clay hives being smoked, honey being pressed from combs, and jars being sealed. An early symbol for Lower Egypt was the bee. The goddess Neith's temple was called the House of the Bee. Her sacred tree is the Red Acacia (*Vachellia seyal*) or Gum Arabic tree, which has globular yellow flowers that attract the sun-loving bees. Recall from the crocodile chapter that Neith is the mother of the sun in some creation schemes. The long prominent thorns of the acacia may relate to another of Neith's symbols: two crossed arrows below two click beetles. Perhaps the thorns also relate to the "arrows" of the bees: their stingers.

In the Bible the Israelites refer to bees as fierce and dangerous. "The Amorites living in the hills came out against you and like bees they chased you."[27] The heroine Deborah, whose name is the Hebrew word for "bee," is a bee on the side of justice in a crucial battle that may have originated as early as the twelfth century BCE.[28] Deborah leads her people in a revolt against an oppressive leader and it is from her victory song that we get the phrase "blessed above women."

Deborah was a very popular girls' name until recently, peaking in the 1950s at #1 on the American charts and falling off drastically by the beginning of the millennium, when bee populations also drastically declined. While armchair theorists are clinging stubbornly to the idea that Colony Collapse Disorder is caused by cell phone towers, and chemical companies are arguing against a mountain of data that show bees harmed by neonicotinoid insecticides, no one appears to have noticed that the bees went away with the Debbies. If you want to save the bees, save the Deb-bees. Name your daughter Debbie. In fact, name all your daughters Debbie.

Beginning in the Roman Empire, there are accounts of bees being used in warfare, usually by catapulting hives into enemy territory. The Irish improved on this by having their St. Gobnait turn the bees into disciplined soldiers and transform their "barracks" into a war helmet. She did this to punish cattle rustlers, which makes the story reminiscent in some ways of the Cattle Raid of Cooley, which features the formidable Queen Medb, whose name means "mead." Irish saints tend to take on the miraculous powers of bees: St. Brigid makes mead appear from nowhere; St. Patrick turns water into honey.

Figure 43: Gold plaque of Thriae bee goddess. Rhodes Island (Greece), seventh century BCE. Photo: Marie-Lan Nguyen/Wikimedia Commons.

Honey keeps forever due to its antibacterial properties and low moisture content, and it can be used as a preservative for some foods, so it should not be surprising that the Egyptians used honey in embalming. Honey's long shelf life made it an ideal commodity of exchange, and a significant part of the tribute Egypt demanded from its conquered territories was paid in honey. Taxes from the wealthy were also paid in honey. Marriage contracts included the transfer of honey. The gods had large appetites for honey, important funerary rituals required honey offerings, and honey was given to sacred animals in the temples. Even the divine crocodiles were fed honey. Egyptian demand for honey was fierce, despite intense domestic production, so it was only occasionally enjoyed by the poorer classes.

Bees are very rare in Mesopotamian texts and iconography, although references to honey abound. Production occurred in northern Mesopotamia and honey was exported to the south, which in other respects was the hive of technology. The keeping of bees, which were considered a type of fly, did not occur in the south until early in the second millennium BCE. Pollination was done by hand. Honey was well integrated into Mesopotamian cuisine, but rarely enjoyed by the less well-to-do, who sweetened their meals with date syrup. The ancestors were offered honey during monthly rites and an account of a divine wedding feast mentions two different honeys. Sexual love and fertility are the places where honey references most arise. The goddess Inanna sings of her consort Dumuzi during their marriage ritual:

My honey-man, my honey-man sweetens me always.
My lord, the honey-man of the gods,
He is the one my womb loves best.
His hand is honey, his foot is honey,
He sweetens me always.[29]

Compare with the Hebrew-Aramaic Song of Solomon:

I have come to my garden, my sister and bride,
and have plucked my myrrh with my spices;
I have eaten my honey and my syrup,
I have drunk my wine and my milk.
Eat, friends, and drink,
until you are drunk with love.[30]

Most biblical references to honey are not as tangy, but honey is extolled as a wonderful thing (*Eat honey, my son, for it is good, and the honeycomb so sweet upon the tongue*)[31] while the reader is cautioned not to overindulge (*If you find honey, eat only what you need, too much of it will make you sick*).[32] I could not find accounts of beekeeping among the Hebrews until the first century, despite contact with beekeeping societies much sooner. Googling "Canaan" and "beekeeping" is useless, because the good Christians who settled in North America named dozens or maybe hundreds of places Canaan, and apparently they all keep bees. Canaan is referred to in the Bible as the land "overflowing with milk and honey," a phrase we now use metaphorically, but in this first instance was meant literally. The area had good grazing along with an abundance of wild bees. There was so much honey that apparently everyone could partake, although the proscription against using it as a religious offering probably didn't hurt the supply.

Figure 44: Ephesus, fourth century BCE. Photo: cgb.fr/Wikimedia Commons.

In Greece gods were usually given honey or honey derivatives as an offering. In some myths the underworld guard dog Cerberus is given a honey cake instead of bread. The priestesses of the sun god Apollo ate honey in order to foretell the future. The Three

Fates were given "sober offerings" of water and honey cake when approached for judgment, but Dionysus and his priestesses loved the fermented drink. The use of mead in ceremony, even in Greece, predates wine, and ritual wine was mixed with honey to make it sweet. Dionysus was depicted with a honeycomb necklace, reflecting his older association with the intoxicant of bees.

Ritual uses of honey in Christianity are rare, but medieval Christian rites did require a great deal of wax for candles. Church rents, taxes, and tithes were usually collected in wax, as Mediterranean kingdoms had collected taxes in honey before the invention of coinage. The pressure to successfully manage hives went beyond enjoyment of the sweet produce, and so a great deal of the surviving signs and superstitions around bees have less to do with messages from the bees about human endeavors and more to do with the affairs of bees themselves. Will it be a productive year for the hive? Will the bees prosper or will they die? Will they swarm? Are the bees disgruntled with their humans?

Irish folklore says bees will not thrive around a family that quarrels, while the French emphasize the importance of talking politely to bees without swearing. Germans say bees can both talk and understand the speech of humans. It seems plausible that bees *would* respond to the emotional energies around them, which are reflected in speech, but not knowing

Figure 45: Lions on sleeve of Artemis of Ephesus. Second century reproduction. Photo: Miguel Hermoso Cuesta/Wikimedia Commons.

German myself I cannot verify that bees can actually talk.

The belief persisted into the early twentieth century that it was important to keep bees apprised of major events, because bees were part of the family and would resent being uninformed. They had to be notified when a baptism occurred. Wedding decorations should not neglect the hive. Not only was honey consumed at a wedding (an almost universal practice wherever bees were endemic), but a piece of wedding cake was set inside the hive for the bees to partake. Most important of all was the duty to inform the bees when a death occurred in the family, particularly the death of the beekeeper. Instructions for breaking the heavy news were often precise, because deeply grieving bees might leave the hive in search of the keeper. The bees would be told that their father (or uncle, aunt, sister) had died but that a new family member had been appointed as their keeper. The bees must not leave their human family, who would continue to depend on them. The hive would be decorated with black crêpe, cakes from the funeral would be set in the hive, and the hive would be turned around so that it was not facing the house when the corpse was taken out. While honey was always present at weddings, mead was liberal at funerals.

The delicate handling of bee feelings when a death occurred reflects beliefs about bees as otherworldly creatures who might return to that other world to follow their beloved human. Virgil said that the bee came from the ether,[33] while in Britain the bee came from the Christian paradise. The Greeks thought nymphs took the form of bees. For the Germans bees came from the underworld, but they traveled to the sky to gather nectar. The association with death meant that the spirit of a soothsayer or healer might leave through the mouth as a bee during trance. In England a bee might fly out of the mouth or ear of a sleeper. While relatively rare, a purported sorceress on trial would sometimes be accused of having a bee familiar or of shapeshifting into a bee.

Since bees are not entirely of this world, magic was needed to attract swarms or to make them land when they appeared. This involved banging metal, which recalls the cymbals that were part of the rites to Cybele. Bees were summoned by banging pots and pans or ringing church bells. There were rules for obtaining a hive from another beekeeper, although these rules varied by locale. A swarm given as a present was the luckiest, though bartering was acceptable, and it was usually considered poor form to pay for a swarm with money. Since bees were members of the family, perhaps this was seen as analogous to buying and selling children.

Beekeeping before the twentieth century was a complicated endeavor. Not only did bees need to be spoken to, pacified, and kept informed, they also needed to be awakened at the end of

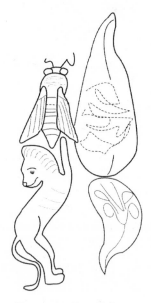

their dormant period. In southern France this happened at Candlemas, when hives were decorated with ribbons and family members sang the bees from their slumber. In the Baltic region knocking on the hives told the bees spring had arrived and it was safe to come out.

Humans and bees have forged an incomparable bond over many millennia. All forms of animal husbandry require labor, but beekeeping has the added burden of keeping bees happy, due to their special semi-domesticated status. Bees can leave at any time and survive on their own. Horses can be fenced, and cats can be seduced with treats, but bees must remain attached by less obvious methods. Humans have learned to improve the survival rate of a

Figure 46: Detail from a gold pin depicting lions, bees, and flower petals. Greece, fifth century BCE.

hive by building good housing, insulating the hive in winter, and providing preferred flowers, but the psychic bond has also been important. This bond makes it easier to communicate with bees when sending out a prayer for a sign.

The Astro-Bee

The following is adapted from the Finnish folk legend, The Kalevala.

The boy loved the legends of the hero Lemminkainen.

The boy told his mother, "Tell again how it was that the great one conquered death.

How the warrior wasted in the void of Tuonela,

How he lay in pieces in the blackness of the whirlpool of death,

How he woke from long uncharted sleep unharmed,

And escaped the fateful waters for the windy plains of home."

"My son, it is as you say.

Lemminkainen entered and escaped from dreaded Tuonela,

But he deserves praise only for finding the abyss.

The nectar of the little bee restored him to his strength.

Shameless and boastful was Lemminkainen til he gazed in the waters of death.

Before bathing in black waters he was filled with scorn and pride.

He resented his wife Kylikki for her strong unfaithful beauty.

He hated the Bride of Bounty for her sullied broken vows.

One night only did he neglect her.

And in one night only did she betray him.

Lemminkainen scorned the counsel of his aged loving mother.

He snorted when the wise one urged him toward compassion.

He argued when she cautioned him against another marriage.

He chortled when she said he would not find a second wife.

Lemminkainen donned his mail and took his spear and sword.

The warrior would win a youthful maiden, more beautiful and more true.

With confidence he parried with the spears and spells of wizards.

With courage he met archers and enchanters and their swords.

He fought onward through the watchdogs to the northern hall of Pohya.

He swaggered to the courtyard of the wizened ruling crone.

He petitioned the Pohya witch to let him wed her fairest daughter.

He challenged her for trials that would win the maiden's hand.

The Northland crone grinned cruelly as she heard the brazen warrior.

Pohya's hostess chuckled as she indulged the reckless stranger.

Far south, in the cabin, troubling signs and smells were brewing.

In the house of the wife and mother dreadful things became apparent.

The frightened maiden showed the mother the hairbrush of Lemminkainen.

Kylikki showed the gray one the wet bristles oozing blood.

One look at the gruesome brush sent the mother for her cloak.

The sight of the gory hairbrush propelled the mother on her quest.

Swiftly raced the anguished parent, across the distant heath.

Like the wind the anguished mother flew past mountains and ravines.

Arriving at the hall of the Pohya, she demanded news of Lemminkainen.

Threatening plagues and sure destruction she demanded

truth from the Northland witch.

Challenged once, and twice, and thrice, the hostess confessed her treacherous ways.

Lemminkainen had been sent to hunt the swans on the stream of death.

Learning this, the worried mother sought the skills of a magic smith.

She made the craftsman forge a rake with long extended handle.

Probing at the shores of slumber, she fished the body of Lemminkainen.

Thrusting in the void she pulled out pieces of the hero.

From the current came his tunic, then his jacket, then his shoes.

Raking the shoals of death she found his shoulder, then his arm, his hand, his thumb.

At last by Tuonela's edge were the hero's pieces gathered.

On the banks of the river of death the nibbled fragments lay.

Now Raven proclaimed the hero lost forever to the living.

He has been eaten by whitefish, by eel, and by pike.

Throw him back, throw him back, back into the deep waters of death.

You will never, you will never, you will never save him now.'

'No! I cannot and I will not abandon my foolish child.

Suonetar the seamstress will repair my broken son.

The goddess Suonetar will knit bones and flesh together.'

So the great seamstress obliged, threading venules through the body.

But still no life fluttered in the heart of Lemminkainen.

The Hero of the Islands could not see or hear or speak.

The good crone called her friend Honey-Wings before her.

'Oh Honey-Wings, fetch the balm that restores the dead to life.

Bright bee, bring me nectar from Jumala's golden meadows.

Bring sweetness to cure my patient's weakness and make him whole again.'

The anxious little bee zipped eagerly away.

The little buzzer buzzed her way into the fragrant garden.

From six bright flowers the winged creature gathered nectar.

From six bright flowers she brought sweetness to Tuonela's bank.

The mother applied the sticky substance to the silent, lifeless form.

The sticky substance was like mead across the fallen singer's throat.

And still the hero lay speechless.

Still he stayed in deepest slumber.

'Honey-wings, my friend,' the mother said, 'Fetch me again a magic ointment.

Fly across nine oceans to the perfumed honey land.

Find the little roofless dwelling with the tiny lidless pots.

Scoop the ointment simmering gently in the little thimble pots.'

Honey-wings boldly sought the secret honey mead.

The speedy bee flew three days over distant murky seas.

Fragrant balm drew the bee through the little roofless dwelling.

The buzzer found the simmering liquid in the tiny open cauldron.

Seven drams she packed against her thorax and her belly.

Six drams she carried in her tiny little hands.

The whirring insect returned with fragrant healing treasure.

In triumph, precious salve was presented to her mistress.

The crone mixed eight ointments and nine magic unguents.

She placed seventeen medicines on her fallen son.
Yet he remained speechless.
He stayed motionless and did not blink.
'My faithful hummer, come to me, and we will try just one last time.
There is one important place that we have yet to mine.

'Fly far into the heavens, toward the moon, but do not stop there;
Soar through the bright moon's aura in the direction of the sun.
Fly to the edge of the sun but do not rest there;
Skirt the borders of the warm-land and aim for the furry lover.
On the shoulders of the Great Bear look to stars that are yet more distant.
Zoom upward through the starscape to the cluster of seven jewels.
But at the seven stars climb higher and higher still.
Climb to the ninth and upmost heaven, little bee, the very ninth.
In this heaven there is nectar, there is balm to cure all ills.
In Ukko's blessed realm are the medicines we need.'

The hummer demurred in fear and said she would not go.
'I am just a little tiny bee; I cannot fly so high.
I cannot pass the rings of the moon.
I cannot skirt the edge of the sun.
I cannot stand on the back of the Bear.
I cannot transcend the realm of the stars.
I cannot soar past the seven great jewels.
I cannot enter the highest heaven.
I cannot reach to Ukko's realm.
I am just a little bee.'

The dogged crone would not accept the little bee's lament.

'Oh Honey-Wings you are so fine, you are so strong,' she crooned.

'You can flit to the rings of the moon and past the edge of the sun.

You can zip through the Bear with ease and surpass the highest stars.

You can attain the ninth high realm where Ukko's nectar waits.

Bring me the unguent tempered there to save my helpless son.'

Strengthened by the mother's faith the whirring wings took flight.

The buzzer zipped by sun and moon beyond the seven stars.

Three days' journey to the farthest sky the little bee endured.

To the ninth of the heavens to the silver kettles, where the sacred lotion lay.

Laden with mead, laden with ointment, the trusted worker returned.

Back to the earth, back to the river, back where the hero lay.

The wise woman dipped her tongue in the salve and said it would suit her purpose.

'This is the balm of Ukko that will save my cherished son.'

Applied to the fissures, applied to the cracks, applied to the joints was the ointment.

Lemminkainen's skin was salved in the middle, in the back, in the head, in the toes.

'Arise my treasured child, arise from your slumber, arise!

Your wondrous dreams are behind you now: awaken, remember, return.'

The fallen man stirred and opened his eyes and reached his hand for his mother.

'Oh sweet were the dreams in Tuonela's land, how happy there was my sleep.'

'Yet you would have slept for a long long time, without the aid of others.

Yes, you would have slept for a lengthy time, as payment for your sins.'

The youth said, 'I am well now, so it's back to the halls of Pohya.

'Now it is time for me to claim my well-earned bride.'

'No! You will not go to Pohya,' the beleaguered crone enjoined.

'You will return with me to Kalevala and fulfill your duties there.'

Lemminkainen resigned himself to heed his mother's counsel.

Tuonela's depths had tempered the brash and proud and reckless youth.

'I thank you, mother, for restoring my life, and I respect your wishes.

With your blessing, I return to my home and to the embrace of my wife.'"

The boy hearing the story vowed to live like Lemminkainen.

"I will visit distant lands and fight accomplished wizards.

I will bribe the keenest craftsmen and employ the greatest seamstress.

With spells and magic weapons, I will travel unafraid.

I will ride to the halls of witches.

I will walk on the shores of death.

And I will listen to the words of my mother.

Her wisdom will clear my way."

The mother then advised him to give great and small their due.

"Even the tiny bee brings health and strength from Ukko's brew."

Sweet Return to Poppy Plateau

Stories of the disappearance of bees are not unprecedented, and legends suggest there may have been a massive die-off in Asia Minor in remote antiquity. Virgil recounts in his Georgics *how the bees disappeared to punish Aristaeus for his attempted rape of Eurydice, and how the bees miraculously reappeared in the carcasses of two bulls he ceremonially sacrificed to them. What follows is an idea of how the bees might have returned. I am not intimating here that the disappearance of the bees was the beekeeper's fault. Tribal societies often required that one member come forward and take responsibility to avert disaster for the entire tribe.*

We rose early and gathered myrtle and pine boughs in the cool dawn. The trees had been chosen by nymphs during the permission ceremonies begun at the crescent moon. The nymphs cut the branches with purified stone blades and used honey to staunch the wounds.

The ravens cawed as we began the arduous trek to the plateau. Everyone carried something, and two of us helped Maiden Kyreen with her robes. We had cleansed and brushed the fur the night before, but it still stank of lion. Kyreen would wear the fur on the outside with the skin against her body rather than the usual way.

Only six dancers made the climb. The swarm dance had been done the night before in the village, and nearly everyone had taken part. The dancers, musicians, and bee speakers who performed this ceremony needed to be strong and fearless, because the contagion of panic could subvert all preparations.

As we reached the height of land everyone stopped to survey the meadow, and we were unsurprised and yet disturbed by what we did not see. There were no honeybees flitting above the poppies, no humming workers bathing in the pollen crowns.

We moved into the little cave and the musicians began setting up their instruments. The floor had been swept the night before and the interior smelled of green herbs. The cleaners had marked with little pebbles a section that contained lion prints. An excellent sign.

The interior of the cave was dim, because Mother Anna did not want smoke in the chamber. She marked a hexagonal space with pollen, and placed on it myrtle blossoms, a sprig of pine, a bowl of water, and six wax figures shaped as bees. The humming instruments vibrated in our ears.

Anna began the honey song. She sang about sweet flowers and idyllic weather; soft breezes and cool water. Her rich voice had a vibration of its own, and as she concluded, with the notes still wandering through the passages, the nectar dancers got on their crouching legs. By this time our eyes had adjusted enough to track their formations. Their dance told of flowers in abundance, flowers with sweetness yet untapped, flowers that would yield great amounts of honey.

When the bee maidens had finished, Father Aristis spoke. His tall frame was bent over because the cavern ceiling was low. He said he was sorry he had offended the bees. He hoped they would forgive, if not him, then the village, which depended upon them. The honey of the bees took the bitterness out of healing herbs and enabled children to take their medicine. The honey encouraged the very old and the convalescent, who had lost their appetites, to eat again. The honey purified wounds and healed sores. He reminded the bees that people lived and worked together in ways similar to them and that our two families were related. He reminded them that the people and the bees had lived in peace for many generations, and that people did not take honey in ways that destroyed the hive, unlike the bear and badger. The people were not greedy and only took a part of the harvest, and they did not expect the honey at no cost. They cleared out little houses on cliff walls inaccessible to bears, houses that faced the warm morning sun. Aristis hoped this ceremony would convince the bees that they were valued and that he personally was committed to living rightly. That the people as a whole had always had this commitment the myrtle trees and the pines would attest. Finally, he would speak for the land itself. The flowering trees missed the bright companionship of the nectar workers, and the fields pined to hear the buzzing music. The poppies ached for the soft tickle of furry bodies against their petals. He begged the bees to think of all who grieved the separation and return to this plateau.

The drums began vibrating softly to signal the welcome dance. The singers began humming at a higher pitch and the soft pipe vibrated above them: one long note followed by five short pips. Maiden Yuri rose and began gyrating, bending up and down repeatedly from the waist. Her dance promised stability and sustenance, with the expectation of a well-fed progeny. When Yuri tired, we sat in the shadows humming until Kyreen growled and growled and finally roared.

The two of us helped the lioness struggle outside, and the others followed but stayed apart. The humming resumed, and we waited.

We heard the buzzing before we saw them. They were dots in the sky, then they were flying near us, then they seemed to be a cloud above us. They settled in a mass on a nearby pine. We waited. When a few landed on Kyreen, we picked them carefully off her fur, placing them in a little basket.

The brothers secured the rope ladder to a tree stump and tossed the other end over the cliff. Bee crevices had been scouted and cleaned in the previous days, nesting sites that could be accessed only by rope or by wing. Aristis took the covered basket and began his descent. At the ledge he would push aside a rock on the stone shelf, leaving a tiny bee-sized entrance. He would coax the bees into the opening. The bees would examine the dwelling, then fly back to the swarm to tell the other bees about their new home.

At the return of Aristis we danced in happiness and celebrated by consuming the honey we had brought. The brothers pulled up the ladder and secured it in the cavern. The rope was too flimsy for an adult bear to descend, but a mother might send her cubs down to raid the hive.

As we prepared our return to the village we noticed the ravens watching us. Father Vergil admonished them not to tell any bear what the rope ladder was for. The ravens broke out in a querulous cawing, and we started to argue with them. We stopped when Anna cautioned that this disagreement could upset the bees. We began our triumphant return to the village and would take up our discussion with the ravens another time.

Bee Review

Magical Qualities: cooperative lifestyle, specialized functions, large communities, complex nest builders, highly communicative, fiercely protective, venomous, sensitive to vibrations, musical, dormant in winter, produce sweet food, create wax, good sense of direction, good color vision, live in caves or tall trees

Magical Applications: healing (especially eyesight, hearing, digestion, wounds, and respiratory infections), wealth, love, beauty, psychic insight, protection

Other Associations: sun, cooperation, flowers, dancing, the number six, sweetness, architecture, caves, music, heaven, underworld, death, gold, marriage

Hex to Perfection

We now continue our numerical journey with the numbers four, five, and six.

Four

Three is a more stable number than two, but it's still an unstable number. The three-legged stool and the three-legged cauldron work, but there's a reason chairs usually have four legs and buildings four sides. I have come to believe that all numbers are intrinsically unstable, even the number one, but four is a relatively stable number, providing a foundation for traditions as well as houses. Four is an even number—the first even non-prime number. Even numbers provide more stability because they can be divided into equal parts; they are not lopsided.

The number two added to itself and multiplied by itself is the same number, four. No other positive integer does this trick. Four objects can be divided into equal rows and columns, which is the characteristic of all integers with whole square roots. $2^2 = 4$, or two rows with two columns. When even numbers are squared, they can be divided into an even number of equal rows and columns, while odd numbers squared produce an equal number of odd rows and columns. $6^2 = 36$, six rows with six columns; $3^2 = 9$, three rows with three columns. Remember, for numbers greater than two, odd numbers are less stable than even.

The square brings us out of the flat world, allowing movement in three dimensions. A triangle is always a face on a single plane. We associate pyramids with their triangular faces, but they must have at *least* four sides. People also associate triangles with the ancient Egyptians, because of the pyramids, but the numerical focus of Egypt was actually the number four. This is somewhat surprising, since orientation to the four cardinal points of the year would not be as obvious in such a warm climate, but Egyptians did have to keep careful track of time to schedule activities around the annual inundation of the Nile. Timekeeping was probably the root of the cult that arose around sun worship. Core beliefs about the sun are usually expressed in multiples of four, in Egypt and elsewhere. (Greece is an exception, as we will get to.)

Egyptian deity relations were usually expressed as four deities or two pairs. The most well-known of these deity groupings are the siblings Isis, Osiris, Nephthys, and Seth. As the Greeks thought in threes, the Egyptians thought in fours. In mummification four internal organs were taken out of the body and preserved in four jars, each guarded by a different deity.

The number four also corresponds to directional points (east, south, west, north), which are delineated by sunrise/sunset and by the magnetic poles. Four is the number of grandparents (the two parents of your own two parents or $2^2 = 4$), which would associate this number with tradition even if it were not already a highly stable number.

Not all aspects of the number four are intrinsic. Some are cultural. I once did graphic design for a man from Hong Kong who had a business in California that was expanding rapidly. He kept ordering more and more phone lines, and he had long arguments with the phone company telling them he did not want any fours in his phone numbers. Apparently the word four in English sounds like the word for death in Cantonese. The phone company insisted they had no control over phone numbers and could not honor his request, but this probably was not true, because somebody started giving him numbers with lots of fours just to yank his chain. This is an example of why you would not want to take the numeric symbology of one culture and apply it to another without reflection. Unless you are bilingual in English and Cantonese, the number four is not going to have these associations.

Five

Figure 47: Pentagram with a pentagon shape in the center boldened.

While the number four is matching, even, balanced, and complementary, the number five introduces disequilibrium back into the
system. It is perceived as an unfortunate number in the tarot
because it comes on the heels of the highly stable four. The
number five brings change. Witches use the pentagram (the five-
armed star drawn with a continuous line) because five is such a
dynamic number, helpful in effecting transformation. The
pentagram is usually pointed upward to invoke heavenly power,
but it can be pointed downward to draw power from earth. The
upward pentagram also represents the individual—head, arms,
and feet. It is often used to represent the physical human body,
well represented by the number five since it is in a constant state
of change. In alchemy the number five corresponds to the
element of ether, which contains the other four elements of air,
water, earth, and fire. It is called the quintessence (the essence of
five) because it is the essence of all things.

The five-sided object in the center of the pentagram, the
pentagon, has an angle of 108 degrees. If you have taken any
yoga, chances are you have been instructed to do certain exercises
108 times, since this is an important number in Vedic philosophy.
Regardless of your belief system, 108 is still an interesting
number, because it is equal to one times two squared times three
cubed, $1^1 \times 2^2 \times 3^3$ or $1 \times 2 \times 2 \times 3 \times 3 \times 3 = 108$.

Five is a prime number, which means that it is irreducible and
cannot be broken into factors except one and itself. The first three
prime numbers are two, three, and five, so if you like to hunt
threes, there you are. In the practice of addition, five is the sum
of the beginning prime numbers two and three. Prime numbers
in metaphysics represent fundamental truths, since they cannot
be divided into any whole numbers except one. Five is a worthy
number for study among alchemists and witches, because it is a
prime among primes.

Six

Figure 48: Hexagram with a hexagon shape in the center boldened.

Six is called a "perfect number," which means that by adding or multiplying its factors you get the same number. What does that mean? It's easier to show than to tell: 1 x 2 x 3 = 6 and 1 + 2 + 3 = 6. Perfect numbers are relatively rare—28 is the next after six—although in the paradox intrinsic to mathematics it is conjectured that there are probably an infinite number of them. Like true love, they are difficult to find.

The building unit of three-dimensional space, the cube, has six faces. Thus, while the number four forms the foundation, multiples of the number six are the actual building blocks.

The six-pointed hexagram, two interlacing equilateral triangles—one pointed up, the other down—illustrates in a beautiful way the principle of "as above, so below." Six is associated with the goddess Aphrodite, probably because her sacred bees make hexagonal cells out of wax. The number six corresponds to the Lovers in the tarot, which is appropriate, since the Latin word for six is *sex*.

The words "hexagram" and "hexagon" are derived from the Greek *hex*, meaning "six." These shapes are used as protection against evil spells. In the common parlance "hexing" means to cause harm through magic, but in Appalachian folklore and among the Pennsylvania Dutch "hex-work" is healing by magic, and "hex signs" are any signs, not necessarily hexagrams, created to ward off trouble. The meaning of "hex" in this context comes from *hexe,* the German word for "witch." If you were going to cause harm with magic, you certainly wouldn't use the number six. It's a perfect number, not permitting the possibility of corruption. Six is the number for love, beauty, protection, and healing. It is no accident that quartz crystals, which have become so important in energetic healing work, are six-sided. Again, six is a perfect number.

The Isle of the Little Cat

This segment from The Voyage of Mael Duin can be found in longer form in Geddes and Grosset's Celtic Mythology.[34] *The hero of this entertaining story is born in a nunnery, the product of rape, and fostered by a queen. Not content to enjoy his comfortable life, Mael Duin pesters his reluctant foster mother to give him the details of his birth. After meeting his biological mother, he pesters her for the name of his father, then goes with his foster brothers to visit his paternal clan, who welcome him but do not tell him the circumstances of his father's death. Eventually a monk reveals the truth, and Mael Duin is off to a far-flung island to confront his father's killer. With heretofore uncharacteristic caution, he consults a wizard regarding the most auspicious way to conduct the voyage and learns that he is to take seventeen and only seventeen companions. Naturally this injunction is disregarded. After weeks of hard travel, the tired and hungry crew land for a sojourn on the Isle of the Little Cat.*

The men disembarked on the sandy beach with weak knees and unsteady gait. The cool dusk seemed pleasant yet somehow strange.

Rising above the cliffs they saw a great fortress with a white tower. Mael Duin proceeded guardedly, reflecting on the travails encountered on former islands: a giant horse with hound's paws who threw pebbles, menacing ants the size of foals, fire pigs who made the ground steamy.

They entered the fortress cautiously. Everything seemed

deserted. The outside walls of the white houses were decorated with necklaces, torques, brooches, daggers, and swords, fashioned from the finest metals and encrusted with jewels. There seemed to be no craftsmen and no guards. The smell of food wafted from the largest house, but upon entering they found no cook, no lord, and no lady. In the great hall a table had been set, and there were numerous cushions, linens, and sleeping pallets along the walls. The place was deserted save for a small cat leaping between four stone pillars that rose in the center of the room. The cat glanced at the men but seemed untroubled by their presence and continued her play.

The wary men stood in silence while Mael Duin considered the scene carefully. Then he smiled. As unnatural as it seemed after the terrible encounters in recent weeks, this situation might be exactly what it appeared to be: a prosperous village whose inhabitants had left on some errand or mission but had laid preparations for the arrival of guests. Perhaps they had been expecting this very crew. The men relaxed and took advantage of the opportunity to wash and enjoy a decent meal. The clean comfortable bedding was enticing. The cat ignored them and continued to play, wash, stretch, and nap.

A long summer day that ends with a good dinner, a soft bed, and a dreamless sleep is the most wonderful of things, yet also the least remarked upon and the least remembered. This incident was destined to be recorded because of what happened the next morning.

As the men leisurely prepared to resume their journey, they inquired of their leader whether it would be appropriate to carry with them the remainder of the prepared food. "Yes, take that and the ale and mead also," Mael Duin replied, "but leave the jewelry and the armaments. We will not raid an unguarded house."

They might or might not have noticed when the youngest of Mael Duin's foster brothers pilfered a necklace, but a companion they had forgotten about completely had been watching their every move. The cat leaped into the air, changing into a fiery arrow in mid-flight as she sheared into the boy. She incinerated him to ashes. It took all of Mael Duin's skill to sweet-talk the cat into resuming her harmless shape.

After soothing and reassuring the cat, the chastened crew returned to the beach. The ashes of their comrade they scattered along the pristine shore. They had encountered many perilous and threatening situations before landing on this hospitable island, but this was the first place where Mael Duin lost one of his men, and it was his own foster brother besides. They left without knowing the owners of the treasure, the fortress, and the fairy cat. She no doubt remains on the veiled island, awaiting future guests.

Questioning the Form

1) Regarding those four pillars guarded by the cat—why are there four and why are they guarded by a cat?

2) Earplugs are yet another object once fashioned from wax. How many things can you think of that are made or used to be made from a bee product?

3) Bees swarm in the sunlight, so why was the first part of the ceremony on Poppy Plateau done in a cave?

4) What interpretation would you give to the birth of four kittens? Five kittens?

5) Think of the stereotypes associated with the following words, as they are applied to people: queen bee, drone, worker bee, hive, hive mind, swarm. Based on your knowledge of bees, are they accurate?

6) What interpretation would you place on six doves? Six hummingbirds? Six squirrels?

7) Contemplate the "four good deeds" of Thoth to "silence evil": creation of the four winds; periodic inundation of the land by water; making all people alike; and instilling in humans a

recognition of the west (ancestors).

8) What does Lemminkainen's dismemberment symbolize? Why is the bee the only creature who can heal him?

9) Here is a honey jar spell for improving interpretation of signs. Honey spells are important in Hoodoo, a magical belief system originated by Blacks in the American South. It incorporates African, Native American, and European magic, with a liberal dose of Christianity. The purpose of honey spells is to "sweeten" something or someone, and it can mean just sweetening your luck. In this spell we are sweetening our education.

For this spell you need:
Baby food jar
Honey
Unbleached paper
Pencil
Scissors
Lavender flowers

Cut a hexagon from a sheet of unbleached paper. I use baking parchment paper, but a thin paper bag will work. Write "sphex," the Minoan word for bee, in cursive in the center. On each of the six sides write "recognize signs" in cursive in one continuous line, linking the first and last letters without lifting your pencil. Go back and dot the i's after you've finished.

Place a pinch of dried lavender flowers in the center of the hexagon. Starting from the top and moving clockwise, fold each of the six sides toward you. You should end up with a packet of flowers an inch and a half or less in diameter.

Pour honey into a baby food jar, covering the bottom with a quarter to a half inch of liquid. Place your packet in the jar and cover it completely with honey. Lick the honey off your fingers. Replace the lid and put the jar on your altar or another special place.

Honey spells work slowly, so expect gradual change. These spells are best used for long term improvement rather than immediate results.

Chapter 5

Under the Rock

Scorpion Security Associates

The road of Ishara is the Scorpion.
—Mesopotamian proverb

מינוזיג

**Figure 49: The Deathstalker, the most venomous of scorpions, is
native to North Africa and the Middle East.**

People tried to warn me about sleeping with scorpions.

I couldn't see the harm in it myself: if I were on top of the
mattress with the scorpion nest underneath the mattress, what
could be the problem? I had no need of the infinitesimal space
between the earth and my bedding, and when the scorpions
emerged at night surely they would not be hunting me.

Years later I met a man who also slept with his bed on the
ground and he had been stung six times in his sleep. He still

refused to consider sweeping out the scorpion nest or raising his futon. I understood. There is something comforting about cocooning with these primordial creatures.

Scorpions have not changed in design in the 400 million years they have roamed the planet. They do most of their roaming at night, capturing small victims in their claws or grabbing onto a mate for a starry courtship shuffle. In the daytime they stay hidden, crouching under rocks to avoid predatory birds or burrowing in the sand to stay cool. Even with these precautions, theirs is a world strewn with enemies: owls, bats, centipedes, shrews, other scorpions. Their venom is mainly for defensive purposes, as their saliva liquefies their victim into a juicy slurp. If they latch onto unmanageable prey, the stinger is there in reserve.

Contrary to popular belief, scorpion stings are not fatal for healthy adults. They are painful, of course, causing swelling and burning at the injection site, and the sting of some species leaves residual migraine headaches. Casualties are typically young children who succumb to respiratory distress, or adults in a weakened state whose bodies react with heart failure.

The discomfort of the venom is one of the reasons scorpions are invoked for protection. Hypervigilance is another. These little critters compensate for poor eyesight with a tactile perception that strikes us less attuned folks as preternatural. Scorpions discern and categorize activity mainly through vibration.

Scorpions are protective mothers. Unlike other arachnids they are viviparous, giving birth to live young. The babies climb onto their mother's back, where she keeps them safe for a few weeks until their first molt. Emperor scorpion mothers have been observed bringing small prey to their scorplings. Some scorpions are parthenogenetic. Gestation is long, between seven and twelve months, with some scorpions giving birth to many dozens of tiny scorplings.

The Egyptians had a scorpion goddess, Selket, who was called upon for protection against—you guessed it—scorpions. Selket

Figure 50: Selket greets the deceased as a woman with scorpion on her head. 1100 BCE.

was one of the guardians of the "canopic jars," the containers holding the pickled remains of four vital organs of the deceased: liver, intestines, lungs, and stomach. The heart, the all-important anchor of the soul within the body, was preserved, wrapped, and returned to the body cavity. The brain was thrown in the trash. Each of the four organs was guarded by a specific deity, and Selket protected the intestines. The guardian deity was depicted on the outside of the jar along with hieroglyphic prayers to invoke that deity's protection. This label also helped the expired prince remember which jars housed his various organs. Labeling funerary objects was an important precaution: not only did the rich take a lot of stuff with them, the world beyond had so many people—as many people as had ever trod the earth—that mix-ups were a potential complication. Thus everything was tagged, and clothing and bedding contained laundry marks. This consistent attention to organizational detail in preparation for the final voyage may strike some people as absurd, but think about it: would you want to root around in someone else's canopic jar by mistake? Selket was entrusted with an important responsibility.

Selket's other major role was helping the deceased draw their first breath in the afterlife. Most "death goddesses" are really death-and-birth goddesses, and breath is the fundamental connection to life. Selket initiated breathing in both worlds. To emphasize this nurturing aspect of Selket's character, she was sometimes depicted without a stinger or as a stingless Water Scorpion. The Water Scorpion is not an arachnid but an insect in a family biologists call the "true bugs." Water Scorpions are true bugs and fake scorpions, and most of them don't even faintly resemble scorpions, but there are a few with pincer-like front legs and long tails that look vaguely reminiscent. The "tail" is actually a breathing tube that sticks out of the shallow water. The Nile species depicted in art has a double-breasted air tube.

Isis was the deity Egyptians invoked most for scorpion protection, particularly as her cult gained prominence. Although many have categorized her as wife/sister to Osiris and mother to Horus, her popular veneration, then and now, relates more to her powers as Divine Physician. She was originally a raptor goddess,

probably a Black Kite, a bird that prefers to hunt in marshy areas. The aggressive kite preys on fish, small animals, and arthropods, including scorpions and Water Scorpions.

Isis was especially valued for her ability to protect and heal children. This geographic region

Figure 51: Ancient Egyptians usually drew the hieroglyph of the scorpion as a Water Scorpion to avoid invoking the venomous varieties.

suffered from a high degree of child mortality that exceeded even what other urbanized societies of the time experienced. Children were in danger far beyond their first year and were usually not named until their fourth or fifth year of life. Isis was venerated as the deity that not only gave children but also helped ensure their survival.

The story of Isis and her seven scorpions, recounted in this chapter at the end of this section, is a part of the longer funerary cycle of Osiris. In this story Isis protects her unborn child from his enemy, the god Seth, who is a deity of the harsh dry desert personified by the wild asses who gallop on the fringes of the Nile Valley. It is the nature of the desert to wage war against the fertile Valley, desiccating vegetation and killing the cereal grasses personified by the god Osiris. It is the fate of the Nile to re-emerge victorious with the summer floods, forcing Seth to retreat to his desert strongholds. If the inundation of water is too strong, however, it results in loss of life and property damage. Seth must be contained but he cannot and should not be vanquished. The Valley and Desert forces must therefore remain locked in never-ending opposition to ensure equilibrium in the world. Since the passive, easygoing Osiris, a vegetation god, is unable to temper Seth, a new protective Valley deity must emerge, which is Horus.

Horus is conceived to do battle with Seth and so Seth's hounding of the pregnant Isis is inevitable. Realizing Seth's persecution will be relentless and implacable, Isis retreats deep into a swampy area of northern Egypt, which the desert has never been able to penetrate. The wetlands have their own dangers, however, and so the god Thoth gives Isis seven scorpions for protection. Thoth is an African Sacred Ibis, a long-legged black-and-white marsh bird. Like Isis he is a physician and magician, and the two have a collegial relationship. The choice of scorpion protectors is significant, since scorpions are typically associated with the desert. There are a few scorpion species who live in damp tropical and subtropical regions, but scorpions are more plentiful in the dry hot regions and this is where the more venomous species live. Some mediation between marsh and desert forces is necessary for the safety of Isis and her child.

The scorpions perform their duty but cause mischief of their own, exemplifying the unpredictable character of the desert with its temperamental dust storms. Isis must monitor the scorpions or they will attack creatures who pose no threat. The vigilance Isis must exert over her scorpion guards typifies the tenuous relationship between magician and familiar. The magician must remain dominant or the familiar takes control. This happens later in the story when the scorpions attack Useret's baby.

Figure 52: Black Kite. Although it is difficult to see from a black-and-white photo, the feathers are not black but variegated shades of brown. Photo: Ashik Musicroom.

The interchange with Useret, Isis, and the poor maiden illustrates the humor that underlies Egyptian perspective. The outline of the narrative mirrors the tiresome morality tales mothers everywhere tell their children to instill an attitude of generosity toward others. This time the predictable framework has a twist. The rich lady, like Seth, is the baddie in this story, since she has resources yet refuses to extend hospitality to the stranger with a scorpion entourage. At the same time, who would do that? The kind impoverished maiden, of course, who fortunately suffers no ill when Isis relaxes watchfulness over her guards, but only because they have another target.

The main purpose of this story is to affirm the origin and legitimacy of the scorpion anti-venom spell and the supremacy of Isis's healing powers. Isis can create a spell to trump the power of any being if she knows their name. The pronunciation of names in the text is unknown to us, however, because Egyptian writing does not record vowels. This is one reason for the many spellings of Egyptian deity names. The lack of a true pronunciation key is unfortunate since Egyptian literature stresses the importance of saying the name correctly in magic. In recent years Egyptologists have started using "e" for all unknown vowel sounds, strictly as a convention and not because this is the most common vowel sound in Egyptian. Under this practice the names of the gods are not only unavoidably inaccurate, they become flat, distorted in resonance, and devoid of poetry. For this reason I prefer Greek names. There is some distortion introduced in the Greek translations, of course, but the Greeks were exposed to late Egyptian dialects, so in most cases we can assume they have given an approximation of a name, a nickname, or a title. Even if the name is quite different, the Greeks did have an ear for vibration and poetic resonance. Where there are different popular spellings and pronunciations of a name, I go with the one that has the most pleasing vibration. If you are an unusually clear channel, you may be able to discover the correct name, although it's very hard to channel a language you are unfamiliar with, and you may distort the sound to fit with your own language.

If you ever have to use the scorpion anti-venom spell, I would recommend going with the scientific names of the scorpions most likely to have caused the sting, on the theory that in this case specificity is more important than pronunciation, which can only be guessed at anyway. Most people when they're stung spout cuss words, and this also seems to work.

For protection against scorpion stings, the son of Isis, Horus, may also be invoked. In another myth a scorpion kills Horus, and

Isis seeks magic from Thoth to bring him back to life. Horus is a protector of children and was probably called upon most frequently in that capacity. Look back at the picture of Horus as a child in the crocodile chapter and notice that he has scorpions in either hand along with four snakes.

Figure 53: Eight scorpions surround four women on this Mesopotamian plate. The women are arranged to form a swastika, a classic sun symbol. Note that the women's arms look like snakes. Samarra 5000 BCE.

While the Egyptian view of scorpions was equivocal and complex, Mesopotamians had a clearer admiration for these creatures. This had nothing to do with the comparative toxicity of the species; the most venomous types are found in both places. Mesopotamians saw scorpions as sacred creatures who should not be harmed even by carelessness or inattention, their stings being the mark of a transgression rather than innate hostility.

To heal the effects of the venom, straightforward herbal remedies were employed along with spells that are poorly understood. One ceremony apparently involved placing the creature in a scorpion-sized temple and imploring her to remember her better nature. My sources do not reveal whether the scorpion-in-a-box was an actual scorpion or an effigy. Information on scorpions in Mesopotamia is sparse in modern texts, but art reveals what patriarchy obscures: only the snake is depicted more frequently. Scorpions appear from the Hassuna and Samarra cultures (6000 BCE) to the Persian conquest (500 BCE). The Scorpio Constellation, which like the rest of our zodiac originates in Mesopotamia, is found in art as early as 4000 BCE.

Perhaps the scorpion's prominence in the sky gave her a special status on earth.

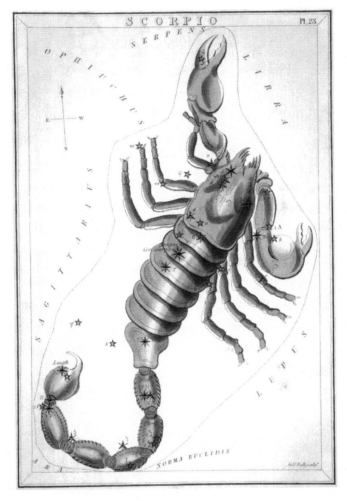

Figure 54: The Scorpio constellation is one of the easiest to recognize in the night sky. Drawing: Sidney Hall.

The tendency for deities to become synthesized due to cultural assimilation and conquest means that we can only speculate about the early scorpion goddesses. Some may have been assimilated with the goddess Nina and others were undoubted assimilated with Ishara. Nina is more of a fisherman's deity, suggesting a conflation or at least association of crayfish and scorpions, which recalls the water-scorpion/true-scorpion personas of the Egyptian goddess Selket. Ishara is a Semitic mother goddess and originally a snake goddess. Eventually the goddess Ishtar acquired a scorpion familiar as she absorbed a myriad of cults throughout the region. Scorpion deities could also be gods or the twin deities ubiquitous in Mesopotamian culture. Unlike the Egyptians, Mesopotamians had no fear of depicting the scorpion stinger and often made it quite prominent. Like the Egyptians, Mesopotamians saw their scorpion deities as protectors and as guardians of oaths. Scorpion goddesses were seen as mother-protectors.

Two Scorpion-People guard the sun tunnel in the *Epic of Gilgamesh*. The excerpt discussed here can be found later in this chapter. The following back story may help you understand this passage.

Gilgamesh is on a quest for eternal life because his friend Enkidu has died and tells him being dead isn't any fun. His ancestor Utnapishtim enjoys endless life upon the earth so Gilgamesh seeks his wisdom. What Gilgamesh already knows but doesn't appreciate is that Grandfather Utnapishtim was shown the secret of life after displaying extraordinary courage, hard work, and trust in divine wisdom. Gilgamesh is endowed with many fine qualities, but by this section of the narrative it is clear that he has not acquitted himself in an admirable fashion. He has been cowardly, selfish, derelict of duty, unsympathetic to others, and above all disrespectful to the goddess Ishtar, who is the patron deity of the city he purportedly governs. His wasted unkempt appearance is an outward manifestation of the present condition of his character.

The fear and trembling with which Gilgamesh approaches the Scorpion-People is in one sense meant to be funny. The Mesopotamians knew well that the only scorpion to be frightened of is the one you don't see, so Gilgamesh's fear is a mark of how ludicrous he has become. Scorpion-People are shown in late Assyrian art as having bird feet and feathers along with pronounced tails and anthropomorphic features. In earlier art, the scorpions occupied the lower portion of the seal and birds stood above them.

Figure 55: Assyrian cylinder seal showing scorpions with wings. Eighth century BCE. Source: Walters Art Museum.

Again, scorpions in their protective role are keepers of the oath. In this capacity they uphold justice and defend truth. That Gilgamesh would tremble before the Scorpion-People at this point of his journey is understandable on a more symbolic level.

The Scorpion-Man asks Gilgamesh: Why is he on this journey? Why is he suffering? Hasn't he heard that the gods have decreed that men must die? Gilgamesh has been asked these questions before and they will be asked two more times along his journey. The questions might also be directed to the listener of the tale: Where are you going? Why are you suffering? Have you accepted that someday you will die?

Scorpions are creatures of death, by their toxic, occasionally fatal, venom and by their time spent burrowed in the ground. They can be seen as emissaries between life and death, because they often venture onto the surface of earth and their venom may bring the victim close to death but not necessarily over the threshold. Scorpions are also creatures of the sun. Not only do they thrive in hot dry regions, they carry venom that burns when injected. Other animals cannot tolerate their fire, but the scorpions themselves harbor intense heat within their tiny bodies with no discomfort.

So scorpions are the perfect guardians of the sun tunnel, the path the sun god Shamash travels in the night. Yet who are they protecting, exactly? The Scorpion-Man affirms that Gilgamesh will be exterminated if Shamash enters before he clears the tunnel. He voices no concern for Shamash, who will presumably dispatch the interloper without distress. The Scorpion-Twins appear to be protecting not the sun or the tunnel but the hapless traveler.

The extreme risk Gilgamesh is taking cannot be appreciated without more background on how Mesopotamians viewed death. Mesopotamians did not practice cremation because the dead body was important. It needed to be buried in an accessible place and marked in a conspicuous manner to help the spirit under-stand that he or she belonged to the underworld goddess Ereshkigal. A proper funeral could not be conducted without a body, nor could the monthly propitiative ceremonies occur without a physical resting place. These ceremonies were conducted every new moon by surviving relatives to bring comfort to those below. Being dead was a bummer, but being dead and forgotten was worse. Most importantly, the dead needed to be reminded periodically who they were and where they now lived. Otherwise, their spirits could wander past the gates of the underworld in a highly confused state, traumatizing the living who crossed their path.

The incongruous juncture that Gilgamesh has reached is this:

he is going down into Irkalla to avoid being sent there, and he is risking an annihilation much worse than death to avoid dying. Also, he keeps being told his journey is hopeless and he will fail. Why not just give up?

Figure 56: Mesopotamian boundary stone. The eight-pointed star of Ishtar hangs above the sky serpent Tiamat. The big hair in the center right is also a symbol of Ishtar. 1000 BCE.

The Scorpion-Woman understands that a person utterly consumed by a goal must pursue it, no matter how foolhardy the mission. The Scorpion-Woman seems the more powerful, with her ability to tap into the void for answers, but we must also appreciate her complementary sidekick, who is able to ask the relevant questions. Both are important. One of the strengths of divination based on signs, as opposed to divination with dedicated tools like tarot, is that it importunes us with questions that might not have occurred to us. The questions are as important as the answers, and usually much more difficult to recognize.

Gilgamesh Challenges the Scorpion Twins

During the Epic of Gilgamesh, *the hero encounters Scorpion-People guarding the tunnel through the underworld, which the sun travels at night. Gilgamesh must pass through the tunnel so he can converse with his ancestor Utnapishtim, who has transcended mortality. As occurs repeatedly during his journey, Gilgamesh is questioned about his reasons for embarking on the hopeless journey for eternal life.*

Figure 57: Twin scorpions protect the symbol of Ishtar in this north Mesopotamian soapstone stamp seal. 3000 BCE.

The scorpion terrified him, but then this was no ordinary scorpion. He (the scorpion, not the bedraggled traveler) was tall as a large man, but he was not a man: his barbed stinging tail curved at the back of him. Like a bird he had feathers folded against his side and scaly talons for feet, but he was not a bird: his barbed stinging tail curved at the back of him. What made him even scarier was that there were two of him: two scorpions rising with curved stinging tails in the shadows of the Twin Mountains.

The Scorpion-Man said, "The one who cowers before me, I think he is a god."

His sister rejoined, "He is two-thirds god, one-third of him is human."

The Scorpion-Man boomed at the shivering supplicant, "Who is this mortal who seeks the underworld before his time? Who voluntarily trespasses into Irkalla?"

His sister answered, "This is Gilgamesh, mighty king of Uruk, who has traveled beyond the paths of ordinary men."

Gilgamesh found his voice. "I have not come to die, but to live forever. I am seeking eternal life upon the earth, like my forefather Utnapishtim."

The Scorpion-Man replied, "Has no one ever told you, the fate of man is death? The gods decreed that each human must ultimately join the mistress Ereshkigal in the world below, lest the population rise until the noisy din again disturbs the naptime of the god Enlil. When Enlil does not get enough sleep, he is cranky."

The Scorpion-Woman said, "He knows all of this, but he does not accept it. He is determined to live forever."

Her brother exclaimed, "It cannot be done!"

Gilgamesh persisted, "It has been done. Utnapishtim, my great grandfather, lives beyond the path of the sun. I will go there, through the tunnel Shamash travels in the nighttime, and find someone to ferry me to that idyllic island where this immortal man lives still with his immortal wife."

The tone of the Scorpion-Man grew more patient, as if he were talking to a child or perhaps a crazy man. "That tunnel is far below the earth, and after reaching its depth the length is twice what you have already traveled. You would only have twelve hours to traverse its entire distance and you would have to run entirely in the dark—at least you would hope to travel in the dark. When Shamash enters the hole you hoped to exit you would be burned alive immediately. There would not even remain a body to be buried."

Gilgamesh said stubbornly, almost stupidly, "I must go to Utnapishtim and ask him how I can live forever."

The Scorpion-Man continued to reason, "You are tired from a

journey already too long. Your clothes are dirty and tattered and you look like a beggar, not a warrior. Is your fear of death that strong, that you could achieve this feat even with a weakened body?"

His sister intervened. "Every man deserves a chance to prove his mettle, however strong the obstacles. Let Gilgamesh pass into the tunnel of darkness. Let him risk what he desires to risk. Let him pass with your blessing."

Into the tunnel of darkness Gilgamesh passed. With the blessing of the Scorpion-Man and the Scorpion-Woman he fell headlong into the void. The terror of running in the blackness was intense, yet the possibility of encountering light inside that tunnel frightened him still more...

Isis and the Bad Little Scorpions

After the god Seth presents Osiris with the dubious present of a coffin, and after Osiris inexplicably lays inside said coffin to make sure it fits, and after the other gods are perplexingly stunned when Seth throws the encased Osiris into the river, and after Osiris gets his weenie eaten by a fish (a carp, in case you were wondering), and after the goddess Isis gets tired of looking for said weenie and just decides to make a new one, and after Isis "breathes life" into her phallic clay creation thereby completing Osiris's resurrection, this long long (some would say eternal) story of friendship, death, and betrayal starts to get really weird...

The mighty Isis, the plucky lady who reduced the sun god Ra into a slobbering fool, who tormented the great light of the world until he was forced to give up his secret name so she could control him—yes, that Isis—was feeling vulnerable and insecure. She could take care of herself against any adversary, but she was not the target of Seth. The life growing in her womb, the child of Osiris, was the focus of the blustering lord's rage. Isis ran to the marshes to hide.

The ibis god of the riverbed, Thoth, observing this uncharacteristic behavior of the formidable queen, concluded that she was in a desperate situation. He gave her a scorpion for protection.

"A scorpion?" said Isis, a bit incredulous.

"Oh, right," returned Thoth awkwardly. "Here's seven scorpions."

"That's probably at least seven times as helpful," mused Isis to herself as she continued her journey. She wandered deep into the wetlands, past the last outpost of the town they call the Two Sandals. The scorpions flanked Isis on all sides, with one on each side, two behind, and three in front. They cleared the riff raff in her path, but she had to keep warning them to refrain from attacking the helpless nonthreatening creatures they came across.

Isis needed to remain hidden, yet she also needed shelter, food, a place to rest, clean clothing. She came upon a rich lady's house, there in the marshes. Isis was not surprised that the rich lady built her house in the marshes, because Isis happened to need, at that moment, a comfortable dwelling in the middle of a marsh. What did surprise her was that the rich lady did not want Isis to come inside the house with her seven scorpions.

"I don't know who you are," said the rich lady rudely, without asking Isis who she was, "but nobody who walks around with seven scorpions can come in my house." The rich lady did not ask who the scorpions were, either, although they all had names. Their names were Tefen, Befen, Mesetet, Masetetef, Matet, Petet, and Tjetet. The rich lady's name was Useret, which means "strong woman."

"I can't just leave these scorpions outside," Isis argued, perhaps mainly to herself. "They were a gift from Thoth and belong to my child as much as to me."

Isis continued wandering through the swamp with her scorpion protectors. Though the scorpions all had different names, they were all of the same mind: the rich lady was crude, mean, selfish, incredibly bad, stupid, ugly, disrespectful—you get the idea. It took a while for Isis to find another house in the marshes, so the scorpions had a lot of time to think up nasty names for Useret. Eventually Isis found a rundown dwelling deep in the marshes.

"Of course you can come in my house and eat my food," said the young girl who lived in the rundown dwelling, "and what lovely scorpions you have."

Isis gratefully took advantage of the opportunity for a few days' rest, but the scorpions neither rested nor reflected on their good fortune. They would be holed up in a fabulous swamp castle, instead of an untidy shanty, if that mean lady hadn't barred Isis from entering. The confreres (and con-soeurs—four of them were female) confabulated over a venomous response. Tefen, the fiercest of the seven, whose name means "damp guy," was elected to enact the retribution.

The six scorpions gave Tefen all their venom so he would be fully charged. Tefen headed out alone and sneaked into the marsh mansion. He stung Useret's baby hard with his sevenfold venom and was gratified when the suffering baby and the distraught mother began screaming very loud. Isis was appalled.

The Mistress of the Great Star, Queen of Magic, and All-Powerful Physician rushed to the home of the howling child. There she asserted her control over the venom of the scorpions. She said:

Flee now from this child, Tefen, and remove your useless poison.
Flee now venom of Befen, flow quickly into the ground.
Flee now venom of Mesetet, fall down to the long below.
Flee now venom of Masetetef, dissolve in the hungry soil.
Flee now venom of Matet, soak into the greedy morass.
Flee now venom of Petet, tumble into the eager void.
Flee now venom of Tjetet, for I am Isis, Speaker of Spells.
I am your mistress, Scorpion Guards.
I draw your poison into the sucking earth.

I command your poison to leave this child.

The child recovered, and Isis fled again into the marshes, wary of attracting attention by her magic. The mother Useret sent rich provisions to the hut of the girl who was harboring Isis. Useret then traveled far, teaching all mothers the spell for healing infants from the evil of scorpions.

Scorpion Review

Magical Qualities: venomous, earth-dwelling, desert-dwelling, prefers night and shadows, mothers protect young, sensitive to vibrations

Magical Applications: healing (especially fevers, migraines, asthma), assessing danger, protection, divination

Other Associations: guardianship, wisdom, death, psychic ability, heat, sun, motherhood, the Scorpio constellation

Nine Worlds I Knew

Our exploration of numbers concludes with seven, eight, and nine.

Seven

If you have even a rudimentary understanding of spellcasting, you know that the number seven is important. If you go into an occult shop or a botanica with a problem, you will often be sold a "seven-day candle" in the appropriate color. If your problem is really thorny, the saleswoman will push a multicolored "Seven African Powers" candle, perhaps with a special prayer. What is so magical about the number seven?

To begin with, seven is another prime number. Split unevenly down the middle, it is four plus three. This is interpreted as the four directions plus the triple goddess, the four seasons plus the maiden-mother-crone, or any other magical representation of four and three. This is expressed visually by the square with a triangle inscribed.

It is believed that the prominence of the number seven is calendrical in nature, corresponding to cycles of the moon and of the star system Pleiades. The moon completes a cycle every 29½ days, and our seven-day week is a moon cycle divided into four parts. It was probably divided into four parts rather than three to chart the two half-moons as well as the full and the dark moon phase. The Pleiades seven-star system can be seen around the world during at least part of the year, and it features prominently in world mythology. The presence and position of this star system has been used from earliest times to orient the yearly calendar. Although there are many stars in the Pleiades system, only seven are visible to the naked eye (and many people can only see six).

There are many correspondences to the number seven, too many to list here, but some that come immediately to mind are the seven-note musical scale, the seven color categories, the seven "personal planets" in astrology, and the Seven Wonders of the

World. Clusters of seven, so common in Western cultures, usually follow from the preeminence of this number rather than from any intrinsic components of the particular category. Why don't we have five primary colors or nine? The musical scale does not need to have seven notes, nor does it in every culture.

Figure 58: The Oswald Wirth 1889 drawing of Justice is faithful to renditions of the card in the older Marseilles decks, with the exception of the Hebrew letter 'het' in the lower right corner, which is an addition.

Eight

In the earlier tarot decks, those created before the Rider-Smith-Waite and similar twentieth century occult decks, the number eight in the major arcana corresponds to the "justice" card.

A bit of background about tarot numerology. The symbolic picture cards numbered 1 to 21, plus the unnumbered "fool" (labeled zero in twentieth century decks) are referred to as the "major arcana," while the numbered and court cards in the four suits are called the "minor arcana." The major and minor arcana probably evolved separately. There is a record of a deck painted for Charles VI of France in 1397 (unfortunately no longer extant), so the major arcana dates somewhat earlier than this. It seems to have been a teaching tool for a breakaway Christian sect—the Cathars and the Waldenses have both been proposed—and it conveys conventional Christian symbolism of the time along with the teachings of a sect that incorporated occult beliefs. The origin of the minor arcana is even more obscure, probably originating in an Arabic game brought home by Crusaders. This game may also have originated as a spiritual teaching tool, and there are similarities to Hindu cards that were undoubtedly painted for this purpose. The tarot is often cited as an authority for pagan philosophy of numbers, but the murky history that is undoubtedly rooted in Christian dogma means it should be approached cautiously as a number theory.

Eight as a number of judgment puts four on either side of the scale. Remember that four is a number of stability and a number of foundation. While we think of judges as powerful people, judges themselves see their role as circumspect, a mandate to interpret given law with an eye to tradition. This is not a creative number, but one for maintaining existing tradition.

It is also a number tied less to the individual and more to higher authorities, a byproduct of its double-four nature. For this reason, eight is the number of the administrator, not just the administrator of justice but any manager obeisant to regulations and material realities.

The mineral fluorite often takes the structure of the eight-sided octahedron. Holding a fluorite crystal in your hand, you may be able to feel the stimulation in the frontal lobes of your brain, which is the section that separates intellect from instinct and attempts to view a situation rationally. Again, the mirrored pyramidal facets of the octahedron suggest balance, in this case perhaps the balancing of left and right hemispheres of the brain. Katrina Raphaell says of fluorite, "It is the stone that manifests the highest aspect of the mind — the mind that is attuned to spirit. From that exalted state of consciousness comes the intellectual understanding of truth, of cosmic concepts of reality and of the laws that govern the universe."[35]

The symbol 8 comes from the shape of the eight-legged spider. The spider is an accomplished builder, the master of one of the most durable structures on earth. She spends part of each day repairing her web from the vicissitudes of wind, rain, and other creatures, understanding and accepting that a valuable possession requires maintenance. Like the spider establishing structure through her web, the textile weaver gives fabric its structure. This is a number that accepts and utilizes limitations. It is often pointed out that the symbol 8 lying on its side is the symbol for infinity, and this infinity symbol is pictured in the number eight card (strength) in the Rider-Smith-Waite tarot. But 8 the number is finite, not lying on its side. It is proudly upright, limited but all the stronger for it.

Eight received its reputation as a bad luck number for its role in miscarriage, not miscarriage of justice, but miscarriage of pregnancy. The eighth month of gestation is a stressful time, with premature birth always a possibility. Eight became the number for well-laid plans going awry, since babies born at the eight-month mark have a reduced chance of surviving past infancy.

Nine

Figure 59: The Ninefold Star is used in Wicca and Ceremonial Magick to invoke the Goddess.

With this number we come full term. It would be illuminating to continue on past nine, perhaps examining the symbolism in the number twelve, walking through fears around the number thirteen, swinging with the twin primes of seventeen and nineteen, or meditating on the "master number" twenty-two. We do have to stop somewhere, however, because numbers go on forever, and the chance of your encountering more than nine animals in the wild who stand still while you count them is low.

Nine is the harmonious square of three: 3 x 3 = 9. It takes the highly unstable yet creative prime number and harnesses it in a way that can be expressed coherently. We think of the creative process as intrinsically unstable, but it takes a modicum of stability to come up with a product.

Nine is, of course, the number of pregnancy. In the early days of creation, the plant daughters of the Mesopotamian goddess Ninhursaga gave birth at a rapidly increased pace, nine days instead of nine months. The absolute amount of time for biological processes is apparently not critical but the number nine is. When the Germanic god Odin receives the runes he must be reborn by hanging upside down (birth position) from the world tree for nine days and nights. There are thus two ways of looking at the number nine: the perspective of the mother and the perspective of the child.

The number nine is the Triple Goddess times three, often portrayed as nine daughters or priestesses. The sea goddess Ran has nine mermaid daughters. In Cornwall a set of nine prehistoric standing stones is known as the Nine Maidens. An early Neolithic rock painting in the Catalonia province of Spain, the Dancers of Cogul, depicts a group of nine black or red feminine figures along with a few animals. There are Nine Muses—not originally tied to the god Apollo, though they may well have had a solar connection.

The association of nine with Goddess is found all over the world. The Hindu Mother Durga has nine manifestations, and the Suseong-dang seaside shrine in Buan, South Korea was originally called the Nine Maidens Shrine. The ocean is often seen as Nine-fold Mother Goddess due to the saline waters surrounding the fetus in the womb. In China, Korea, and Japan there is folklore about the Nine-Tailed Fox, who shapeshifts into a woman.

Numbers are among the first things taught in primary school, and names for numbers are one of the first things taught in foreign language study. Understanding numbers is a basic part of priestess training. Numbers are literally in the blood, because mathematical systems grew out of a need to anticipate menstruation, control fertility, and chart the course of pregnancy. Yet even though women gave birth to math, numbers should not be considered intrinsically masculine or feminine, with the exception of the number one as all-that-is, which by its parthenogenetic nature is always female. Meditating on numbers—not just your personal associations and the associations you've learned but the core qualities of numbers themselves—will bring your divinatory powers to a new level.

The Snowshoe Queen

The following is a sequel to a myth related in Invoking Animal Magic,

where the Norse gods of Vanir are forced to kill the eagle giant Thiassi
to save the goddess Idunn. After Thiassi is killed, his formidable
daughter Skadi appears at the Vanir council demanding restitution for
the death of her father. The gods agree she is entitled to compensation,
and one of her requests is a husband of her choice…

Nine moons a child grows in the womb, and these nine moons rule the nine worlds of the gods. Each is rooted in the Tree like an umbilical cord in the many-veined placenta. Nine nights the god Odin hung from this Tree, his feet bound and his head reversed, enfolded in the wisdom of the Tree. Nine daughters the sea goddess Ran brought into her world, each riding the crest of a different wave. Nine mothers, all of them sisters, raised the god Heimdell, who guards the Bifrost Bridge between worlds. Nine nights, the newly married Skadi and Njord agreed, were necessary but sufficient to assess the success of their marriage.

The start of their life together was not auspicious. Njord did not warm to the snowy terrain of Skadi's beloved Thrymheim. He hated the howl of the wolves at night. He hated the roaring waterfalls; the ice cracking; the thunderous avalanches; the wind bombarding the firs; the yowling, growling, whimpering wolves. He suggested the couple retire to his own estates.

Skadi had been given—no she had demanded—her choice of the gods of Vanir. She had chosen the god with the most beautiful legs, who turned out to be the sea god Njord. Skadi herself had developed powerful calves through daily snowshoeing, so from the standpoint of legs this couple was admirably suited for one another. Skadi could not understand why things were not going well.

She agreed to try living in Noatun, which Njord assured her was an idyllic place. During those nine nights Skadi was as unhappy as she had ever been in her life. Her peace of mind was disturbed by the shriek of seagulls, the pounding of waves, the stench of seaweed, the constant battle between sea and rocky shore, and the jarring call of the gulls. The marriage was not working out.

They parted amicably. Nine nights in both places was a thorough test, and Skadi loved her wolves more than any husband, if she had to make that choice. There are those who claim she eventually found a consort more like herself, but this cannot be proven. With her mountains, her snowshoes, and her wolves, she is happy enough.

Questioning the Sentinels

1) Would you want to have scorpion protectors? If so, how many?

2) Why would a scorpion goddess have power over breath?

3) Why seven scorpions? Why scorpion twins?

4) Scorpions emit a mild florescence, which shows up well under black light. What magical quality would this bring?

5) Are you, in any small way, like Gilgamesh? Specifically: Do you expect things you have not worked for or earned? Do you discard the advice of experienced people who try to help you? Do you ever become so driven you forget to eat, rest, or play?

6) If you had already been stung six times by scorpions, what would the significance of a seventh sting have?

7) What things do you associate with the number seven?

8) What qualities would the eight-sided star or octahedron have?

9) Why does a cat have nine lives, as opposed to eight or ten?

Chapter 6

Seeing the Puzzle

Quoth the Raven, Evermore!

Ghastly grim and ancient Raven wandering from the Nightly shore—
Tell me what thy lordly name is on the Night's Plutonian shore!
Quoth the Raven "Nevermore."
—Edgar Allan Poe, "The Raven"

Figure 60: Ravens yelling in an aspen tree. Photo: U.S. National Park Service.

At the end of my trail run I wearily transition to a walk as I cross an open field. I hear a barrage of croaking as I pass a tree where three ravens monitor my movements. I break into a run again because the ravens tell me there is a message waiting at home. A great deal of pondering goes into the interpretation of a raven's message, but for me the message of the raven is usually that there is a message. *Head's up! There's somebody trying to get ahold of you. You have a package! Have you checked your email? Notice the blinking red light by the phone when you get inside.*

It's almost always good news. Really, I don't know what the naysayers are talking about when they try to make the raven negative. Ravens are alert and curious creatures, they love to gossip, and they stick their beaks in everybody's business. If there's good news coming, they have to be the first to tell you. *Croak croak croak*: it means you have a visitor, a promotion in the works, a godchild on the way. *Croak croak croak*: it means there is no privacy in this world, and there's always somebody around to spill the beans.

The various species of corvids—including ravens, crows, magpies, rooks, and jays—have complex and highly varied social lives. Variations in social organization have at least as much to do with environment as with species, and it is difficult to avoid conflating members of this group, particularly when we move into folklore. Ancient cultures in many cases do not appear to distinguish between them.

We tend to think of corvids in groups. Poe's raven was ominous before she ever opened her beak, solely for being solitary. A single raven speaks without speaking of isolation. I am not suggesting that you necessarily read something unhappy into the single raven, only that you recognize her as singular. By the way, if Poe's raven really was "tapping gently rapping," then she was female, not male as the poem suggests, as this is part of sexual dimorphism of the species.

Let's examine the social behavior of corvids more closely. A baby corvid is hatched in a tree or cliff nest with three or more siblings. Her father and mother guard her fiercely and cater to her gargantuan appetite. While adult ravens quarrel between themselves over choice morsels, parents share food of highest quality with their offspring. Sometimes the hatchling has an older sister or two helping to feed and protect her. As the youngsters fledge, the family remains together for weeks or months or years, congregating with others of their kind in the winter months. When the young adult finally flies out on her own, she may or may not remain close by, but she will almost certainly join a flock composed of corvids who have not nested, either because they are too young or because they have found no open territories. The size of the flock will vary from about a dozen to more than a hundred, depending on species and availability of food. Within that group the young corvid will likely find a special someone to share her life, and she and her mate will groom each other and roost side-by-side. At dusk the flock will resemble lunch tables at a middle school, with everyone jockeying to sleep close to their favorite friends.

If the couple is lucky enough to find an open territory, they will defend it vigorously while nesting, although once their youngsters fledge they may be tolerant or even welcoming to select visitors. The parents may take a late summer vacation with friends and they may congregate with others during the winter months.

There is a correlation between high social interaction and what biologists define as intelligence, although the correlation is not a strict one. The complex social organization of bees, for example, is dismissed as "instinct," with instinct posited as the opposite of intelligence. We humans seem to be born with so little innate good sense that it is not something we value. Perhaps problem-solving in novel situations, as opposed to instinct, is difficult

Figure 61: Bronze crow statue from Romano-Celtic temple in Oxfordshire, England.

to document and replicate in a laboratory setting, and so by defining intelligence this way we set other animals up for failure and can reassure ourselves that most "intelligence" belongs to us.

However intelligence is defined, corvids have broken through investigative barriers and convinced biologists that they are very smart, shoring up conventional folk wisdom. Wherever this family of birds is found, which is in most of the world, they are portrayed in local folklore as highly intelligent, usually outsmarting all the other animals. Biologist John Marzluff makes the interesting point that since corvids developed their current brain power about eight million years ago, judging by cranial size, while the human intellectual leap began two and half million years ago, early humans "came face to face with savvy crows and ravens who could easily outwit them."[36]

A lot of people would maintain that they can still outwit us. People in many large cities are plagued by crow thievery and vandalism. Stealing laundry, scattering garbage, snatching jewelry, vandalizing cars—the anecdotes are endless, and while humans devise ingenious ways to foil them, crows devise ingenious ways to circumvent all obstacles. They truly are the worthy opponents of *Homo sapiens*.

In terms of objective measures of cognition, a few of the tests crows have passed are noteworthy. They not only play and use tools, they can *make* their own tools and toys. They can recognize their own mirror reflection. When the communication code of prairie dogs was broken in the 1990s, revealing the code to have some qualities of language, it was the intelligence of nearby wild ravens that truly stunned the researchers. Ravens already understood the conversations of prairie dogs and responded accordingly. Ravens have their own distinct calls—eighty or more—that are context-specific in meaning and vary by region.[37] In other words, they also have a language of sorts. It is not as complex as human language, but crow and raven pets often do learn a few human words or phrases that they are able to use in context. This is in addition to the famous corvid mimicry, which can cover a wide range of human-made sounds (trucks, laughter, sirens) and the calls of other birds. The use of other bird calls may be used strategically, such as when Blue Jays mimic the cries of Broad-Winged Hawks to scare other birds away from food.

Ravens communicate with each other with a wide variety of postures, flight patterns, and wing gestures. Flight movements and wing gestures of wild ravens have been used by northern indigenous hunters to locate caribou. Here the line between divination and interspecies communication becomes blurred, because ravens sometimes rely on human hunters to help them gain access to the carcasses of large animals. Yes, animals read the signs of humans, too.

In the science of augury, the direction a bird flies from and to is critical. The associations with each of the directions vary according to religious tradition and whether you are in the northern or southern hemisphere. Pay attention also to what is, physically, in that direction where the raven flies. By this I mean, is the raven flying from town? Towards a lake? Towards your house?

Whether the raven lands near you, appears to recognize you, or acts hostile toward you is significant. While ravens and crows all look alike to us, they can tell themselves and us apart based on visual clues. We don't know why their eyesight is more discerning than ours, but it may have to do with their tetrachromatic (four-cone) vision, a trait they share with others in the Passeriformes order. Raven feathers, after all, are not uniformly black but blackish brown, green, navy, or purple, and to more discriminating eyes this variation may be consequential. From an evolutionary standpoint, color vision is all about discernment. Ravens and crows recognize human facial features, a trait biologists take advantage of when applying color bands and tracking devices. The birds strenuously object to being captured and banded, so researchers wear masks when handling them to discourage aggressive corvid behavior toward ordinary citizens. Ravens even teach their children to avoid the people in the masks.

No matter how much research is funded and how many papers published, ravens and crows will always understand us better than we understand them. Their survival depends on becoming familiar with our behavior, exploiting our weaknesses and avoiding our traps. They are now so attuned to our ways that they are aware of variations in speed limit along the roads they scavenge and have learned the basics of picnic etiquette.

Though our interactions with crows and ravens have changed as we have changed, the symbiotic relationship between us is ancient. Since they know so darn much about what is going on, it would be surprising if they had not been designated creatures of prophecy. Are they truly omniscient? Do they really know that

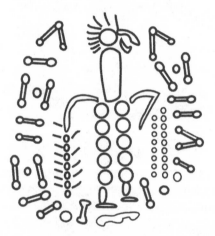

Figure 62: Coin from the Balkan peninsula depicting raven goddess with her bones. Possibly Celtic. Bulgaria, first or second century BCE.

you will have unexpected guests for dinner, and that the light on your answering machine is blinking? This seems like a bit of a stretch, even for me. The thing of it is, in divination it does not matter what the raven knows; what matters is what *we* know when we encounter the raven.

When Alexander of Macedon saw ravens quarreling at the gates of Babylon, the emperor knew this was an evil sign, though he continued into the city. A few weeks later he was on his deathbed. Ravens portended calamity to this man in this place at this time in his life. The association of ravens with death and ill fortune is the most widespread and pervasive in Western cultures. In folklore of southern Spain, for example, one croak of the raven means misfortune and three croaks means death. Franco-Americans will sometimes refer to nuns (in a derogatory way) as "crows," a habit that began in long ago France, where superstition had it that wicked nuns became crows after death while priests became ravens. Swedish folklore portrays ravens as the disturbed souls of unfortunates denied a Christian burial. Like the priest-raven connection, this is a probable distortion of a pre-Christian belief.

But is disaster necessarily the message of the raven? When Alexander was lost in the deserts west of Egypt, after torrential rains wiped out the road, two ravens appeared, and the emperor understood they had appeared to guide his party. Soon the conquerors had found the oasis at Siwa. Ravens portended salvation to this same man in this other place at this other time in his life. Whether Classical historians were embellishing or accurately reporting is not important here: the contradictory interpretations show a nuanced view of raven symbolism, dependent on circumstantial variables.

In Mesopotamia, where Alexander died, the raven plays a pivotal role in the culmination of The Great Flood, a story of Sumerian origin that most people know as the "Noah and the Ark" story of the Bible. In the version presented in *The Epic of Gilgamesh*, the boat called "The Preserver of Life" runs aground on a mountaintop soon after the rains cease. The hero Utnapishtim releases a dove seven days later, but the bird soon returns. Utnapishtim releases a swallow to the same effect. When the raven does not return, Utnapishtim has received confirmation that the floodwaters are receding. He frees the livestock and other animals he has brought on his boat, and the family performs ceremonies of gratitude to the gods, at least to the friendly ones who did not cause the flood. The goddess Belet-ili is angry with the perpetrator, the god Enlil, and the god Enki brokers a deal that involves some concessions from the storm god: never again will he attempt to annihilate humanity, and he will confer upon Utnapishtim and his wife immortality.

Ravens generally have large territories, especially in desert regions, so the raven's disappearance counterpoised with the return of the dove and swallow may be related to finding or not finding a suitable place to land. Yet the boat is, after all, already stuck on land. The story probably invokes an omen well known to early listeners of the tale: raven disappearance signifying ebbing of floodwater; raven arrival predicting rain. Another possibility is that Utnapishtim's raven fled because the carrion-eater knew that the disaster was finished and flesh would not be available for harvest.

Mesopotamian raven predictions tend toward acquisition of wealth, especially unexpected windfalls (which in a way ties into the idea of raven as rain omen in that dry climate). Raven associations with death are well documented in Celtic and Germanic lore. The Irish goddess Morrigan changes into a crow to foreshadow the death of the hero Cuchulainn. When he dies in battle she alights on his body to signify that she has taken him. The name of the goddess Badh Catha is often translated "battle crow." The name Bran, which means "crow," is given to a Welsh hero who voyages into the land of the dead and another hero who reincarnates as a crow. The Continental Celtic goddess Cathubodua, whose name means "battle raven" is portrayed riding a horse, which you will recall from the earlier chapter is often another war symbol. This is just a sample of the Celtic raven battle/death divinities. They are ubiquitous.

A caution about the Celtic "warrior goddess." The majority of Celtic goddesses found in glossaries, most of whom we know little about, are given this appellation. This is not necessarily wrong, but it is misleading. The Celts *were* prone to military skirmishes to send messages and settle accounts, but the period in which the Celts emerged into recorded history was characterized by prolonged battle fueled by desperate efforts to fight off Roman subjugation. All people take their gods into battle with them. The legends that were meaningful during this period were prominent in the memory of later historians, usually monks, who recorded them. Contemporary accounts from Roman invaders emphasized military culture and had their own biases. It's also unlikely that early historians knew much (or cared much) about women's stories and culture. Add to this mix the recorders' desire to exalt a pre-Christian past while remaining sensible to the authorities of the times, and it's easy to see how warrior culture could play an outsized role. The problem is one not of accuracy but of emphasis and omission.

Figure 63: Ravens and magpies compete with a wolf for an elk carcass. Photo: Jim Peaco/U.S. National Park Service.

The cautions about the fierce Celts and their fierce goddesses with their fierce ravens apply as much, if not more so, to the Norse. In fact, there has been a backlash in recent years against the marauding Viking stereotype by practitioners of Norse paganism, especially since the Germanic religions seem to attract people who romanticize warfare. We must keep this in mind as we turn to the Valkyries, bloodthirsty maidens who ride on white horses above the battlefield, waiting to carry off the souls of the slain. They have a special relationship with the raven, who is sometimes sister, sometimes child, sometimes friend—leading to speculation that the raven is really a form of the Valkyrie goddess herself. The Valkyrie maidens are usually referred to as a multiplicity, with nine being a favored number.

Raven and crow behavior supports the battle symbolism. Both are scavengers who cannot feed on large unrented corpses, though they will peck out the eyes of the dead. Ravens did haunt battlefields at one time, waiting to feast on the fallen, and even today they shadow hunters. They tear off pieces of the carcass to cache, flying back and forth to get more beakfuls, and if you didn't know any better you would think they were carrying the soul off to that other place. In pre-Indo-European cultures that practiced excarnation, ravens would have feasted on the dead after bodies had been torn open, perhaps by owls. Neither the Celtic nor the Germanic tribes disposed of their dead in this way, but this was probably a part of the symbology of the earlier cultures they absorbed.

Despite being extremely social, ravens and crows squabble quite a bit between themselves, fighting over food and territory. They even, rarely, perform "executions," a practice poorly understood though well documented. Corvids do not routinely harm members of their posse who are ailing and will even protect the disabled and bring them food. The dominant theory is that solitary birds with no allies eventually excite territorial instincts. Whatever the reason, the flock becomes very noisy as a number of birds execute the offender. Once killed, the cacophony abates suddenly and the birds abscond, leaving behind the corpse.

More common than executions of their own kind is mobbing of raptors. Any songbird might take part in a mobbing, but jays and crows are the most enthusiastic, while the larger and less vulnerable ravens seldom bother. Ravens do buzz and snap at eagles, perhaps to draw eagles away from nest sites (although this does not totally explain things). Some ravens hang out around wolf packs, waiting to devour leftovers from a carcass. In the meantime they enjoy teasing the wolves, pulling their tails and scampering off.

The raven-wolf pairing is more conspicuous in Germanic lore than the raven-horse, although both can be found. Two wolves sit at the feet of the god Odin, while two ravens flank his shoulders. The names of these ravens are Huginn and Muninn, usually translated as "thought" and "memory." Odin the Allfather "sends them out at daybreak to fly over the whole world, and they come back at breakfast-time; by this means he comes to know a great deal about what is going on, and on account of this men call him the god-of-ravens."[38] There is some controversy over the translation of "Muninn," who is mentioned less frequently than his sidekick in extant Germanic lore. Two pertinent questions usually not entertained would be 1) Are these ravens really guy-ravens or is this a case of default male bias? and 2) Why *two* ravens?

The sex of the ravens does matter, since ravens are Odin's servants and the Valkyries, called the daughters of Odin, serve him on the battlefield as well as in Valhalla. In the *Poetic Edda* the battlefield is referred to as "Huginn's grove,"[39] so one or both of these same ravens are hovering alongside the fight like the Valkyries. Perhaps Huginn and Muninn are the culmination of a process beginning with a dominant raven-goddess, changing to a raven-goddess subsumed under rule of the Allfather, culminating with a subordinate raven deity stripped of feminine association.

That *two* wolves and *two* ravens flank Odin is curious. Why not one raven-wolf pair? Why not nine ravens? Two is not an automatically recurring number in Germanic lore; nine, and occasionally three, are the most prominent numbers. If this were a story of Semitic origin I would attribute the pair of ravens to cultural emphasis on complementary halves, but that is unlikely to be the case here. When Odin says he has two ravens, he means that the ravens are two, and we do have to ask, why *two*?

The idea that the mind of the God is divided into thought and memory is suspect, since this is a dualistic concept that, if it existed at all, would most probably have arisen through Christian influence. The translation of Muninn's name as "memory" is contested anyway. There are marriages between gods and goddesses, which might explain the raven-pair, as marriages are often ways of blending the pantheons of conquerors with those of

Figure 64: Bracteate of Odin with a horse and a raven. Sixth century.

indigenous people. There are other deities that are commonly thought of in pairs, such as the goddess Frigga and her son Baldur, and the boar-goddess Freya with her boar-brother Freyr. Could Odin's winged familiars be brother-sister raven deities?

Where the number two arises most frequently is in reference to the Aesir and Vanir, the two branches of pantheons that came together under the reign of the Odin. Feminist scholars theorize that these groups represent an indigenous Old European pantheon (the Vanir) linked to a conquering Indo-European pantheon (the Aesir).[40] We could also call them two allied Indo- or pre-Indo-European pantheons—the point is that they represent the confederation of two tribes. This would explain why Odin has two ravens and wolves at his command: they represent the raven-wolf totems of each of these tribes. This is supported by Odin's revelation in the *Prose Edda*, "Over the world every day fly Hugin and Munin; I fear that Hugin will not come back, though I'm more concerned about Munin."[41] To me this speaks of a ruler trying to maintain control of an unruly alliance.

The references to Apollo, Odin, Lugh, or Arthur as corvid deities abound, while references to corvid goddesses with specific, longstanding, and proven associations are harder to find outside pagan texts. This is not merely because the feminine was de-emphasized and distorted in patriarchal antiquity, although it was; the process of culling continues today, with mythology in Western societies becoming increasingly masculine in character.

Apollo is the god most often cited in modern texts as a crow deity. The cult of Apollo grew at a fantastic rate in the centuries before the Common Era. Apollo overtook religious centers throughout Greece, western Anatolia, and the Aegean, including the most famous shrine at Delphi, and in the process became the god of oracles, healing, music, all the arts, the sun, history, philosophy, mathematics, all of scholarship, husbandry, archery, youth, truth, politics, moderation, and ecstatic prophesy. In the process he acquired the lyre, the laurel tree, the pillar, the bow, snakes, wolves, dolphins, cattle, sacred stones, scores of healing and oracular sites, the number seven, the number nine, the number ten, the number twelve, and of course crows. Before he colonized so many things and became the god of colonists (true), he surely had some original sphere in function, region, or personality. The oldest association that has been found is Apollo as mouse-god, and it's possible that this deity of a nocturnal underground creature had a complementary role as god of light, particularly if his mouse cult had a Semitic origin as Robert Graves maintains.[42] I discuss Apollo as mouse god in my earlier book *Invoking Animal Magic*.

Figure 65: Apollo with a crow.

I had assumed that a few disgruntled priests decided to award Apollo the crow as symbol of thieves because he had stolen so many things, but I discovered in my research that Apollo appropriated oracular shrines of the crow god Cronus, so the irony may have been unintentional.

Cronus is vaguely familiar to most people as somehow tied to the family tree of the Olympians. This genealogy arose out of a need to put merging pantheons into a coherent framework while at the same time justifying the dominance of the cult serving the ruling class, and so should be treated with some of the cynicism in which it arose. There are conflicting stories about how Cronus came to be born and to rule, but by any account he was one of the old guard who was overthrown by the newer gods. The name Cronus has been linked to the Greek "korax" (meaning crow) from which we get the English words "crown" and "corona." Speculative etymology is an insufficient foundation to build a relationship, but there are other clues. The sickle belongs to Cronus, which ties him to the curved bill of the crow. I was skeptical of this link until I looked at Neolithic sickles of the region, which are slightly curved and unlike the short-handled crescent sickles used where grain is still harvested by hand today. Crows are only too happy to harvest the grain as it ripens, so the old sickles are readily reminiscent of a crow head.

Cronus was worshiped at his cult centers for divination and for rain. Accepting Cronus as a crow deity or the sickle as a crow emblem makes the corvid/rain connection more logical. The crow deity brings rain to protect the vested interest crows have in the grain harvest. Cronus also has an association with death, as the ruler of the idyllic part of the underworld known as Elysium.

A less familiar goddess who has an explicit rather than strongly inferential link with crows is Coronis. She is one of the Hyades, the seven sisters of light who are rain-makers. Olympic genealogy makes her a parent with Apollo of the healing god

Asclepius. She is also tied to Apollo in a story where the mistrustful Apollo sends a crow to spy on the goddess, and she does indeed cheat on him with another god. Apollo has Coronis bumped off by his sister and punishes his crow for not halting the liaison by changing him from white to black. This story accomplishes three things: 1) it solidifies Apollo's ownership of the crow while denigrating the crow at the same time; 2) it explains why the god of light would have a black emblem; and 3) it justifies usurpation of the goddess's cult by making her demise a result of her own betrayal. Reading into this story a bit, I would guess the unruly priestesses of Coronis resisted the cult of Apollo effectively for a while.

The goddess Athena is believed to have turned Coronis herself from a white crow into a black crow. This is why the raven rests

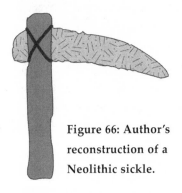

on the bust of Pallas in the Poe verse quoted at the start of this section. Pallas is another name for Athena. The story goes that a crow named Coronis brought Athena some bad news, and the goddess in a rage changed the feathers of Coronis from white to black and banished her from the Acropolis. I disagree with those who categorize the crow as a familiar of Athena on the basis of this story. I think crows and ravens were banished from Athena's temples because her priests wanted owls to nest there. Crows like to nest in high places (hence the term "crow's nest"), and they mob owls. The purpose in the mobbing is to defend chicks and eggs from owl predation, and yet crows seem to pursue owls with an unnecessary vehemence, seeming to attack them on principle. At any rate the two birds could not have cohabitated, so crows would have to be banished from Athena's domain. In addition to firmly linking Coronis with the crow, this story again makes the crow an

Figure 66: Author's reconstruction of a Neolithic sickle.

oracular bird, in this case a bearer of bad news.

Sometimes the truth is not what we care to hear, but whether the corvid's message is welcoming or sorrowful, the truth behind her message is that she is concerned with us and places herself amidst our affairs. The lives of corvids and humans are inextricably tied together, making them ours forevermore.

Raven-Kin

The troops of the hero Owain, son of Morgan Le Fay and nephew of King Arthur, take the form of ravens to counterattack Arthur's men in The Dream of Rhonabwy. *This internecine war is fought through a game board, with the two chiefs maneuvering game pieces to direct the combat. Each game defines a battle. The game is called* gwyddbwyll, *and we don't know how it's played. It is not a precursor to chess, nor is it derivative, but it is analogous in superficial ways. The game board represents the land, which is also the embodiment of the goddess.*

Cast of Characters

Arthur: A king of Wales.

Owain: Another king of Wales.

Blond Page: Curly-haired with blue eyes, wispy beard. He wears a yellow tunic over chartreuse leggings and shoes of particolored leather with gold buckles. His sword has three edges and a golden hilt. The black leather scabbard of the sword is also trimmed in gold.

Auburn Page: Large and muscular with a sunburned face. His curly hair is auburn and he has large eyes. He wears a yellow satin cloak embroidered in red silk. His black boots lace high over his white linen trousers, and they have golden buckles. He carries a three-sided sword, with a red gold-edged scabbard made from the hide of a roe deer.

White-Haired Page: He has rosy cheeks and large glinting eyes. His green satin scarf is fastened with a gold brooch and he wears fine wool leggings. His multi-colored leather slippers have gold buckles. He carries a tall sharp lance with a flag attached.

Leopard Knight: He is heavily armored and carries a single-edged sword with gilt handle and green scabbard trimmed in brass. The sword is secured in its sheath with a belt of dark green leather and a black leather clasp inlaid with ivory. On the prow of his gold helmet sits a gold leopard with ruby eyes. His horse is dapple gray and wears a scarlet caparison and yellow stockings.

White Knight: Rides a white horse sporting a black caparison edged in yellow. The horse has black stockings. The knight wears a yellow robe of quilted satin bordered in green and he has heavy green armor. His three-edged sword is housed in red leather. The belt securing the sword is gold trimmed deer leather, with an ivory and black leather tongue for a clasp. On the gold sapphire-encrusted helmet of this knight crouches a lion with malevolent carnelian eyes. The lion's flaming red tongue lolls.

Black Knight: Rides a black horse with red caparison and white stockings. The horse also wears a blanket that is half black, half white, trimmed all the way around in red gold. The knight wears a mantle of the same fabric. Both knight and horse carry speckled brass armor. The knight's sword is three-edged, with gold hilt and gold leather belt, the belt fastened with a black whale-bone buckle. The knight's helmet is yellow brass inlaid with crystal, with a menacing griffin on top. The griffin has a huge glittering eye that sparkles many colors.

Game One

Setting: In front of a white tent with red trimmed canopy. Owain and Arthur are seated at a table with a board game.

(A black serpent with glinting red eyes and crimson flaming tongue emerges from the tent's crown. Blond Page emerges from the tent.)

Blond Page: King Owain! Horses are tormenting your ravens. Help!

Owain (to Arthur): I think that message is for you, lord, not me.

Arthur: That page in the yellow tunic was addressing you. I have already heard from my messenger.

(Horses and ravens scream.)

Owain: Surely not, lord! He said my ravens are tormented.

Arthur: It is your page with the green stockings and hence your message.

(Ravens silently fly overhead en masse.)

Arthur: Hahaha. You should have taken heed. My game.

(Blond Page returns to the tent.)

Game Two

Setting: Outside a bright yellow tent. Owain and Arthur are seated at a table with a board game. A vermilion lion crouches atop the canopy.

(Auburn Page emerges from the tent.)

Auburn Page: Do you know the king's horses are again harassing your ravens? We are doomed!

Owain: You cannot play in this manner, sir! Desist with this extemporaneous movement.

(Horses and ravens scream.)

Arthur: Is that genuine Roe leather on that young man's scabbard?

Owain: I will not employ your method, sir.

(Ravens silently fly overhead en masse.)

Arthur: I believe gold-edged triangle-swords could not triumph in this instance. It is again my game.

(Auburn Page returns to the tent.)

Game Three

Setting: In front of a huge speckled yellow tent are Owain and Arthur seated at a table with a board game.

(A golden eagle with carnelian eye lands on top of the tent.)

White-Haired Page exits the tent. The White-Haired Page salutes Owain.

White-Haired Page: Lord, hundreds of your ravens are slaughtered.

Owain: Please stop this, sir.

Arthur: No my dear Owain. Cease parlaying with this page in the green neckwear and play the game.

Owain (to White-Haired Page): Return to the battle, and raise the flag you carry at the thickest part of the fighting.

(The flag is raised and the ravens flap their wings in fierceness. The ravens descend in cacophony.)

(Leopard Knight on horseback approaches King Arthur. The tip of the knight's green lance is stained with blood.)

Leopard Knight: Your horses are being slain by the ravens. They are suffering.

Arthur: Time to scatter your ravens, my lord Owain.

Owain: Oooooh. A horse in a red dress. With yellow stockings. Impressive. Now play the game.

(Leopard Knight exits. There is screeching of horses, croaking of ravens.)

(The White Knight approaches the gamesmen. The silver tip of the lance drips blood.)

Arthur: I beg of you, Owain, you are slaying the best men and horses of Britain, and this island will become impossible to defend. Stop at once.

Owain: If things are so dire you must desist in idle chatter with your lion lidded knight. Play this game, lord.

(Horses thunder past in a group, no longer shrieking.)

Owain: Wait, I believe it is my game now.

(White Knight exits.)

Game Four

Setting: Owain and Arthur seated at a table with a board game.

Figure 67

Tent is collapsed and surroundings are disheveled.

(Horses screech; ravens scream. Black Knight comes racing up to Arthur. The knight's azure silver-tipped spear is covered in blood.)

Black Knight: The ravens are routing us, sir!

(Arthur crushes all game pieces into dust.)

Arthur (to Owain): I believe the time has come for a truce.

Owain: You mean that I have won.

Arthur: No, the game is suspended.

Owain: You have conceded then.

Arthur: No, I do not concede. Your move.

(Owain looks down at the table, which has no game pieces to move.)

Owain: Let the flag be lowered; this game is suspended.

Cache and Release

This fable is based on a story in Jewish Fairy Tales, *collected by Gerald Friedlander.*[43]

There was a young man devoted to his father, we'll call him Samuel, who promised the old man at his deathbed that he would feed the fishes.

"Always I left bread on the water after I had removed my nets," said the father. "I did not lay bread over my nets to trick the fishes, that would be mean. I took my day's catch and then I gave bread to the ones who were left."

"Yes Father, I will continue as you wish," said Samuel. And he did just that, tossing bread in the water at the end of every day's fishing. It developed, however, that one fish, more aggressive and selfish than the others, ate most of the bread and grew very large. One day this fish jumped out of the water and swallowed Samuel.

The big fish did not swallow the man who brought his daily meals in order to consume him; he swallowed Samuel to bring him to an even larger fish—a whale—for a consultation. The whale was curious to find out why Samuel was leaving the daily bread rations, and the greedy fish hoped to divert attention from his self-centeredness by bringing the man to the whale.

So the big fish ejected the fisherman deep in the water, and the whale in turn swallowed the fisherman. Deep in the caverns of the gargantuan stomach Samuel heard the echoing voice of the whale, inquiring about the daily bread delivery. Samuel explained that he was continuing a kindness that had been started by his father. The man and the whale then conversed about the prophet Jonah, because apparently the ancient story of the prophet trapped for three days in the whale's belly is also told among whales. Finally the whale announced that before releasing Samuel on shore, he would give the young man the gift of understanding the speech of animals. Samuel already understood the speech of animals well enough to discuss scripture with a whale, but he was in no position to negotiate.

When Samuel reached dry land, he felt dizzy and had to rest under a tree before walking home. Drowning does not occur when men find themselves deep in the ocean if they are part of a fish story, but they can still find themselves woozy when they return to the open air. Samuel felt woozy.

A fledgling crow noticed Samuel under the tree and said to his father, "That man is dead. I will peck his eyes out."

The mature crow said, "You naughty little bird. He is only asleep."

The little crow hopped on the Samuel's shoulder, undeterred. "His eyes are closed, so maybe he is dead."

Samuel, who was only resting, not asleep, and certainly not dead, had overheard this conversation. He reached over and grabbed the little bird by his little bird legs.

"Oh no! Don't hurt my crow boy!" said the father crow.

"He was going to peck my eyes out," responded Samuel.

The father flew over to the tree branch above Samuel. "Let my son go, and I will lead you to a magnificent treasure."

"Lead me to the treasure," said Samuel warily, "and I will release the crow."

The father sailed to the ground and began scooping dirt with his bill. "It is right here where I buried it," said the crow.

Sure enough, there was a large treasure chest cached below the tree. Samuel released the bird as he filled his pockets.

"What a lucky escape!" said the crows as they flew away.

"What a lucky discovery!" said Samuel's family when he returned home with his loot.

"What a lucky break that the big fish isn't eating all the bread anymore," said the fish who were lucky enough to escape Samuel's nets the next day.

But Samuel understood that all this good luck was the blessing of his late father, and he remembered to say his prayers of gratitude.

Raven Review

Magical Qualities: black, scavenger, intelligent, noisy, good at mimicry, social, unpredictable, drawn to novelty

Magical Applications: shamanic visioning, healing (especially vision, exhaustion), money, eloquence

Other Associations: wisdom, rain, conflict, thievery, mischief, wealth, death

Visionary Know-How

Superior visual ability is one of the key characteristics of the superhero. Superhuman vision can mean seeing through walls and buildings, seeing across galaxies, seeing past and future events, seeing in total darkness, seeing with perfect recall, seeing the other superheroes who are invisible to everyone else, and shooting laser beams through the eyes. No living creature on our planet can do any of these things, but still we dream. Moving into the realm of the more-plausible-if-you-don't-think-too-long-about-it, is the 1970s television show *The Six Million Dollar Man*, where astronaut Steve Austin sports a bionic replacement for his injured eye that has 20.2:1 acuity. No one seems to know what this number means, except that it is much better than the eyesight of an eagle, who can discern a rabbit from two miles away. It is supposed to convey the idea of better-than-perfect acuity. Austin's bionic eye can also see in total darkness by translating infrared heat sensors into visual images, and he can form images at high speed to apprehend things that are moving too quickly to be grasped in detail by the normal human eye. The eye also shoots lasers.

If I were to devise the perfect eye it would have, like Steve Austin's eye, great apprehension of detail over a very large range. It would be equally astute at close and far distances. It would perceive colors from the infrared to the ultraviolet, and it would distinguish small nuances within the whole color spectrum. It would register clear true-color images in total darkness and in dazzling sunlight. It would have a 360 degree stereoscopic field of vision at all times, and detail within that entire field would be perfectly in focus. It would be able to detect pinpoints of distant starlight. It would be able to track the position of the sun on a cloudy day or in thick fog. It would be able to form images at a few hundredths of a second, so that nothing could speed by too quickly to be noted in detail, yet it would be able to hold in focus stationary objects. Moving from near to far vision, and vice versa, would be instantaneous. Visual memory would be photographic, and depth perception would be superb. Pattern and form recognition would be complex. There would be no blind spots, and no breakdown of image or color integrity. It would see equally well in water and air mediums. It would be well protected from cold, heat, sand, dryness, ultraviolet radiation, predators, and any other conceivable source of injury. Last but certainly not least, it would be lightweight and energy efficient, requiring little physical nourishment.

I'm probably forgetting something important, but you're also probably getting the idea that this kind of perfect eye is unknown in the animal world, and that some of these characteristics are as mutually exclusive as running fast and slow at the same time. Not that Mother Nature has given up. She has responded to the challenges by not only modifying the structure but also by reinventing the basic design more than once. The octopus and the orca both have good eyes for underwater vision, but octopus eyes developed from the skin while orca eyes, like those of all vertebrates, are part of the brain. Nature gives her creatures two or more eyes, since a single one won't do the job, and scorpions can have as many as twelve. Always there are compromises. The widely spaced eyes of the deer allow constant monitoring of the environment but preclude binocular depth perception beyond sixty degrees. This is why a deer must turn her head to see you clearly, despite her wide visual field. The owl has very good binocular perception and can form a clear optical image in dim light, but only at the expense of huge forward facing eyes that cannot move in their sockets; hence her need to turn her head frequently. Human eyes move constantly, which is a good thing, because only a small portion at the center can form a crisp image. Still, outside the clear picture zone the human eye can detect motion reasonably well and can form images in low light. In fact, though the idea of "which animal sees the best" ultimately makes no sense, if I *had* to pick a winner I would choose humans.

Now wait a minute. I am aware that most people think humans have poor eyesight. It is true that our kitty cats see much better than we do in the dark. A hawk can see about eight times farther. A honeybee would view film at 24 frames per second not as a "moving picture" but as a series of snapshots. A goldfish discerns colors in the near-infrared and some snakes discriminate into the ultraviolet. Butterflies can distinguish close detail much better. Rabbits react to visual stimuli instantaneously. Wild geese can navigate in the clouds while we get lost in a fog. We could go on and on. There are two areas of vision in humans and other apes, however, that are impressive. The first is good color vision combined with passable night vision. Some moths combine these characteristics better than we do, but this is a rare combination in the animal world. The other is pattern recognition, at which humans excel. It was through pattern recognition that our brain-power evolved, and recognition of animal signs requires close attention to patterns.

Let's move away for a moment from comparing visual abilities and look at two important things that all creatures have in common. The first is that they can see. Every multi-celled motile animal has visual organs. The most primitive developed from the cilia, the part of the cell responsible for movement. Vision emerged very early in evolution and outside of single-cell animals it is nearly universal. The exception is those animals who became sightless after adapting a niche in total darkness, such as cave spiders. Even these animals have vestigial non-functioning ocular organs. This brings us to the second point about vision, which is that it is perception of light. Always and by definition. "Seeing in the dark" is an oxymoron. Pit vipers do have thermal sensors near their eyes that allow them to locate prey in total darkness, and information from these sensors is conveyed along the optic nerve and processed in optic centers of the snake brain, so they may be translating this information into an image. But we're beginning to split hairs. Eyes are organs that perceive light waves. Light and vision go together.

Another universal characteristic of animal vision is visual memory. In superheroes, this means a perfect detailed photographic image that can be recalled without effort. Animal visual memory (including that of humans) is the opposite of this. The eye perceives aspects of the environment already recorded and the brain does not register this old information. Animal vision is selective and filtered; it ignores familiarity and is drawn to novelty. What is acknowledged as a sign also depends on filtered information. The novelty of your encounter turns an animal appearance into a sign.

Since we can't explore the vision of a wide range of animals here (that would take more than a hundred pages and about a thousand years of research on my part), it might be useful to consider various visual environments and apply these to animal signs.

The most obvious place to begin is in the ocean, where vision on earth began. Our planet being unusual for the amount of water it contains, the earth perspective is a watery one. Water changes light and thus perception. Water refracts light, meaning it bends light and slows it down. At the surface, the scattering light waves make it challenging to form an image. We perceive this as glare. As we move further down in the water, the longer and the shorter wavelengths of light, which we perceive as red and purple, become filtered out, until by about fifty feet under all colors are in the blue-green spectrum. By about six hundred feet, there is no longer enough light for photosynthesis, so there is no plant life. At three thousand feet, no light is coming through at all. By a process called bioluminescence, fish in this region make their own light to see, which makes them kind of like people.

In addition to the distorting effects of water on sunlight, water is often clouded by plankton, decaying material, and silt. The visual challenges of life underwater do not mean that fish necessarily have poor vision, however. Some detect and distinguish colors better than we do; others have the best low light vision of all vertebrates.

Water has the effect of making things appear closer than they really are, which is partly why fish tend to be nearsighted. Looking up from below the surface of the water, objects appear smaller; looking down from above they look larger. Birds who dive for fish underwater and marine mammals who live part of their lives on land have especially versatile powers of accommodation: they can see well in two worlds.

Predatory birds who search for prey from the air need the keen far-distance vision we so admire. Diurnal birds have good color vision, usually tetrachromatic (four cone) vision, a step above the trichromatic vision we have. The purpose of color vision, from an evolutionary point of view, is to detect contrast. Color vision requires a great deal of light, which is why most birds are active in the day and roost at night.

Nocturnal animals have fuzzier vision than day travelers. Their challenge is to form images quickly, and seeing in low light simply takes longer. They take advantage of every bit of light available with a reflective structure called the tapetum, which gives night animals their eyeshine and also sacrifices a bit of detail. The eyes of nocturnal animals tend to be proportionately larger. These eyes are concerned with concentrating light, not filtering it, so damage from ultraviolet light waves may occur in bright daylight. Still, nocturnal animals can usually see well enough to function in the daytime, while the reverse is usually not true for diurnal animals. I regularly see bats hunting in the daytime in spring. Most mammals and marsupials are nocturnal. Diurnal color vision evolved in fish and was retained (for the most part) in reptiles and birds. Early mammals became night creatures to escape predatory dinosaurs who, without the mammal's thermoregulation, could not function in cooler nighttime temperatures. In embracing the night, mammals lost their color vision. As mentioned earlier, we apes have to a large extent regained color vision, although the mechanism through which we see colors differs somewhat from non-mammals.

Vertebrates with eyes in front of their head have an overlapping visual field, which allows for good binocular vision. In general, predators have this type of vision. The exceptions include diurnal predatory birds or fish-eating whales. Animals with eyes on either side of their head sacrifice binocular vision for a larger field of vision and may have blind spots in front.

Some animals have the ability to track the direction of the sun in diffuse light, which we call polarized vision. Honeybees, who navigate using the angle of the sun as a guide, are a prime example of this. Homing Pigeons, spiders, and many other diverse creatures have polarized vision.

Birds and mammals tend to be farsighted, except for domestic creatures, who are almost always nearsighted. Humans tend to be nearsighted, in contrast to the wild apes who are slightly farsighted. Environment and visual habits play a significant part in how vision develops, sometimes permanently. Deer and other ungulates have a habit of scanning the horizon for predators, to the detriment of clear focus at closer range. There is a phase early in life in which stereoscopic depth perception develops in the human brain, and this perception depends on exposure and practice. A person who gains eyesight after childhood will have poor depth perception.

Certain acquired habits are the root of common vision problems in humans. One of these is inhibited eye movement. It is natural for the human eye (as well as the head and the rest of the body) to move constantly. When eye movement is repressed a variety of vision problems ensue, some of them paradoxical. People who habitually stare or otherwise do not allow their eyes to move naturally will perceive non-moving objects as stationary, which of course they are, yet poor vision is the result of this. People with good vision do not inhibit the "optical illusions" that make stationary objects appear to move. Vision pioneer William Bates[44] proved this through a series of experiments designed to register the illusion that as the eyes moved, stationary objects moved (or appeared to move) in the opposite direction. In these experiments, people with good vision noticed the optical illusion right away. People with near or far sightedness or astigmatism reflexively compensated and initially had difficulty recognizing the illusion. As vision improved, subjects began to detect movement in exercises designed to emphasize the phenomenon.

In sign interpretation, as in all forms of sight, it is important to relax enough to allow sensory data to register. This does not mean that we have to believe absurdities or accept illusions; it does mean that we need to allow data to reach consciousness without pre-filtering it to conform to our own paradigm. Otherwise, we become divinatory myopics, seeing the world "correctly" but seeing less and less of it over time. As you look for animal signs in an open, relaxed, and interested manner, your eyesight is bound to improve as well. I believe that seeing is visionary, and that attention to signs translates into better sight.

The ability to notice and categorize color is not necessarily different for men and women, although *colorblindness*—the inability to see red-green shades—is sex-linked and hereditary. Color discrimination for most people appears to be learned rather than innate. A few hunter-gatherer cultures only have words for black versus white, while even in developed countries numbers of words for color and ideas about the "basic colors" differ. Even without cultural emphasis on color differentiation, humans are able to distinguish contrast quite well, which biologists assure us is the primary purpose of color sight. In my opinion the superiority women exhibit in distinguishing colors comes from the importance fabric plays in female socialization. Male visual artists seem to have good color recognition and vocabulary, reinforcing the idea that color discrimination can be developed.

Children like bright colors. I decorated my child therapy waiting room with strong uncomplicated colors and was gratified to hear the squeals of delight from young children and to watch their eagerness to sit in the brightly colored chairs. (Adults, when they commented at all, said they found it a bit much.)

The English language has a rich color vocabulary, and it should come as no surprise that color plays an important role in Euro-shamanism. Here are a few ideas to consider when interpreting color.

Green shades are discriminated by human eyes better than any other, naturally enough, since we didn't climb down from the trees all that long ago. Green is the color of your favorite foods: lettuce, broccoli, cabbage, Brussels sprouts, kale, celery juice, spinach, asparagus, scallions, avocados, honeydew, pears, peas, and pistachios. Take a look at the vegetable section of your grocery and notice how green it is. Green was labeled a "fairy color" by early Celts, leading to the surmise that pre-Celtic peoples favored the color, perhaps as camouflage. Green is the color of the heart chakra and of the planet Venus. Remember that Venus is the planet of love and of abundance. The association of green with abundance colored the decision of the United States government to print green money. Only in the deepest oceans, the driest deserts, and the most desolate winters is the color green subdued. Green can also mean unripe or young in the sense of immature. The color green will probably not register with you on your daily walk because it is so pervasive, but if you are alert you may see a green bird, a green snake, or a green bug. Are you thinking about a trip to the Emerald Isle? Signs involving the color green may indicate that, in this instance, the time is ripe. Gods associated with green include the Green Man, Baldur, and Osiris. Female deities include Venus and the Dryads.

Blue is the color of the ocean. This is by default, as longer and shorter wavelengths of light become scattered and filtered by water molecules during the endless voyage to the deep. Blue is the color of the sky because molecules in the atmosphere scatter and absorb a good deal of shorter wavelength light (ultraviolet and violet) while scattering the slightly longer blue wavelength. Both of these effects contribute to the earth appearing blue from outer space. Blue is the color of the throat chakra and hence associated with communication. Deep blue was highly favored by the Sumerians, who developed the world's first written literature. So prized was this color of blue that a great deal of lapis lazuli was imported to that country, most of it coming from Afghanistan. Ancient Egyptians were partial to the much lighter shade of blue that today is painted in the bottom of swimming pools. Blue is a calming color that is associated with serenity in its paler shades and sadness in the realm of gray-blue. Clear shades of blue indicate truth. Blue is a protective color. The deities Isis, Inanna, Ishtar, and the Virgin Mary are associated with blue.

Red is the most important color in Dianic Witchcraft. Together with white and black, it forms the sacred triad of colors for most traditions in the Craft. Red is the color of menstruation and of birth, since both involve bleeding. Red is the color of motherhood and of the Mother phase in a woman's life cycle. The full moon once looked redder from earth, and it still has a reddish cast if you look at it closely, so red is sometimes regarded as the color of the full moon while the waxing moon is white and the dark moon is black. Contrary to popular belief, red is a low—not a high—

energy color, and its usefulness in magic stems from this fact. Looking at this from a physical angle, the wavelengths in the red spectrum are longer, slower, and have less energy. Shorter wavelengths in the upper violet spectrum have the most energy. Often a witch does not try to create from the upper spectrum because the energy is moving too quickly to be malleable. I liken it to hopping a freight train to go cross country. You might think that you would want to jump on a high-speed train to get to your destination sooner, but that train is moving too fast for you to mount. In spellcasting red can be diverted, molded, and transformed, and hence it is the most creative color. Red can also manifest as anger and sexual desire. Despite being lower, not higher, in energy, red is a stimulating color for humans. The god Mars is associated with red, as are the goddesses Diana, Hestia, and Freya. Celtic triple goddesses like Morrigan and Cerridwyn are linked with red, black, and white.

Yellow is an intellectually stimulating color guaranteed to keep you alert. The association of yellow both with fear and joy, two mutually exclusive emotions, is puzzling. Yellow as the color of fear goes back at least to medieval times, when yellow was associated not only with cowardice but also with other negative emotions such as resentment, jealousy, and betrayal. The dominant theory is that this arose from beliefs about jaundiced skin. I interpret yellow as a sign of elevated mood. Yellow coming into your environment might also presage a new field of study. The god Apollo and the goddess Brigid are associated with the color yellow.

Purple became associated with royalty through the rarity and expense of purple dyes, thus linking it with power. The bluer color of violet facilitates psychic activity and lighter violet expresses divine union. For this reason, purple is important in New Age philosophies and in some pagan priesthoods. Purple is also prominent in Christianity, used in liturgies of the advent and lent seasons. Purple was the color of the early twentieth century women's suffrage movement and lavender is the color of the gay rights movement. Thus the color carries a flavor of liberation. Whether we're talking about the color combination (red + blue) or the monochromatic prism violet may (possibly) be relevant for spellcasting, but for interpreting signs the distinction is unimportant. Purple can be associated with the god Pluto and with the lesbian goddess Artemis.

White light contains wavelengths across the visible spectrum. In bright (as opposed to low light) settings humans perceive white when all three types of color sensors (cones) are stimulated. Though we tend to think of white as the absence of color, it is in fact the presence of all colors. White clothing is valued in hot climates because it is somewhat reflective of light, and in dry Mediterranean regions clean white clothing has been reflective of economic means or social status. The reflective properties of white make it a good color for protection. Pure white signifies purity in the sense of being unadulterated, but white as a symbol of chastity is a patriarchal notion. White as the Maiden's color signifies the young waxing moon. Rare white animals that are usually dark-colored are considered emissaries from the Otherworld and held sacred. The white deer and white pigeon are prime examples. Animals that change from brown to white in winter symbolize transformation. Even animals that are usually white, such as the mute swan or the domestic white sow, are often linked with important goddesses. Both white and black are associated with death; in Old European graves statuettes of the Death Goddess are painted with chalk. In Celtic legend death appears to the hero as a very pale-skinned woman. "Death" signs are not necessarily about physical death and can mean transformation, change, or metaphysical journey.

Black is the complement of white and the absence of color. Black absorbs light and attracts power. In fact, black attracts just about everything: think of the lint drawn to black upholstery. Witches like to wear black and use black in magic for its attractive power, but the down side is that black attracts surrounding energy without discrimination, so its use calls for judicial application. Habitually wearing black can lead to depression. Black is a birth as well as a death color, the void that gives birth to light, the darkness in which seed germinates. In ancient Egypt black was associated with the fertile soil of the Nile inundation and thus with the generation of plant life as well as rebirth in the Afterworld. Black cats, snakes, dogs, and birds have especially strong links to important goddesses. The goddess Hecate is often seen as a black-haired black-eyed young woman with luminescent white skin. The god Anubis is a black-headed jackal. Black is associated with the god Saturn. There is an ancient tradition of black meteor worship from Anatolia through Mesopotamia to the Arabian Peninsula, and Cybele is a black meteor goddess. Black is the color of the dark moon and the Crone phase in a woman's life cycle.

Some mention should be made of cryptic coloration. If you happen to notice an insect or lizard standing perfectly still and blending into the environment, the concepts of camouflage or invisibility might go into your calculation about the significance of your meeting.

Seeing invisible things is a concept that edges us back into superhero territory. In the contrived landscape of superhuman faculties, superb color differentiation, which could plausibly be linked with seeing things that are camouflaged, is never mentioned. The ability to detect small shifts in color is one of those perfect vision qualities I enumerated earlier, so it's interesting that, to my knowledge, no superhero demonstrates this— no ability to view an object and give the corresponding 64-crayon name or the six-digit number from the RGB palette, much less the light frequency. But I guess a superhuman feat like that has no application in fighting crime.

What about laser beams shooting from the eyes? I was going to tackle this issue, but it's really not a visionary trait, and I decided it would take us too far afield. Not that it isn't important, but it will have to wait for another time.

If you are developing vision it pays to have at least a crude understanding of sight. In the realm of divination, we are such visual creatures that we tend to translate our extrasensory perception into visual images, and our divinatory language (words like vision, foresight, second sight) is based almost entirely on visual metaphors. Any sign in nature that points to vision itself can be thought of as a sign that is underlined, highlighted, and placed in a bold font.

Vision is complex, and all animals see a bit differently. While the ideal of perfect sight appeals to visual creatures like ourselves, even in speculation the image starts to break down. Perfect eyesight, like perfect intelligence, is an elusive proposition: we all have a piece of it. When you encounter an animal sign, you are being invited to view your world from another perspective.

Leaves of Gold

The vision that disappears when shown to others is a common fairytale. This story is loosely adapted from several versions, including the one in Josef Baudis's collection of Czech folktales, The Key of Gold.[45] *I like that the fox in this story is a reliable source of information rather than a mendacious trickster. I do not agree with the adage that a vision should never be shared, but sometimes it is wise to be circumspect.*

The heart-shaped leaves spun circles through the air as they sailed to the eddy of the stream. The girl studied the floating discs for a long time, thinking they looked like gold coins. Gradually she became aware of a red fox staring back at her through the pool. She whirled around.

There was a boy her own age standing behind her, a boy with strawberry blond hair. "I'm trying to see the fox!" she said, still crouching on the flat rock, peering behind the muddy legs of the boy.

"If you are looking for the fox with the gold coins, that is I," said the boy. He was bedraggled and dirty, but he used correct grammar.

"Change into a fox again," said the girl, delighted.

"In a moment," said the boy. "Don't you want to see where the gold is hidden?"

He led the girl to a glade littered with gold and gave her two leather pouches to hold the coins. "Do not show these to anyone," he admonished her. "They belong to you and only to you. Do not share them."

She turned to ask if she could share them with her parents, but the boy was gone, and there was a fox scampering into a thicket.

The girl decided it was time to return home. As she walked along the road approaching her house, there was her mother — and a very angry mother she was, too. "You naughty girl. You have been gone three hours!" said her mother. "This is the longest yet, and I thought you had been hurt."

"No, I'm perfectly okay," the girl protested. She did not think she had been gone three hours, but she decided not to argue. To calm her mother down, she said, "I have brought you some gold coins. They were given to me by a fox." The girl stopped. "Or maybe it was a boy."

"A boy?" Her mother tensed again. "Were you with a boy out there?"

The girl considered. "I think it was a boy fox."

Her mother relaxed. "Let me see what you brought."

The girl handed a pouch to her mother, and her mother pulled out a small handful. "They are very pretty leaves," her mother said. "They do have a golden color."

The girl looked in the pouches again and she saw that her mother was right: they were filled with leaves, only leaves, and not gold coins.

The girl took the heart-shaped leaves and scattered them into the garden behind her house. She cried as they twirled to the ground, not because her mother had yelled at her but because she had wanted to share the gold coins with her mother, and that had not been possible.

Questioning the Shades

1) What war games analysis focuses on what the participants are wearing? The long commentary on the attire of the pages and knights (and their horses!) seems to detract from the action in the battle between Arthur and Owain. Why is there so much emphasis on the appearance of the messengers in this story?

2) At the end of the fourth game, when he is obviously losing the battle, Arthur requests a truce. Why is the conclusion of the game called a suspension of conflict rather than a loss for Arthur (and win for Owain)?

3) Seeing a nocturnal creature in the daytime is considered a significant sign, although in my experience it is not a rare occurrence. How would you interpret the daytime sighting of an owl? Would the frequency of your own nocturnal ramblings affect the significance of the daytime sighting?

4) What aspects of "Cache and Release" reflect common crow behavior?

5) Some friends mention to you that earlier that day they "saw some ravens," and knowing you to be an expert on animal divination they want to know "what that means." What questions would you ask your friends before venturing an interpretation?

6) While running an errand you find yourself in an unfamiliar waiting room for several minutes. The room is dominated by a large tank of beautiful tropical fish. What interpretations might you give to this animal sign?

7) What would iridescent colors, like those on a pigeon's neck, signify?

8) You encounter a Bluebird on a walk in the country (or at any rate it's a bird and it's blue so you'll call it a Bluebird). None of the books on animal spirits list a "meaning" for Bluebird. How can you interpret this sign?

9) The color symbolism outlined in this chapter is hardly exhaustive. What meaning would you give the following colors: taupe, turquoise, peach, mauve, fuchsia.

Chapter 7

What's With That Noise?

Hunting and Pecking

Why do the Latins revere the woodpecker and all strictly abstain from it? Is it because, as they tell the tale, Picus, transformed by his wife's magic drugs, became a woodpecker and in that form gives oracles and prophecies to those who consult him?
—Plutarch, *Roman Questions (21)*

Figure 68: Gilded Flicker at a Saguaro nest. Photo: Jean-Guy Dallaire.

The tinny clattering invariably woke me at daybreak. My first thought during my first month in the Sonora desert was always: those stupid woodpeckers. Apparently they didn't understand the difference between a tree trunk and a chimney vent. The acoustics in a desert valley favor the amplification of sound, but this does not account for the sleep-shattering intensity of the racket. The Gilded Flicker, the usual culprit in the dawn ruckus, puts a great deal of muscle into venting. He is the undisputed champion of the morning metal banging circus, overpowering the Gila and Ladder-Backed Woodpeckers and punctuating his hammering with a piercing shriek and a uniquely penetrating version of the woodpecker yaffle. His is an undeniably rude introduction to the desert, but in a remarkably short time his presence becomes one of those comforting yet vaguely noticed sounds of the desert, like a coyote chorus in the evening.

When I decided to include a chapter on sound for this volume, there was no question in my mind that the animal I would explore would be the woodpecker. Even living today in the northern forest, where the irascible Gilded never ventures, woodpeckers are an omnipresent feature in my life. They stick around through the winter. They sport an attention-grabbing plumage. They flit from tree to tree in a conspicuous manner. They make noise incessantly: pecking, chipping, drilling, hammering, cackling, squealing, yelping, wheezing, screeching, and just plain yelling. There are so many of them and so many different kinds. Just in my neighborhood, there are Downy Woodpeckers, Hairy Woodpeckers, Pileated Woodpeckers, Yellow-Bellied Sapsuckers, and Northern Flickers. They compete in signature shrieks that are remarkably distinguishable from one another. How could I *not* write about an animal that tries so hard to be noticed?

And I assumed that once I began pecking in earnest I would find a plethora of folklore and myth to sort through. I was in for some disappointment. Though always in the past my instincts have been correct when identifying an animal with historical significance in Euro-shamanism, even in those cases where the animal was commonly reviled or dismissed as exceedingly humble, this time I was up a tree. Stumped. In a hole. Confronted with all the lack of evidence, pragmatism pressed me to abandon the search and examine a bird with a less obscure magical pedigree. There were certainly other respectable choices: the musical wren, the delightful cuckoo, the illustrious eagle. But I could not let go. I clung stubbornly to the bark of this tree with a hunch pounding me like the *ki ki ki ki ki* of the Pileated Woodpecker. I was sure I was onto something.

For one thing, North American aboriginal lore is rich in story and folklore about the woodpecker. This wisdom is usually absent in Native animal-spirit books targeted to a mass audience, a testament to the lack of interest most English speaking people have in this bird. In an Algonquian tale Rabbit is invited to dine with the twelve Woodpecker Girls and is impressed with the gourmet meal of grubs they offer him. He is envious and determined to outdo them. Rabbit is very talented—he molded the clan animals from the animals who died during the Great Flood—but unfortunately his pride in this instance is greater than his own ingenuity. He invites the Woodpecker Girls to dine with him and attempts to re-create the grub delicacies with disastrous results. The Woodpecker Girls laugh at him, and the Woodpeckers are laughing still.[46]

In a myth attributed to the Hasinai-Caddo (Texas), people become woodpeckers after abusing a mescaline producing plant. Elders warn that only those initiated in medicine ways should touch the plant, but most people ignore the warnings and spend their days caught up in visions. They forget about their children and one day notice that the children are missing. Creator hears the distraught cries of the parents and changes them into woodpeckers so they can hunt for their children. This is why woodpeckers tap at trees and poke into holes: they are looking for their offspring.[47]

The woodpecker can also be found in Japanese and Hindu mythology, albeit not in abundance. Why is legend of this bird in

Western cultures so sparse?

The usual suspect where there is an absence of animal lore is Christian suppression. Christian authorities inveighed heavily against the remnants of animal worship, in some cases documenting all that survives of these and other pagan practices. Where there was Irish influence on early Christianity, animal beliefs were deliberately introduced into the new religion, and in some cases Church fathers grudgingly allowed animal beliefs to be syncretized. The hare and the deer come to mind as examples of this. Other times sacred animals would be vilified for a supposed affiliation with the Devil, as was the case with the snake, wolf, bat, toad, pig, and goat. In this regard it is interesting that the few fairytales that include woodpeckers are negative. A red-haired woman is changed into a woodpecker for her stinginess against St. Peter. A woodpecker mother is easily tricked into sacrificing her children to that other villain, the fox. A woodpecker becomes a nemesis to a human community with his pecking and tricky ways, and an innocent dog and horse are killed in the process. These stories appear coded and may carry political messages. They bear little resemblance to real woodpeckers, who are generous, intelligent, protective of their children, and generally indifferent to humans.

Indifference of modern humans to the woodpecker could be another explanation for the dearth of literature. The public has a decided preference for apex predators, such as wolves, bears, wildcats, and raptors. The threat of extinction plays a role in popular veneration, a corollary to the aphorism that "familiarity breeds contempt." Americans are rightly proud of the comeback of the Bald Eagle from her precarious threatened status, although some question the wisdom of this bird as a national symbol, arguing that the country's tendency toward militarism can be traced to the influence of this large efficient hunter. In this instance as in so many, Benjamin Franklin is given credit for prescience because he argued that the turkey was a better symbol for the American republic. This was not, as many suppose, because the turkey is a ground forager but because, in Franklin's opinion, the eagle was a "coward" and a lazy hunter who chased other animals off their kill. He held the Wild Turkey in higher esteem as a more aggressive "bird of courage." I do not share Franklin's derision of the majestic Bald Eagle, but I do have to admit that the Bald Eagle has always flown away as I approached, while I have actually been charged by a Wild

Figure 69: Black Woodpecker with chicks. This common Eurasian bird has the red cap typical of most woodpecker species. Photo: Alastair Rae.

Turkey. This rather makes sense, since the Eagle nests in a high tree or cliff while the Turkey has chicks on the ground that are more vulnerable. Status as apex predator does not necessarily dictate aggression or courage. Be that as it may, the Bald Eagle was chosen primarily not for her character but for the eagle's affinity with the Roman Republic, reflecting the country's early romanticism toward all things Greek and Roman.

The eagle is the bird of Zeus-Jupiter, the Father God of Greece and Rome, and therefore classically linked with these two Classical democracies. The eagle featured frequently, though certainly not exclusively, on the coinage of the two empires, and a pervasive Roman issue had an eagle on one side with the god Mars on the other. The eagle was not, however, the animal most closely associated with Mars. That animal was the woodpecker.

The woodpecker, like Mars, is busy, purposeful, vocal, preoccupied with romance, and eager to confront rivals. The same can be said for most birds, of course, but the woodpecker is so darn *loud* about it. He becomes active before the migratory birds return, performing an aerial display made more conspicuous by his red coloring. He punctuates this theater with cries that make up in volume what they lack in harmony, and with that incessant tap tapping. He is not subtle.

The red markings link the woodpecker with the "Red Planet," the ruler of the first sign of the zodiac. The woodpecker has defined many of the astrological characteristics of Mars the planet. It is associated with not only red things and fiery energy (pretty self-evident), but with the head (the woodpecker's red cap), dentistry (sharp prominent beak), frustration (banging of the head), surgery (partly red blood but also incising the tree), and carpentry (of course).

Go to any compilation of world deities and you will find virtually nothing about the god Mars other than that he is the "god of war." I have shared my suspicion about warrior deities elsewhere, so I will only say a little about this. It makes sense that the woodpecker god would be associated with the spear, as Mars undoubtedly is, on account of his sharp beak. But spears are not exclusively instruments of war—more commonly, they have been used for hunting large animals. The affinity between Mars and battle speaks more of the high regard the Romans had for this deity combined with *their positive view of warfare.* Ever-increasing territorial expansion was the source of Roman opulence as well as, ultimately, the seeds of the Empire's destruction. In the same vein, the Greeks, who saw war as an instrument of economic collapse, assigned warfare as the purview of a Thracian deity, Ares, whom they wished to malign. That Mars was not exclusively seen as a warrior deity even at the height of the Roman Empire is illustrated by the British and Continental Celtic gods who were syncretized with Mars, often more closely associated with grain or healing than with war.

Mars is not the only Classical deity associated with the woodpecker, although here the mythological record becomes sparse and confused. There is a hero named Picus, a son of Mars, who is changed into a woodpecker by Circe, the witch of the Aegean. When he returns to his manly form he has acquired awesome powers of prophecy due to his ability to understand the speech of woodpeckers. Picus later becomes the father of Faunus, the Roman equivalent of the wilderness god Pan. Alternatively, Picus is the first king of the central Italian Peninsula and the son of Saturn. A female woodpecker lands on his head one day, and the Etruscan augur interprets this as a sign of a disastrous armed conflict for the country. Picus personally wrings the neck of the messenger bird, thereby diverting the misfortune onto himself. This self-sacrificing act is more in line with that of a tribal chieftain than a stereotypical king, indicating that this story goes quite a bit back in time.

Along the subject of female woodpeckers, there is a Greek Dryad deity named Dryope, whose name according to Graves means "woodpecker."[48] In one story she is transformed into a Lotus Tree and in another into a Black Poplar. Both times she is trying to escape the dastardly clutches of the god Apollo, which is a theme you are no doubt associating by this time with the usurpation of a goddess cult by the priests of Apollo. Dryope is the mother of the god Pan.

If you are feeling muddled at this point, so am I. Various

aspects of these woodpecker stories are mixed and matched in contradictory and confusing ways, always with key details omitted. The legend of Mars and the founding of Rome, told later in this chapter, is the only tale with any coherence, and even here the storyline is thin. Woodpecker myth from Etruscan, Greek, and Latin sources—all of it obscure and esoteric—has been jumbled together in a problematic mess. There are clues indicating that the woodpecker is indeed important, but how?

It might be helpful at this point to return to North America, specifically to the northeast, where in recent memory the woodpecker has been better acknowledged in folk belief. At the time of European contact, eastern North America was filled with the mature forests woodpeckers need to thrive, most species being dependent on dying trees. Iroquois and Algonquian peoples were farmers and hunter-gatherers who depended on forests for meat, plant foods, medicine, clothing, and many other things. The only domesticated animal was the dog. People maintained a close and conscious symbiosis with the forest.

Europeans depended on forests for lumber and fuel, and one of the primary reasons for the exploitation of North America was to obtain hardwood lumber that was scarce in the spent forests of Western and Central Europe. Even where forests were managed for timber, they would not have supported woodpeckers well, since woodpeckers prefer rotten standing wood. There are a few species that survive woodland destruction, such as the European Green Woodpecker, who eats ground ants and can nest in orchards, but settled farmers probably did not interact in a significant way with woodpeckers. As I explained in my earlier book, *Invoking Animal Magic*, one of the ways an animal becomes integral in shamanism is through economics. An animal such as the mouse is destructive to food stores and must be propitiated. An animal such as the cow provides milk and must be encouraged to propagate. Woodpeckers become destructive when their habitat is destroyed, pecking houses, fence posts, and furnishings, but this may have been gradual enough for farmers to effectively respond by killing the birds. Woodpeckers are able to torment homeowners in suburbia today because they are legally protected from harm. Woodpecker feathers continued to be used as decoration and in haute couture until consciousness about endangered species became widespread in the nineteenth century, but domesticated birds also filled this niche.

Where woodpeckers might be expected to have a material role in the community would be in hunter-gatherer cultures. Tail feathers of tree-boring woodpeckers are significantly stronger than those of other birds because the woodpecker must stabilize her body while pounding the tree at speeds of 15mph or more. I don't know whether these feathers make better fletching—turkey or goose wing feathers are used for arrow fletching today—but there was probably a use for stronger feathers when they were used for utilitarian purposes. Obviously the red or yellow feathers would have decorative value. Woodpeckers would also have led gatherers to sources of grubs and other edible insects.

The archaeological record for woodpecker magic in pre-agricultural Europe is sparse. Woodpecker bones are found with other bird and animal bones at a Mesolithic site in Serbia and I found reference to an atlatl (a primitive spear throwing device) that had a decorative White-backed Woodpecker from an unspecified European site. Where the archaeological woodpecker record is rich is again in North America. Woodpecker skulls and bills were apparently traded. Woodpeckers are found on pottery and shell engravings. Of course, archaeologists in North America have contemporary Amerindians with tribal memories to help them interpret findings and ask the right questions. Some woodpecker designs are stylistic and might be missed without this insight. Another factor is that the archaeology in North America we're discussing here typically goes back about a thousand years while Paleolithic Europe was ten thousand years ago. Finally, it should be considered that since pecking wood is the sine qua non of the woodpecker, effigies of the bird might have been carved in wood rather than more durable bone or stone.

So is the woodpecker important in Euro-shamanism in a traditional sense? I'm not sure, partly because I seem to be the only person asking the question. Here's why I think she should be very important.

Woodpeckers in the Northern Hemisphere tend to be black and red or black, white, and red, colors that are potent in witchcraft, especially when used together. This is true of woodpeckers in the tropics as well (woodpeckers in South America are even more brilliant), but since birds in the north tend toward the drab, woodpeckers stand out here. Then there is the drumming. Human drumming is used in musical worship and in trance induction, but in woodpeckers drumming is speech. Not only do different species have signature drums (which may be difficult for untrained ears to distinguish), but they vary their drumming when communicating with others of their species, including rivals, potential mates, and family members. The metal vent banging that bemused me in the desert is done deliberately by the male to attract a female with the loudest sound possible. He thinks it's sexy. Though today computers are used to analyze recordings of woodpecker drumming to break communication codes, it is not far-fetched to assume that some people living intimately with the forest could differentiate woodpecker taps. This puts a new slant on the ability of Picus to foretell the future by listening to woodpeckers. In modern parlance Picus would have been a "woodpecker whisperer," although it makes more sense to call a person fluent in woodpecker speech a "woodpecker tapper."

What would woodpeckers have been saying to the human tappers and what are they saying to each other? There is a Central American woodpecker called *La Telegrafista* because her relatively short taps sound like a telegraph machine, but I am not suggesting that woodpecker language is anything as complex as what we would have sent over a telegraph. Woodpeckers are saying:

"Hey babe!"
"Good morning."
"Danger!"
"Where are you?"
"Get out of here!"
"What do you think of this nest site, dear?"

Territorial and romantic drums sound the same to us, though woodpeckers themselves know the difference. Woodpeckers are careful listeners. They get information from echoes and vibrations in materials they tap. Sometimes they strike a piece of wood and listen for the scurrying of insects. They can be induced to start drumming when a human nearby begins tapping, for example on a typewriter.

As for what woodpeckers told the human tappers, North American folklore says that woodpeckers predict the severity of the coming winter and that woodpeckers disappear in anticipation of extreme cold. A pervasive belief found in both Eastern and Western Europe is that the pecking is a sign of rain on the horizon, perhaps because the loud pecking of some species can resemble a distant thunder roll. In this regard, it is interesting that the woodpecker is the bird of the redheaded Norse god Thor, who wields the hammer and lightning bolt. More obscurely, the woodpecker is said to lead an observer to treasure. I have found that birds who bring rain are very often considered treasure birds.

The most thrilling treasure of the woodpecker is the springwort, a reddish root believed to draw down lightning. It can open any closed or locked door. To find the springwort, magicians would seal the entrance to a woodpecker nest. The woodpecker would then fly off to find a springwort sprig, but would be induced to drop the plant when he returned and found that the seal had been removed. The springwort sounds like a valuable herb, but nobody really knows what a springwort is. Jacob Grimm tentatively identified it as the Caper Spurge or *Euphorbia Lathyris*.[49]

If the woodpecker is starting to resemble the raven as a rain-bringer/treasure- finder/oracle/friend-of-the-shaman, consider this: both ravens and woodpeckers deal in death and decay. The raven cleans the bones of dead animals while the woodpecker forages in dying trees. Since animals associated with death help the healer in her work, it seems like the tree-worshiping witch would naturally gravitate to the woodpecker.

Witch-healers in the Ozarks, who are called "goomer doctors," use various portions of the Pileated Woodpecker in their healing work and give the Pileated the appellation of "Lord God Peckerwood."[50] Also in relation to witches, it seems like woodpeckers, being peckers of wood, would have some link with wands or staffs. In this regard the report that Cretan Zeus stole the scepter of the woodpecker is tantalizing. Zeus is not every-where the Indo-European thunderbolt god, but is sometimes an unrelated local god whom the Greeks referred to under that name. On Crete "Zeus" was probably a Minoan god worshiped before the Mycenaean invasion. Was he also a woodpecker god?

Also, what are woodpeckers doing in the Aegean islands? Those of you reading this are probably thinking, "They came on boats as sailors, and once they got ashore Circe or some other witch changed the crew into woodpeckers." I agree that this is one explanation, but I did some research to see if I could find additional data to make the "Zeus of Crete with the woodpecker scepter" story even more plausible. It turns out woodpeckers can fly great distances, even though you would never guess that by looking at their undulating flight pattern. A few species, such as the Yellow-Bellied Sapsucker and the Eurasian Wryneck, are true migrators.

The Wryneck is a drab black-and-cream bird in the woodpecker family without the woodpecker's typical coloring, long bill, or pecking habit. She forages on the ground and appropriates abandoned tree cavities. She twists her neck in an uncanny way and for this reason she is used in reversing spells, especially spells to win back an errant lover. In one of the Greek epics, the unwilling heart of Medea, a witch-protégé of Circe and priestess of Hecate, is won using a Wryneck spell. In another myth the goddess Hera changes the nymph Iynx into a Wryneck in retaliation for messing up Hera's love life. Iynx's name is the root of the English word "jinx." Although the Eurasian Wryneck sounds like a woodpecker and is placed in the woodpecker family by modern taxonomists, it is unclear how the ancients linked the two. Pan, son of woodpecker goddess Dryope, is father

of Iynx, so they seem to have some relation. At any rate, we do not need the Wryneck to put the woodpecker scepter on Crete. There are several species of woodpecker on Crete, and apparently one of them once had scepter before it was stolen by Zeus.

Woodpeckers are related to that other witchy animal, the bat, because they live in caves. Not rocky caves, but dark hollow rooms in trees with narrow openings. They are like humans in building shelters out of solid wood. I would find a house carved in rotten wood a bit buggy, but I guess if you eat insects that is not a deterrent. The male does most, but not all, of the excavating. Mom and Pop live in separate dormitories except when nesting.

Figure 70: Etruscan soothsayer with bird. Italy, fourth century BCE.

In very few animal species is the male as involved as the

woodpecker in raising young. The male broods eggs and hatchlings as much or more than the female. Both parents continue to feed the fledglings after they leave the nest. Young woodpeckers depend on their parents longer the most birds, for periods up to several months, variations depending on the species and the availability of food. In some species independent young will hang around to help parents with a second brood. The Acorn Woodpecker is the most social species, with several generations living in multi-unit apartments and storing nuts in communal granaries. They often raise young in collective nurseries.

Like most birds, woodpeckers are highly territorial. Hostile interactions between woodpeckers center around flight displays, tapping, and shrieking, but actual physical fighting does not usually occur, nor do quarreling siblings pierce each other with their sharp bills. Piercing, stabbing, and impaling are reserved for predators at the nest site. Parents battle fiercely to protect eggs and nestlings from squirrels, martens, foxes, crows, and starlings. Adults must also fight to keep their sleeping cavity from being appropriated. Though fledglings are vulnerable as they learn survival skills, adults can easily defend themselves with sharp bills and a habit of hopping around the tree trunk that confuses raptors. Woodpeckers alighting on the ground to eat ants are more exposed, but this is not a timid bird. If we were to go by Ben Franklin's system of assigning respect to a bird according to his valor, the woodpecker would be a contender.

The question most people have about woodpeckers is how they manage to drill like they do without getting a headache. There has actually been a fair amount of research on this, with the aim of designing helmets and automobiles that minimize brain trauma during collisions. Woodpeckers hit the surface of the tree trunk at about 15mph, analogous to the average downhill skier plowing into a tree, and they do this repeatedly. With each strike they sustain an impact about ten times that which would cause injury in a human. The answer lies in design, proportion, and duration of impact. The lighter brain of a bird can sustain a greater collision. The woodpecker's brain is oriented differently than a human's, with little surface at the forward part of the brain and most brain matter in the back of the skull. There is less fluid surrounding the tightly packed woodpecker brain, so the brain is not bouncing inside the skull. Also the duration of the impact is slight. Human accidents resulting in brain injury (car crashes, football collisions) typically last between three and fifteen milliseconds, with shorter duration causing less injury. The impact duration for a woodpecker striking a substrate is less than a millisecond. There are various shock absorbing features in the beak, head, and neck, which we won't delve into here, that operate as safety backups. It has been pointed out that if the woodpecker displaced all the impact of her drilling with her body, she wouldn't be applying that force to the tree, where it needs to go.[51]

Something you may not have wondered about, which turns out to be significant, is why the woodpecker pounds furiously at her target for a few seconds, then stops to rest for a few more seconds, then goes back at it. You probably thought she got tired. As it turns out, all that pecking builds up heat, not only in the point of contact but also in the woodpecker's brain, so she stops to let that heat dissipate.[52]

So the woodpecker is a hothead, in addition to being coura-geous, territorial, effective in protection of dependents, and equipped with a sharp beak that ancients considered spear-like. Maybe Mars was a warrior deity in pre-history, although I think it makes more sense to look at his pursuit of insect prey and call him a hunting deity. Hunters as well as warriors need courage and protection. I surmise that woodpecker deities were somewhat important in hunter-gatherer and early agricultural communities and became attenuated in importance as societies became less forest dependent. Specialized healers and seers would have retained a connection with the woodpecker gods that was not transmitted in popular folklore. Much of my speculation is generalized from classical sources, not because such information is prominent in these sources but because obscure data is more readily available there. I have a feeling that single-minded dedication would reveal widespread traces of a woodpecker cult in other places. Leland speculated that folklore about the Redcap goblin, found throughout northern and central Europe, is really about the woodpecker.[53] In some stories that seems like a possibility; in others it seems unlikely. Without more data it's hard to tell.

In cases where the trail is faint, it's probably best to dispense with folklore and rely on the original source: woodpeckers themselves. From studying woodpeckers I have learned that they are intelligent birds who drum for many surprising reasons. The morning metal banging is not an exercise in futility but an attention-grabbing signal that has a purpose. Woodpeckers drum to communicate, hunt, excavate, and obtain information. For the diviner they can bring a cornucopia of messages about topics related to the home.

The Woodpecker and the Horse

Folk stories of God-and-the-Devil or God-and-the-saint are often recycled legends from pagan times placed in a Christian context. Frequently they relate historical events and remote but significant political conflict. To decode the following story, which comes from Poland, recall that the horse was a latecomer to Neolithic Europe. Horses were hunted to extinction during the Ice Age and returned with Indo-European migrants from the east. Early agriculturalists farmed without ox or horse or even plow, instead poking a sharp stick into the dirt and dropping a seed. Ground feeding woodpeckers such as the European Green must have looked like they were doing the same thing as they poked their long bills in the earth for ants.

The woodpecker was once God's bird, but he was badly harmed

by the Devil. Here's how it happened.

God and the Devil used to be friends—you didn't know that, did you? They aren't friends now. Back when they used to like each other, they farmed adjoining fields, the Devil with his horses, God with his woodpecker. God noticed that the Devil was plowing more efficiently than he was, so he secretly borrowed the Devil's horses one night. Back then, God was as tricky as the Devil.

When the Devil visited the field next morning, he was astonished to see that God had finished plowing in just one day. The Devil decided that, after all, God's woodpecker was the better farming assistant and asked God to swap animals with him. God readily agreed.

The Devil found plowing with a woodpecker slow and cumbersome, especially since he was used to the assistance of his horses. Not realizing that God tricked him, the Devil struck the uncooperative woodpecker hard on the head, causing the woodpecker to bleed. This is why the woodpecker's crown feathers are red.

Woodpecker Review

Magical Qualities: black/white/red coloring, drums with bill, social, builds in wood, courageous, lives and forages in decaying trees, both sexes highly nourishing and protective of young

Magical Applications: shamanic journeying, money, romance, weather prognostication, healing (especially head trauma or headache), finding or building a home

Other Associations:

Bird Dreams

One night while camping with a friend, I heard snarling, growling, and snapping noises outside our tent. They continued sporadically for more than an hour, although I didn't time the disturbance and I certainly didn't go outside to see what animal was making such a ferocious racket. Camping at this park worked a bit differently than most: you hiked into a designated multi-site area rather than erecting a tent at a solo location. One of the campers, an older gentleman, actually did poke his flashlight outside the perimeters of the campground to satisfy his curiosity about our snarling neighbor. He identified her as a Gray Fox, and he insisted that she did not seem rabid. According to North Carolina Wildlife Resources Commission, "Foxes are very vocal and people are most likely to hear a fox during the breeding season. Gray fox vocalizations range from mews and coos, to growls and snarls, to barks and screams."[54]

A few years ago a music video asking, "What does the fox say?" went viral.[55]The premise of the question, that nobody knows what fox vocalizations sound like, was really an excuse for some clever singing, but it's a good idea to learn animal-speak if you're studying animal divination. You might be able to hear, but not see, the animal hiding in the foliage, or you might be cowering in your tent afraid to come out. In thickly forested areas, including temperate as well as tropical rainforests, most of the animal activity is happening upstairs. Even the Gray Fox climbs trees.

Figure 72: We think of a typical wave as moving like this, but this is conceptually closer to how a light wave behaves, not a sound wave.

Before analyzing various animal sounds, let's look at sound itself.

Sound is a vibration conveyed through a medium, usually air. When you speak, your vocal cords create changes in air pressure. The patterns of these changes move in a wave. In waves information, rather than matter, is moving from one place to another, so the same glob of air doesn't actually move from your mouth to someone's ears like it was a spitball. In sound there is a temporary displacement of matter moving through the air (or other conduit).

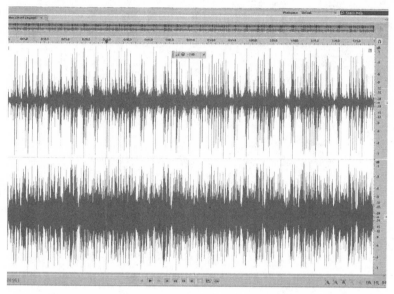

Figure 73: My audio software gives me this picture of sounds graphing higher and lower frequencies. This is useful for editing audio tracks, but does not represent how sound waves behave.

Because we are such visual creatures, we usually try to "see" the mechanics of sound in order to understand it. This is a contradiction in terms, but we'll try to do that nonetheless. Let's look at waves again. If you and a friend hold the ends of a bedsheet stretched between you, and you jiggle your side, a wave will move across the sheet in an up-and-down motion. This is how electromagnetic waves move, including those electromagnetic waves in the visible light spectrum. But light waves, as we know, can move through a vacuum, which is why we can see stars across galaxies. They don't need a bedsheet or anything else to move in. Soundwaves do need the bedsheet (or something else).

The tricky part to understand, though, is that they're not moving up and down along the sheet: they're moving straight across.

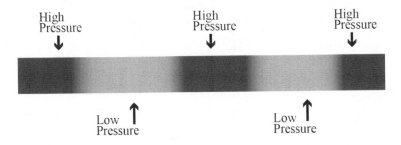

Figure 74: A sound moving through the air alternates between higher and lower pressure.

It helps to visualize the soundwave as a gray bar with gaps of lighter gray representing the areas of lower air pressure, and the darker gray bars representing areas of comparatively high pressure. The wave is moving, but it is not moving in a ripple; it is moving directly through the medium.

Waves are described by two variables: amplitude and length. Amplitude readily makes sense when we're talking about light waves. It can be measured as the height of the peak of the up-and-down wave. Amplitude in sound is loudness (and we certainly understand that!) but how is it explained in terms of the sound wave? Go back to the concept of changes in pressure. As a sound wave moves through the air, the areas of higher pressure are labeled as *compression* and the areas of lower pressure are labeled as *rarefaction*. When we have a greater amount of compression, we have greater amplitude. Using the grayscale bar analogy, a pictured soundwave with a greater amplitude would have a darker gray bar and a much lighter gray gap.

Wavelength is fairly intuitive for both light and sound. It is the length of one complete cycle of a wave. Shorter wavelengths correspond to what our ears perceive as higher pitch. Shorter wavelengths also correspond with higher frequencies, which is

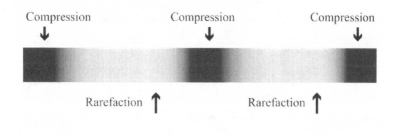

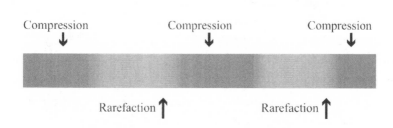

Figure 75: A visualization of amplitude for sound. The wave on top, with tighter compression, is louder.

the number of waves traveling through the air (or other medium) per second. Shorter waves = more waves per second = higher frequency = higher pitch.

Figure 76: A visualization of the length of a sound wave. The top image has a shorter wavelength, which corresponds to a higher pitch.

If this isn't making sense, look at the pictures. If it still doesn't make sense, skip it and move on. The important thing to understand is that there are two important variables in sound: amplitude and wavelength. Amplitude corresponds to our perception of loudness; wavelength to our perception of pitch.

Since sound can be reduced to these two variables, it seems like it should be easy to determine which animal hears the best. But not so fast. Sound may be simple, but hearing is complicated. We could be talking about hearing high frequencies (wax moth), low frequencies (pigeon), or faint noises (rabbit), but maybe we're talking about the ability to map surroundings using echolocation (bat), or the ability to memorize and reproduce sounds (mockingbird). Dogs are known for their uncanny ability to distinguish and categorize all sounds associated with their owners. The ear tufts on the lynx enhance the excellent sense of sound direction all cats have. Water is a better conduit of sound than air, which creates its own set of problems for mammals, but dolphins and whales are still able to navigate in water using echolocation.

Hearing evolved in separate ways for vertebrates and invertebrates. Hearing organs on insects and other invertebrates may be located anywhere on the body, not necessarily close to the head, and can be simple sensory hairs, antenna receptors, or more complex organs. Though auditory organs evolved on different tracks for vertebrates and invertebrates (and for different types of invertebrates), these organs are important in any case for maintaining equilibrium as well as detecting sound. Remember that sound is always the detection of vibration.

A few animal sounds deserve special mention.

Many of the high-pitched squeaks of mice are at frequencies beyond our range, but cats can hear high-frequency vibrations coming from mice and other small creatures. This is one of the reasons why your kitty often seems to be responding to stimuli for no discernible reason.

Some birds speak by moving their wings. You are probably most familiar with this phenomenon in pigeons. The anatomy of the pigeon wing partially explains the high-pitched sound at takeoff, but pigeons manipulate their wing song as a form of communication. One of the most alluring sounds in the woods is the drumming of the Ruffed Grouse. The male finds a fallen tree log to beat his wings against, and the high-speed flapping of his wings, which sounds a bit like a motor, carries for some distance. Biologists believe he is flapping for romance and to establish territory.

The splash of a beaver is the bane of canoers and kayakers, and believe it or not the sound is not the accidental coincidence of the animal's swimming away. She consciously plunks that wide flat tail to startle a potential predator.

Songbirds have a special vocal apparatus called a syrinx, which unlike the larynx we possess is able to express two notes at a time. The only way a human can do this is with a musical instrument. You may be familiar with the word "Syrinx" as a beautiful composition for flute by Claude Debussy.[56] In Greek mythology Syrinx was a wood nymph who tried to avoid the amorous pursuit of the god Pan. She ran into a riverbank and disguised herself as a reed. Pan could not distinguish her from the other reeds, so he tore several from the riverbank and fashioned them into his signature flute, the panpipe. The wresting of music from the reed goddess Syrinx through allegorical rape suggests forcible theft of a women's tradition.

But getting back to the syrinx of our feathered friends, the same species of bird can be found over a wide geographical area yet have regional variations in song, called "dialects," which can add to the challenge of differentiating birdsong. Over the years I have devoted painstaking effort to learning several dozen songs and calls of birds in my region, but not everyone will have the time or opportunity to do this. It doesn't take familiarity with nomenclature, however, to recognize a sweet song. The clear haunting echo of the Wood Thrush is a gift in and of itself, but a lovely song could presage another form of sweetness coming into your life. The song can also bring insight into present circumstances or facilitate a change in outlook.

According to biologists, birds sing *to attract a mate* or *to defend territory*. Understanding birdsong as divination is pulling it into our world, but even in the context of their world this is an oversimplification. Birds sing for many different reasons, including just to hear themselves sing. Why does any woman sing or speak? And here's a sobering thought: when men speak, is it always to impress women or to mark territory with other men? Maybe it is, and that's why biologists interpret birdsong in only these two ways.

Another assumption that deserves some scrutiny involves who exactly is singing. It used to be axiomatic that singing in female birds was rare. They wouldn't be impressing anybody, and territory is for males to create and defend. Reinforcing this bias was the fact that male birds are easier to study. Female birds are often drabber and harder to spot than males, and they tend to hang closer to the nest site. The consensus still is that males sing more than females, but perhaps the singing imbalance is not as pronounced as originally thought.

The relationship between birds and humans is a true cultural exchange, with lots of imitation moving back and forth. Captive parrots or lyrebirds exhibit the most impressive display of human sounds, such as cell phones and camera shutters, but even wild mockingbirds, magpies, and ravens will produce sounds like creaky gates, car alarms, or (my favorite) flushing toilets. A surprising number of birds imitate other birds, not just these champions, and for birds mimicking can play a part not only in romance but also in parasitic or predatory behaviors. Still, these explanations don't explain everything.

Songbirds dream in song: their link to the Otherworld is an auditory one. Scientists believe bird brains are processing songs learned in the daytime during sleep. Of course birds do learn their song language from listening to other birds, but might they also be flying into etheric spirit realms at night to learn new songs, perhaps from their bird ancestors or deities? Could they be eagerly sharing these songs during the dawn chorus?

Birdsong can not only foreshadow events, but also directly influence them. The line between divination and magic is sometimes thin. When I was very young, I used to go up to my bedroom when I was sad and listen to the Mourning Doves outside my window. They understood my little girl troubles, which no adult could, and their cooing sympathy put me in a better mood.

The connection between music and trance states is well known, and birdsongs are a powerful portal into shamanic realms. The flute was developed to guide the seeker into the receptive states generated by birds, and it remains a reliable tool for helping the priestess into other dimensions. Human musical harmonies and birdsongs sound similar to our ears, and mathematics confirms that the logic in birdsong and human music is the same.[57] Music inspired by birds has been invaluable in the important shamanic tasks of foretelling the future, connecting with ancestors, healing, preparing for death, and helping women to conceive. The appropriation of the reed pipe by Pan suggests not just a theft of music but also of shamanic practice connected with music that was once women's province.

Birdsong and less melodious noises in the environment can carry important cues for divination. If you hear a sound you can't identify, you can still note the qualities of the animal sound and the circumstances in which it arose. Then you can connect it with other signs to decode the message.

The Booger 'Coon

I got the shell of this story from a book called Witches, Ghosts and Signs: Folklore of the Southern Appalachians *by Patrick W. Gainer.[58] I've added a few things about witches I remember from my childhood and recounted the tale from a skeptic's point of view. This story conflates two popular legends that probably came to the North American continent from Ireland: The Witch Hare and the Black Hound, both of which I discuss in* Invoking Animal Magic. *In America the Black Hound is called a Booger Dog. The story incorporates a belief found in some Native American tribes that raccoons have special magical powers.*

Now here's a story I been tryin' to figure out an' maybe you can help. My neighbor Martha was talkin' about it when she was by earlier on account of the dogs a-barkin', but she didn't remind me of it. I was thinkin' about it anyway, 'cause it ain't somethin' anybody'd be likely to forget.

Real spooked howlin' it was, an' Martha said it was a bad sign, 'cause it reminded her of when Wilma got shot for turnin' into a 'coon. An' I said, "Come now, I don't believe that story," an' she said it were a bad sign anyway.

But I 'spose I gotta tell you the story 'fore I can tell you why I don't believe it.

Lester Duffy, who never can be trusted even when he's a-swearin' up an' down it's the truth, says he was huntin' in the night when his hounds tree'd a 'coon, an' he shot five times an' couldn't kill that 'coon. So he says he got a silver bullet outta his pocket, an' then he shot at that 'coon an' she screamed like a hant an' took off 'cause she was hit.

Then later Leon Corey come for the doctor 'cause his wife Wilma was doin' poorly an' everbody said she must've got hit by that silver bullet on account of she was a witch. Wilma! She ain't no witch. She is one of the nicest women in this county an' 'fraid of everthin'. Real mousy she is. I can almost picture Wilma turnin' herself into a mouse jus' from shiverin', but she ain't no 'coon or no witch.

I know what maybe you're a-thinkin', that I got no cause to be inferrin' nothin' on witches, with my Aunt Sal bein' a witch an' healin' lots of folks. She probly could witch Wilma well again, but

Wilma's scared even of Aunt Sal. You might say my own Gramma was a witch—I reckon some folks do. She always knew when people was gonna die. Got so everbody got petrified when she saw 'em on the sickbed—thought she was come to tell 'em they was ready for the Lord, even though she'd never come right out an' say it. Folks put two n' two together when they noticed people dyin' a day or so after Gramma came to see 'em, but Gramma said she never got no messages that people was gonna die, jus' that she had to see 'em quick. Gramma never got no urge to see Wilma when she took sick, which was good, 'cause that would've put Wilma under for sure.

So I ain't inferrin' nothin' on witches in general when I say Wilma's too nice to be a witch, 'cause there are witches an' there are *witches*, an' if you don't know the difference...well, some day you might find out.

Now to be fair, Lester never said Wilma was no witch—other folks done that after they heard Lester's story an' started figurin' things. But she didn't have no bullet hole in her side where she was a-hurtin', let alone a silver bullet, an' anyway, you'd think if she got shot she'd of gotten better when she didn't die right away. She's still lingerin', an' she told me what the doctor said she got but I don't remember the name of it.

Everybody heard those hounds though. Loud an' spooked they were, eerie. That's the part of the story that can't be made up. But here's the thing—what was Lester a-huntin' in the night-time, with dogs an' a rifle, unless he was after 'coons? An' in that case why would the dogs chase after a 'coon that weren't a real 'coon, an' one that they was scared of besides? An' why didn't Lester show us that silver bullet 'fore he shot the witch with it? You have to take my word on this, it weren't at all like Lester to have somethin' like that an' never show it to nobody.

I don't think Lester was huntin' at all that night. I think he was up at the house, an' he heard the dogs a-barkin' outside, an' he got his gun an' his lantern an' went out to see. I think he didn't want to explain why he couldn't get a 'coon in five shots, so he made up that part about the silver bullet. An' I don't think that 'coon screamed like a hant—I think it *was* a hant. I heard it too. That wasn't Wilma. That was somethin' that weren't alive to begin with so it couldn't get kilt even by Lester, who I have to say is a pretty good shot.

Lots of folks is avoidin' Wilma now, which is not right, an' the 'coons have got it easy 'cause nobody's a-huntin' with the lanterns. I wouldn't be 'fraid of Wilma even if she were a raccoon, but a Booger 'Coon—I might be scared of that. The dogs are sure scared. They've started that 'sterical howlin' again. If you don't believe me an' wanna take me up on a bet, go out there right now an' see what it is. Don't take no silver bullet with you, though, 'cause if Martha's right an' I'm wrong I won't have you shootin' Wilma again.

Wish those spooked hounds would stop howlin'... They got me spooked too.

Questioning the Vibes

1) Go to the "Woodpecker Review" page and fill out the last section.

2) In the Woody Woodpecker episode, *Termites from Mars*, Woody is tormented by termites who have arrived from that planet in spaceships and are destroying his house. After suffering much damage, he discovers he can foil them with sticky scotch tape. A Woody Woodpecker cartoon doesn't have to make sense, but why is the premise of this episode all wrong?

3) Here again is my list of the characteristics of animals important in magic. How many does the woodpecker have?

a. Complex social/family behavior

b. Economic value

c. Danger to humans

    d. Behavior or appearance that suggests androgyny

    e. Association with death

    f. Characteristics that appear human

4) Why would there be a close mythological relationship between the woodpecker and the wolf?

5) Identify five birds in your area and learn their songs. (If you already know five, great: learn five more.)

6) Mars is believed by many to have been an agricultural deity before he was a war god. Does this make sense?

7) Pick a time to listen, not to look, outdoors. Pay attention to how birds and animals react audibly to your presence.

8) A snake usually announces her presence by the sound of slithering in the brush. A snake has no outer ears, however, and hears through vibrations that are channeled from her mouth to her auditory organs. What magical power would you ascribe this?

9) During the course of your day, a bird (we won't specify what kind) startles you by a song reminiscent of the ring tones on your cell phone. Your cell phone is turned on and is not ringing. How would you interpret this?

Chapter 8

Into the Mist

The Oenoe Doe

Artemis Parthenos, Tityoktone
golden clad in armor and belt
you yoke to a golden chariot
your golden bridled deer.

From where did your horned team
first set out?
Thracian Haimos,
where Boreas' hurricane blows
his evil frost on the cloakless.
—Callimachus, "Hymn to Artemis"[59]

Figure 77: Reindeer in Sweden. Photo: Alexandre Buisse/Wikimedia
Commons.

My kindergarten teacher, Mrs. Greiner, was the fattest woman I had ever seen, up until that stage of my limited life experience. She had the kind of fat where her second chin was bigger than the first, where even her wrists and fingers were fat. Perhaps in nostalgia for leaner times, she told the class that when she was born she only weighed three pounds. I didn't believe her and neither did the most of the other kids. That made us even, because Mrs. Greiner didn't believe I'd been to the North Pole.

The North Pole, as you probably know, is very far away. My family and I had to travel several days to get there. As expected, it was cold when we arrived, and we had to wear sweaters, even though it was summer. The concessionaires sold Christmas cookies in July, because that's what Santa eats. Elves were busy making toys, which makes sense, because how could they make enough for all the (good) children if they didn't work year round? The Pole was white metal, tall and cold to the touch.

"You couldn't have been at the North Pole," said Mrs. Greiner. "How did you get there?"

"In a car!" I said. How did anybody get anywhere? Did she think we went on a horse or on a reindeer?

"You can't get to the North Pole in a car," said Mrs. Greiner. "You must have been somewhere else."

But I knew for a fact we were at the North Pole. *Mrs.* Claus was there, and everyone knows she doesn't travel. Also, there were reindeer. They had antlers and they were smaller than regular deer, and once a day they pulled Santa around the North Pole in his sleigh, which had to be hooked up to a train track since it was summer and there was no snow. The reindeer were tame and let us touch them and they had a reindeer smell. Reindeer do not smell like cinnamon mulled cider or gingerbread cookies or wintergreen. No.

But although the reindeer passed the smell test, a few years later, as my awareness of geography expanded, there were a few things about that experience that didn't quite fit. There is no land mass at the North Pole, and even the frozen cap is surrounded by open water in the summer, not to mention that there are no gas stations or bathrooms along the way. I *couldn't* have been at the North Pole. Santa and Mrs. Claus and the Christmas cookies and the reindeer and even that white pole could not have been at the North Pole either: I had been the victim of an elaborate hoax.

And Mrs. Greiner was probably telling the truth about being born three pounds.

Figure 78: Woodland caribou from northern Idaho. Photo: Steve Forrest/US Fish and Wildlife Service.

There was one thing about that experience at the "North Pole" that turned out to be correct: the reindeer. They do exist, and they're not at the tippy top of the pole, but they are close. Migrating wild herds today live in or near the Arctic Circle, while semi-domesticated herds reach only a bit further south. In North America, migrating caribou species, which are similar to reindeer, live in northern Canada and Alaska.

Reindeer migrate in late spring from taiga to tundra, where they have their babies relatively isolated from predators. After giving birth, the females shed their antlers. Males by this time have long disposed of their heavier antlers, which would make the dangerous spring migration across hundreds of miles cumbersome. Females and juveniles keep their antlers through the winter to dig through snow and brush seeking nourishment. Therefore Santa's reindeer, still antlered at Christmas, must all be girls.

An elder doe leads the herd on the trek north. Reindeer hooves are well adapted to ice and slippery bog, and reindeer are strong swimmers. In the northern territory the calves fatten with the rest of the herd on lichen and other tundra vegetation. During the fall and winter, in the scrubby forests of the taiga, they will also eat berries, willow, birch, grasses, and other forest plants. Their eyes undergo structural changes as the year darkens, allowing them to utilize the light waves they screened out during

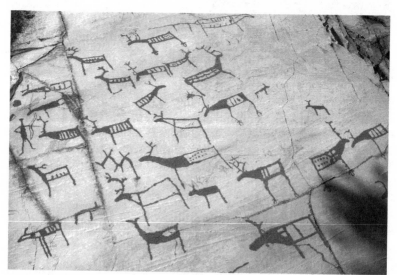

Figure 79: Reindeer on restored rock painting near Alta, Norway. 2000 BCE. Note disc and half-disc on far left and the dots, squares, and slashes on the deer.

the glaring arctic summer.

Not all reindeer migrate. The non-migrating species live at slightly lower latitudes, and include the Boreal Woodland Caribou, which extend into the southern Canadian provinces, and the Wild Forest Reindeer, found in the Russian Altai-Sayan region (bordering Mongolia). They are endangered and rare. Reindeer of all species were once plentiful and widespread. In the Ice Age, reindeer habitat spread over much of Eurasia, in Europe extending just north of the Mediterranean coast. North American reindeer, which eventually diverged into the subspecies we call caribou, lived as far south as Tennessee and Nevada.

Paleolithic Europeans utilized reindeer for food, clothing, and implements. The skull of a sixteen-year-old reindeer doe, mounted on a pole, graced the site of a lake in northern Germany where reindeer were corralled and slaughtered about 15,000 years ago. Perhaps she represented the ancestor to which the deer would return in order to be reborn. Reindeer and other deer species were important culturally, judging by the abundance of deer imagery in cave paintings. There was probably no single motivation behind cave art, any more than we can give a single reason why witches today cast spells, but one plausible motive was to increase animal populations through magic. This would explain why cave artists were usually women, as evidenced by signature hand prints often found with the art. People usually assume that the horned animals depicted are male, but female reindeer also have horns, as do many other female ungulates. Alexander Marshack[60] posited that cave art is linked with calendars, judging by the dots and slashes on or around the images. Even today, indigenous Siberian herders mark calendar time by the cyclical behavior of reindeer. Calendar-keeping in early societies was a woman's function, based on the need to track fertility.

The question of when reindeer were domesticated is a thorny

one. Domestication is technically defined as the point at which a species living close to humans has diverged genetically from the wild population. Reindeer typically have not been fenced or corralled, and up until the last century feral animals were incorporated into managed herds. From a human standpoint, reindeer have not required much genetic engineering. They tolerate each other and they tolerate humans. They are easy to tame, to the point of acquiescing to milking and accepting a harness. They mitigate predation on newborns by migrating to give birth. The case can be made that reindeer are not entirely domesticated even today, and yet humans have probably been following the reindeer for many thousands of years.

Figure 80: Heracles captures the Ceryniean Hind as Athena and Artemis look on. Greece 430 BCE. Photo: Marie-Lan Nguyen/Wikimedia Commons.

In antiquity the deer familiar of Artemis was a female reindeer, which is often confused with a stag. Both horned and hornless does are depicted driving the goddess's chariot. These does are magical and can run faster than an arrow. A fifth doe, called the Ceryneian Hind, was too fast even for Artemis to catch, but that doe was later given to her by one of the Pleiades sisters, Taygete. The third labor of Heracles involves capturing the Ceryneian Hind and bringing her alive to Mycenae, a city in the Argolis region of the Peloponnese. This quest, which takes exactly one year, begins at the temple of Artemis in Oenoe (the Oenoe located in Argolis). Though the journey begins and ends in about the same place, Heracles chases the Hind through the upper Balkan region and into Hyperborea, a vaguely defined place in the north. The indomitable Hind then leads Heracles south to the temple of Artemis atop Mount Artemisium, where she allows herself to be captured. This is a shaman's journey, an initiation into the cult of Artemis. The giant Hind, with her gold antlers and brass hooves, may have been a statue in the temple with those features.

The stag of Artemis being in fact a reindeer raises questions about the four stags who nibble on the branches of the Germanic world tree, Yggdrasil. This is the tree that holds the nine worlds, three each in the lower, middle, and upper regions. A snake nibbles at the roots of the tree, an eagle claims the high branches, and four deer browse the foliage. These animals create balance by tempering the growth of the ever-growing tree. The deer are identified as stags in the only source that mentions them, the *Prose Edda*, so this is not a case of a picture being misinterpreted, at least not in modern times. It is curious that reindeer would not be prominent in the mythology of the Norse, when reindeer memory survives as far south as Greece. Another stag, called Eikthyrnyr, lives atop a tree called Laerad in Odin's upper realm of Valhalla. Eikthyrnyr munches the leaves of Laerad along with a nanny goat named Heidrun. From the udders of Heidrun flow mead; from the antlers of Eikthyrnyr flow the waters that make up the rivers of the worlds. Eikthyrnyr could also be a reindeer doe. Default male bias being the pervasive affliction that it is, assertions of maleness in animal deities must be entertained with skepticism. The presence of so-called stags where we would expect to find reindeer, amid the absence of mention of any does, suggests either naiveté or a patriarchal rewriting of mythology.

Although few people reading this book will casually stumble upon a real live caribou or reindeer, and are much more likely to interact with Whitetail, Mule, Fallow, Red, or Roe Deer in the wild, I am emphasizing reindeer in this chapter because a great deal of Euro-shamanic understanding of cervids evolved through interaction with this specific type of deer. Ironically, people in highly urbanized environments often have more symbolic contact with reindeer than with any other type of deer, because reindeer images are so ubiquitous during the Christmas holidays. There is a great deal of overlap in symbolism for all deer, but

Figure 81: Detail from seventeenth century Icelandic manuscript showing four deer browsing on the foliage of Yggdrasil.

historically reindeer herds have lived in closer proximity to people, increasing economic dependence and creating a closer bond.

At the Winter Solstice, when the sun is at its nadir, the desire to connect with the reindeer goddess is particularly acute. Slavic peoples worshiped the mother goddess Rozhanitsa with her reindeer familiar at the Solstice up to the twelfth century, and today echoes of the ceremony are found in reindeer embroidered linens displayed at Christmas and white-icing reindeer-shaped cookies. The Saami worshiped the reindeer sun goddess Beiwe at both solstices, sacrificing white does. Butter was smeared on thresholds at winter solstice to help Beiwe regain her strength, and the goddess was entreated at this time for protection against insanity. Living in a cold northern climate myself, I can attest to the dangers of cabin fever. Solstice reindeer and caribou ceremonies are continued today throughout the arctic region by Samoyedic, Evenki, Inuit, and other indigenous peoples.

The Scottish goddess Cailleach Bheur roams the hillsides herding giant deer and drinking their milk. Cailleach, under various spellings, has been characterized as a deer, hare, cat, grain, serpent, gray mare, mountain, stone, and hag goddess, or as a hag goddess alternating with a maiden alter-ego. The pervasive characteristics of this deity are: female, old, and very large (even giant). I believe Cailleach is a word for a pre-Celtic concept of ancestress, and hence we should expect to find many Cailleachs. The deer Cailleach may be a reindeer, since milk and herding are part of her lore. Reindeer were indigenous to northern Scotland up to the thirteenth century. Alternatively, the deer Cailleach may be linked with Red Deer, who also live in groups and are larger than other European deer species. Another possibility is that the deer Cailleach could be an Irish Elk, a huge species of deer (not elk) that inhabited much of western Eurasia through the Ice Age. It is speculated that the changing climate could not support the Irish Elk, but the species was able to survive in isolated pockets throughout the Neolithic, documented in the foothills of the Ural Mountains even in historical times. The male Irish Elk had beautiful, formidable antlers.

The Scottish word for shape shifting, *fith-fath*, literally means to take the shape of a deer. It is easy to see why deer, having such a fey quality, would be equated with this concept. Deer are crepuscular creatures, active in the gray periods of the day, and seem to appear and disappear at will. I once stood next to a doe in an open forest and did not see her, so invisible did she make herself. It was almost like she transformed herself into a tree. I have heard many anecdotes about women changing themselves into deer—always women for some reason—and I have even witnessed this phenomenon myself.

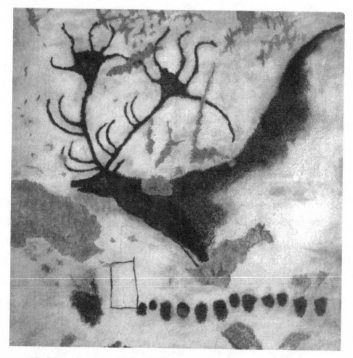

Figure 82: Megaloceros (Irish Elk) from Lascaux Cave. France, 17,000 BCE. Note the square and dots beneath the drawing.

The Irish mythical maiden Sadb is turned into a white deer against her will by her enemies, and her son Oisin is born with human form but a tuft of fawn hair on his head. Sadb's transformation into a *white* doe suggests a possible link with the reindeer. The Irish deer goddess Flidais also seems to have some reindeer qualities. Flidais keeps herds of deer and cows that deliver abundant milk. Reindeer does are referred to as cows by herders and biologists, a designation I have not used here to avoid confusion. Perhaps Flidais's cows are the reindeer kind, especially since she has a wagon drawn by deer. Flidais has the title "fair-haired," which might refer to the golden summer coat of the Roe Deer or to the white mutation common in reindeer.

An increasingly popular conception of the Deer Goddess goes by the name of Elen or Elen of the Ways. Knowledge about this goddess was disseminated through the research of Caroline Wise[61] on Elen of the Hosts, who appears in a short section of the Welsh *Mabinogion*. While researching ley lines in Britain, Wise discovered this passage:

...Elen thought to make high roads from one stronghold to another across the Island of Britain. And the roads were made. And for that reason they are called the Roads of Elen of the Hosts, because she was sprung from the Island of Britain, and the men of the Island of Britain would not have made those great hostings for any save for her.[62]

The "hosts" refers to the army that utilized Elen's roads. Elen of the Hosts is a historical figure, the queen of a usurper in the Gaulish Empire who assassinated the Emperor Gracian. Also known as Saint Helen (and not to be confused with the Saint Helen who is mother of the Emperor Constantine), she is reputed to have established Christianity in Wales. Wise theorized that the roads of Saint Helen were created by migrating reindeer, and that the Elen of the Hosts described in the *Mabinogion* is conflated with an older deer goddess. The most convincing part of her argument, from a scholarly point of view, is the prevalence of deer words sounding like Elen in many European languages. My Google translator confirms that "eilit" is Irish for "doe," while "jelen" is Polish for "deer" and "elen" is Bulgarian for "deer." "Elain" is Finnish for "animal." *The Dictionary of Word Origins* has this to say about the English word "elk":

The Indo-European base *ol-, *el- produced a number of words for deer-like animals—Greek *elaphos* 'stag,' for example and Welsh *elain* 'hind,' not to mention English *eland*.[63]

"Elen" may be a root Indo-European word for "deer," and if so would be an appropriate appellation for the Deer Goddess. If the roads of Elen were established by reindeer, however, it is doubtful that a reindeer goddess was worshiped on the British Isles at that earlier time by that name, since the large scale Indo-European migrations, unlike those of the reindeer, were fairly recent.

The most compelling case for Elen as a deer deity is the number of people who attest to connecting strongly with a deer goddess by this name. Chesca Potter seems to be the first modern artist to channel Elen as Reindeer Woman in the 1980s, but Elen is probably now the most commonly depicted Horned Goddess.

The flying reindeer that became incorporated in the Santa Claus myths are conjectured to originate in shamanic visioning with reindeer. Flying is a common sensation in this state of consciousness. My impression of the Heracles pursuit of the Ceryneian Hind is that this describes an initiatory journey of altered consciousness for devotees of the Deer Goddess as well as a legend of pilgrimage. The visionary flying reindeer hypothesis has been bolstered by the taste reindeer have for the psychotropic Fly Agaric mushroom. Eighteenth century explorer George Stellar is credited with documenting the practice of the Siberian Koryak of slaughtering intoxicated reindeer to attain a visionary state by eating the meat.[64] The Koryak also apparently drank urine of men who had eaten Fly Agaric to recycle the psychotropic alkaloids.

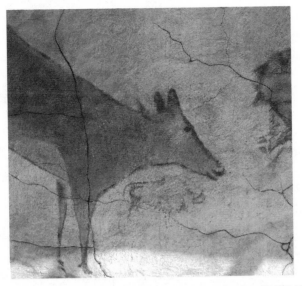

**Figure 83: Doe on ceiling of Altamira Cave, Spain. 17,000 BCE.
Photo: HTO.**

It has been reported that indigenous peoples consume the urine of reindeer intoxicated by Fly Agaric as a way of experiencing the mushroom's psychotropic effects. I could not find documentation of this anywhere, however, until serendipity led me to the work of Andrew Letcher, who researched the question exhaustively, found no reliable sources, and concluded this was bunk. Then a few years later Letcher debunked his own debunking when he learned from an indigenous Saami herder that urine from flying reindeer is indeed consumed for its hallucinogenic effects.[65] Dedicated scholars have gone to great lengths to bring you the truth about reindeer urine tripping, but understand I am not endorsing the practice.

Inspired by flying reindeer, many believe the red-and-white costume of Santa Claus comes from the coloring of the Fly Agaric mushroom, a conjecture that cannot be proven or disproven. I tend to give credence these speculations, having witnessed the predilection of some animals for this mushroom and effect it has on them. It is implausible that pre-historic humans were unaware of this mushroom's special powers.

Though some find psychoactive botanicals a useful way of gathering wisdom, people differ in their ability to physically tolerate Fly Agaric, San Pedro, Damiana, and other substances, which may be illegal or difficult to find. In lieu of substances (or in conjunction with them) some use sleep deprivation or fasting to obtain psychic messages, but this can also be physically taxing. Reading animal signs is a safer and more comfortable system for obtaining messages from the spirit world.

Because deer are abundant in many places, it is possible to put together a series of significant interactions, sometimes spanning many years, thereby arriving at a deeper or more overarching message. I will close this chapter by illustrating this through my own deer interactions.

1. In 1986, driving off the mountain with a few other women after a full moon ritual, I braked at a three-way crossroad as my headlights shone on a beautiful stag with huge antlers. The animal glowed under the moonlight. He remained centered in the intersection for several minutes before lumbering into the darkness.

As I was a neophyte, I did not tie this to the number of women in the car (I think there were three, including me), nor did I take note of the compass direction in which the deer retreated. I did notice that he showed us all four sides of his body, a sign that the animal encounter was momentous and should be pondered seriously. I probably did not know at the time that the threefold crossroad signifies a significant life turning point. We took the stag as a gift from Diana and a sign that our ritual had pleased her. Though my formal initiation would not occur for many more months, looking back I recognize that this deer was presaging that initiation. The meaning of an animal encounter changes as you travel further down the road.

2. About ten years later, I was traveling a desert highway outside of Tucson when I had another significant encounter. I was going the speed limit, more or less, which is way too fast to be driving at dusk on a rural road. A stag ran in front of my car, a very large stag with a huge rack. In some parts of the United States it is uncommon to see male deer with multi-pointed antlers, because so many succumb to hunters before they are fully mature. I slammed on the brakes, and—every driver's worst nightmare—I plowed into the deer. The stag was so big that the front of the car scooped him up like a cow catcher and he landed on the hood, his face a few inches from my eyes. We stared at each other for several seconds through the (still intact) windshield, his large brown eye locked on my blue ones. Then he recovered himself and scampered away. I parked and followed him into the brush, worried that he might be injured. An owl hooted. I searched in the gloom for some trace of my deer, but evidently he had made a clean getaway, unharmed. My car was also undamaged.

This interaction was not as joyful as the one previously mentioned—in fact it was downright unnerving—but it was no less significant. Deer represent a journey into the mystic space between the worlds, a function they underscore by bringing so many motorists into the land of the dead. Since I had been forced into an intimate encounter with this animal, I took it as a sign that I needed to do some thoughtfully planned work on a psychic plane, moving deliberately into the mystic landscape instead of being thrust there. At the same time, this too was a gift. I felt like I moved inside that brown eye and came back with something powerful, though myste-rious. The spectacular antlers on the deer drew my thoughts back to the crossroads deer of long ago. Notice this is a second impactful encounter with a deer while traveling a road, albeit separated by many years. Deer are a part of the road I travel.

I am not one to draw dire warnings from Horned Owls, but the owl hooting in this instance was a caution. The desert is a dangerous place off-trail in darkness. I needed to regain the road and slow down.

3. Another unusual interaction with deer happened recently, on a warm restless night as I tried to sleep. I was on the sofa, not in my bed, for reasons I will not go into other than to assure my readers that I was not in the doghouse. I noticed my cat was staring out the window, and though she was completely still I sensed she was excited about something. I tiptoed over to the window to see what she was looking at. It was a young deer, legs splayed and head down, peering into the window. The deer stared at me. I stared at the deer.

This was a young deer, indicating a project underway, not a maturity of process. I mentioned earlier that a familiar is sometimes employed to attune a psychic to otherworldly information, but in this case my psychic attunement to my cat drew me into a happening in the physical world. I wondered if this visitation between the young deer and the cat might be a regular thing, so a few nights later I made a point of checking. Sure enough, the two were checking each other out at three o'clock in the morning. The animal became aware of me and then I became the recipient of the faunal gaze. I don't think that the cat and the deer had a Bambi-Thumper relationship, nothing so intimate, but a regular visitation for observational purposes was occurring. I suddenly felt like a participant in an inverse zoo, enclosed in a safe box with a window open for viewing by the free animal population. I realized this was the third deer with which I had locked eyes through a window. I was having this interaction at home, at night, pulled out of my sleep to meet a creature symbolic of shapeshifting and shamanic visioning.

Through gazing deeply in the eye of the deer, I gained a path for moving between worlds. I think I began receiving this pathway on that full moon night years ago when I met the stag in the crossroads, but realization of power is the ability to recognize it and use it consciously. Animal divination is a transfer of knowledge, animal to human-animal.

The Antler Wagon

The Saami sun goddess Beiwe and her daughter Beiwe-Neida travel the sky enclosed in reindeer antlers. I chose a repetitive poetic form to tell this story because the rhythms of animal herds ruled by the sun are repetitive, as are the rhythms of people who depend on the herds.

She rides across heaven in antler wagon.
She rides across heaven in antler wagon.
Holding her daughter, she defines the day.
Holding her daughter, she defines the day.
She crosses antler heaven holding her daughter,
defining a day in the wagon ride.

Bring peace to hearts in the blackness.
Bring peace to hearts in the blackness.
Offer red blood of white reindeer.
Offer red blood of white reindeer.
In the heart of the blackness offer red blood.
White reindeer bring peace.

Bring light to wake forest in springtime.
Bring light to wake forest in springtime.
Make rings of birch branches.
Make rings of birch branches.
Birch forest light rings, bring branches, make
time wake the spring.

Her reindeer daughter brings heart. Her reindeer
antlers hold the light of day. In the
forest she wakes blood in birch. Time
branches, crosses heaven, makes
an offering. Black, red, white define
the wagon ride. Peace.

The Unfortunate Hunter

This tale is recounted in Monica Kropej's Supernatural Beings from
Slovenian Myths and Folktales.[66] *It's the kind of story that usually
carries a moral, so I have tacked one on at the end. Ember Days are days
when certain activities normally allowed are prohibited for religious
reasons. They were absorbed from pagan Rome. Slovenia was
Christianized by the Roman Catholic Church, not the Eastern
Orthodox.*

The man pulled back his bow and aimed the arrow.

The man was right where he wanted to be. His mother had
told him not to do this, his Church had forbidden it, and perhaps
God Himself had deemed it wrong. He was not cowed. He would
do as he pleased.

It was a fine autumn day, Ember Sunday in fact—the best day
to be in the woods. He had pretended to be sound asleep when
his mother tried to wake him. The second time she came to his
bed she had sounded cross, and the third time she had realized
he was only feigning sleep. The family left for mass without him,
and the minute they were out the door he put on his green shirt
and trousers.

Now he had a deer in sight. A beautiful antlered deer with—

"Jesus!" said the man, dropping his bow.

The deer had a golden chalice between his antlers and he was
wearing priest's robes. Priest's robes were on the deer's back. The
deer was dressed as a priest, and he had a chalice on his head, the
deer was holding a chalice, the deer was dressed like a priest

and...

The man ran quickly home to his mother. Mass was finished, but the man told his mother she must go back to the church and fetch the priest. He needed a Catholic priest now. He must confess in time before...

But when the mother and the priest returned the young man had been ripped apart. Torn in pieces, right down the middle. The Two Black Dogs, who do the bidding of the Devil, had come for the hunter and they had taken his soul. Now he was in Hell.

Hunters: obey all hunting laws. The laws of your family, the laws of your religion, the laws of your government, the laws of your hunting club. This is what happens when people don't follow the rules. The deer put on clothes, the Black Dogs come up from Hell to get you, and everybody's Sunday dinner is ruined. You have been warned. Also, don't pretend to be asleep when your mother tries to wake you.

Deer Review

Magical Qualities: antlers, docile, adaptable eyesight (reindeer), migrating (reindeer), crepuscular, excellent at staying hidden

Magical Applications:

Other Associations:

Tracking the Signs

There is a disturbing navigational hazard known to airplane pilots and cave divers as *spatial disorientation.* As the term implies, it is a state of directional confusion caused by the absence of any reference point. The sufferer can unknowingly be flying upside down or be deep underwater with no idea where the surface is. Under these conditions, even a small miscalculation can move a plane off track until it is flying in a wide circle. Like those rare individuals with perfect pitch, a few people hav unerring equilibrium that is up to this challenge. Othe eventually encounter a reference point if they remain ca though obviously this is the territory where panic reigns.

We all have experienced disorientation on a less extreme level, such as driving in whiteout or heavy fog conditions. Nobody likes it. The other day I found myself in this situation while I was in the woods circumventing a large patch of blowdown. I discovered I had lost the path, and though I could have approximated my location on a map, and I have a pretty good sense of direction, I felt disconcerted until I regained the trail.

We commonly think of divination as a tool for clarifying our journey, but when divining with the world at hand we can find ourselves pulled from a secure state into confusion. I won't present confusion as an unqualified boon—sometimes it is the result of poor choices or irresponsible behavior (*I knew I should have packed that compass!*)—but you can be doing everything correctly and still find yourself in a morass. Your divinatory signs are either alerting you to the nature of your predicament or intentionally leading you into unfamiliar territory. To find forsaken treasure you must become lost.

At the time I found the blowdown that got me somewhat lost, I was on my way back from a jewel of a lake in the wilderness. A friend of mine had inadvertently found this place a few summers back while leading a pack of peak baggers. The group strayed onto a faint herd path that took them a few miles off their intended course. Bowled over by the beauty of this idyllic spot, my friend wanted to spend the rest of the day there, but the others were determined to reach the predetermined summit and ɔt a little annoyed at the detour. They betrayed a singularity of ʋose that might be called a disorder, though they would ɪbtedly have characterized the strength of their resolution way. By becoming too focused on a goal, you can miss the the world is giving you, and sometimes even getting ɪough to get you on track.

ʻting of all signs are the ones that appear to throw ɘ out the window. The bewilderment caused by data that doesn't fit can be a good thing, though, because there must be a dissolution of ordered connections for a better theory to emerge. A paradigm shift cannot occur without the disintegration of beliefs and the subsequent disorientation. Temporary confusion paves the way for new insight. The most profound animal signs are not the ones that tell you where to go next or what to expect in the year ahead. They are the signs that open the world, allowing you to see something new, even to realize a deeper level of truth. The animal is not only bringing you a sign; the sign is leading you to the animal goddess.

There may be some confusion generated by what I've presented about goddesses and animals here and other places. I've called Neith a crocodile goddess, then referred to her as a bee goddess and mentioned that she's also a click beetle. I've linked her with the acacia tree. I've categorized Cybele with the bee and the lion, and Isis with the scorpion and the kite, and just to confuse things further I'll tell you Isis is also the star Sirius. Ishtar is linked with the lion, the owl, the planet Venus, the cedar tree, and the bull. Artemis has more associations than I care to mention here: deer, bear, dog, quail, hare, moon, bow, rivers, forests, mountains, and many more.

Tables of correspondences will often list an animal, bird, tree, herb, stone, element, planet, color, and flower for each deity. Where there is no obvious candidate, they will choose the one that seems to fit best, and where there is more than one animal they may either list all in that category or choose the one most widely reported. There's a neatness to this approach, and if you believe that only belief matters then you might want to go with a clear invented approach.

Another approach is to search through a confusing disarray c information until you get your bearings. By consciously steppi into the place of spatial disorientation, magical revelation occur in the grayness of indeterminate light.

The goddess with her confusing array of corresponde

which don't quite fit in a table, can be conceptualized as a riddle. Riddles are powerful tools for imparting spiritual wisdom. Think of the troll under the bridge in fairytales, who demands the answer to his riddle as tribute for crossing the bridge. The purpose of his riddle is not merely to demonstrate the prowess of the heroine but also to place the listener in a space of questioning. Any troll worth his token will pose a question that at least temporarily discombobulates the listener, and the answer will be remembered and perhaps pondered on different levels.

The tracks of animals can also be a riddle. The focused tread of the coyote versus the erratic ramble of the dog. The bouncy stride of the weasel versus the regular step of the fox. And is it a Gray Fox or a Red Fox? A Gray Fox has partially retractable claws typical of tree climbers, and the nail imprint is usually missing in the snow. Red Fox claws show up unless the snow is very deep, and this fox is not a climber. I once tracked a fox with clear claw prints to the base of a tree, where the tracks disappeared, introducing some ambiguity in identification. Sometimes you have to admit you're outfoxed.

When identification is easy, it's easy to lose interest. *It's just a deer.* But how many deer? Were they young or full grown? What did they do in this spot? Where did they come from and where did they go? Sometimes the record of the animal's movements completes the message.

There can be other signs of interest when the animal herself is ~ent, and the animal usually is absent or unseen. There are marks in trunks, there are feathers, there is animal hair, scat. Moose browse can sometimes be distinguished from ~e height of the torn branches. The angle of the chewing ~tiate muskrat from beaver. Owls and raptors will ~ckages called pellets that contain animal skeletons ~ through their digestive track. The size, content, ~ellets can indicate species, and if you pull the ~tick you can sometimes find a skeleton.

After noting the diagnostic details of size, shape, and placement of scat, you can pull the feces apart to see what the animal ate. The smell contains all kinds of special clues, but you probably don't want to investigate the evidence this thoroughly. I was once on a tracking expedition where some members of the group knelt around a pile of scat in the snow, blowing air on the treasure to warm it up so they could get a clearer scent. Others took photos for later reference, though I was not ready, yet, to start taking pictures of poop. Trackers are a breed unto themselves.

Tracking is a language that reveals a story. Sometimes the signs can be baffling, but even then—especially then—there is the danger of filtering out pertinent data. The tracker learns to hesitate and observe, then organize information. One clear indicator of the novice tracker is a facility for drawing fast conclusions. The goal is to be accurate; there is no need to race.

In the same way, the augur remains in the gray area for a spell, allowing the picture to coalesce. I follow this principle in the next example, which describes a casual stroll down an unpaved road after a snowstorm. The signs are noted in a spirit of curiosity, and an interpretation emerges spontaneously.

I head out in the brisk sunlight on a woods road. Half a foot of snow has fallen the night before, and tire marks show that this road has been traveled within a few hours. Now it is deserted. The morning after foul weather is a good time to meet wild animals, but today I see only tracks. The first ones are tiny— maybe a little rodent, but a small bird hopping along the ground can leave a similar trail if the prints are indistinct. These twin prints are aligned as if the animal were hopping, reinforcing the idea that this is a bird, but mice also have a hopping gait. It helps to know that many birds will leave at least an occasional smudge in the snow from tailfeathers, and birds will fly a few feet when they meet an obstacle. This track is unbroken, so I return to my surmise that this is a small rodent. The lack of a tail mark is significant: maybe a Short-Tailed Shrew.

Further down the road are slightly larger tracks with an almost identical hopping pattern, this time with the telltale tail impression. This is probably a mouse. I'm almost tempted to follow the trail because I like mice when they're not in my house eating my food. Woods mice doing their mousey thing can be fascinating, but I'm out for a casual walk and I don't feel like bushwhacking over boggy terrain.

Still further along the road I find slightly larger, well-defined tracks with prominent nails: a squirrel, either Red or Gray. The Red Squirrel is a tad smaller than the Gray, but there is an overlap in size and I'm not good enough to tell them apart.

These little animals are speeding across the road, not ambling along it, because they can't afford to be exposed to raptors and other predators. Even the rabbit, which I encounter next, is too vulnerable to ramble outside the brush. I would love for this to be a Snowshoe Hare track, but the prints are too small and the hind paw is narrow, not splayed. Cottontail. This is my first positive identification of the day, but I'm beginning to notice a pattern in the patterns. The prints are teensy tiny to begin with and they move up by increments. I imagine that if I continue down the road I will find my Snowshoe Hare prints, then maybe a moose track, then eventually the enormous print of a Sasquatch. Since it's time to return home, I'm not able to test this theory, but the message is not abstruse. Small steps: start as small as you can and soon you will be leaving a larger print. I apply this message to a project I'm currently immersed in.

The same process of linking signs is involved in another animal encounter, this one occurring in the summer. This story begins high on a mountaintop, at the conclusion of an exhilarating climb.

The view above timberline is panoramic as I lay back against a boulder, careful not to disturb the alpine vegetation. I allow my attention to float upward to the hawks circling on the air current.

I love gazing at the sky and noticing the textures of clouds. Looking at the sky from down below can make you feel small and humble, sometimes a worthy perspective, but the sight of a hawk lifts you off the ground and draws you into heaven. Suddenly you feel very large.

I spend the next day very much down to earth, walking down the main street in my village. The village is bisected by a temperamental brook with a high bridge. I enjoy looking at the water here, which is sometimes roiling and fierce, sometimes barely a trickle. Today in late summer the water is low and the bank is lush. Waddling along the shore is a pregnant muskrat. She is unconcerned about my presence and intent on scurrying up a muddy slope, but she's so preggo that she keeps slipping and rolling back in the brook. It's considered bad form to laugh at the clumsiness of a pregnant woman, but a muskrat doesn't bother to take offense, so I let loose a giggle.

Muskrats are fertile aquatic mammals who may birth two litters even in the short summers of the Adirondacks. They burrow along stream banks or build dome shaped huts with twigs and mud. They often live in colonies, sometimes alongside beavers. Despite being numerous they are not easy to spot, though their signs are unmistakable. They eat a lot of vegetation and shovel a lot of mud.

I have a soft spot for the muskrat because I associate her with the sultry voice of Toni Tennille singing "Muskrat Love."[67] The muskrat's fertility and her flair for mud-molding can be related to my own creative processes, so my initial interpretation is that I, too, am preggo (in a different way).

"Muskrat" is an anglicized Algonquian word, and in a Lenape creation story Muskrat helps to form the world. Creator asks the animals to pack mud on the back of Turtle to form the first land mass, but only Muskrat can dive deep enough to gather the mud. Muskrat's creative energy delves beneath primordial waters to the earth's core.

The muskrat appears to be the exact opposite of the soaring hawk, yet my hunch is that these two sightings back-to-back are connected to the same deity. The air stream and the mud stream carry the same energy, manifesting as a blissful high and an earthy belly laugh. *Floatin' like the heavens above, it looks like muskrat love.*

Taking our tracking skills a step further, let's examine the jumbled and contradictory clues that surround the mythology of another animal deity. There is certainly a fog surrounding the goddess Hera and the confusing data and allegations we have received about her. Hera is known to us through high school mythology as Zeus' jealous termagant wife, which makes her appellation "Goddess of Marriage" somewhat ironic. We are told she is the daughter of Cronus and Rhea, and she is said to have been "nursed by the Seasons" (Greek Hours or Roman Horae). Other stories say she was nurtured by the old water Titan deities Oceanus and Tethys, while still others name different water gods. "Hera" may actually be the title "Lady." Hera is sister to Zeus, Demeter, Hestia, Hades, and Poseidon and mother of Ares, Hephaestus, Hebe, Eris, and the Cretan birth goddess Eileithyia. Her attributes are the cow, cuckoo, peacock, pomegranate, water lily, fig, apple, orange, willow, myrrh tree, chaste tree, lion, snake, sky, stars, wind, water, scepter, golden throne, and crown. This much data seems to obscure rather than define her. Who is she?

As wife of Zeus, Hera is defined within a patriarchal system of worship. Rarely, a goddess in a matriarchal society will have a consort, but that will not be an important relationship unless he is also her son. Matriarchal mythological relationships can be: divine mother only; divine mother with son or daughter; divine mother with twins (male or female); divine sisters; or divine sister-brother. Husband-wife or divine father are patriarchal inventions.

The mythological record paints Hera's relationship with Zeus as contentious, when not outright combative. This indicates a reluctant syncretism of the cult of a patriarchal god with the cult of a goddess. Graves describes the political strife behind this union as the subjugation of a matriarchal culture by a patriarchal one.[68] Hera's worship in Greece far predates the arrival of Zeus. We can surmise that she was herself a divine mother goddess of a matriarchal society.

The Greek family tree obscures more about Hera than it reveals. Complex genealogies are always the result of two or more pantheons being consciously combined. This sounds like cynical manipulation on the part of the priests, but family relationships in ancient societies, even ancient patriarchal societies, were not firmly set. Family adoptions between adults were common, had the same status as relationships through birth, and might even be formalized by contract. If people can establish family relationships by agreement, why not gods through their priests? A combined pantheon would not necessarily have to come through patriarchal takeover —a matriarchal society absorbing refugees could adopt relationships among their gods as well as their peoples—but in this case we know that the Greek pantheon, like so many others, was the result of conquest and subjugation.

Though Hera is given a specific origin in the new genealogy, her birth in water, demoted to a fostering relationship, has not been completely obliterated. Hera's yearly ritual rebirth through her water-bath speaks to self-creation from water, as does her water lily association. What is significant about this, to me, is that it establishes Hera as a primal mother goddess. Early Greeks, like the early Egyptians, believed life emerged from water.

One of Hera's most vibrant centers of worship was at Argos, a port city on the Peloponnese Peninsula, in southeast Greece. Archeology shows it to be among the first cities in Neolithic Europe, and it is believed to have been established by people from Asia Minor. Hera's temple flourished there long before the arrival of Zeus, but much of what we know of her worship comes from male writers during historical times. We know, for example, that Alexander of Macedon took two hundred peacocks to Hera's temple at Argos after his conquest of northwest India. This does not preclude the idea of peacocks gracing Hera's temple much earlier than this, but, since peacocks are not indigenous to the region and the people who established Argos came from a place without peacocks, we can assume that the peacock is not an original attribute for Hera. This does not allow us to entirely dismiss the peacock, because we do need to account for the assumption in antiquity that the peacock would be a bird beloved of Hera. One explanation is the "eyes" on the male peacock's feathers. The eye in creation schemas can sometimes be the source of life. Recall the Eye of Ra in Egypt. One of Hera's heroes, Argus, is known for being all seeing or "having a hundred eyes" that Hera gave him. There is a myth that has Hera taking the eyes of the slain hero Argus and placing them on the peacock. Hera's association with eyes again makes her the mother of life.

Figure 84: Hera. Taranto, Italy, 450 BCE. Photo: Nemracc/Wikimedia Commons.

Another striking thing about the male peacock is the amount of gold in his feathered display. Hera's famous statue at Argos, no longer extant but described in the literature, has her seated on a golden throne. In surviving statues from other places Hera is typically depicted seated on a gold throne with her arms extended to welcome worshipers. Deities with an emphatic gold association are typically sun deities, so I am going to tentatively assert Hera here as a sun goddess.

Most birds are monogamous for a season, if not for life, but not the peacock. Female peacocks make the rounds between the male territories, and males do not establish harems. This polyamorous behavior recalls the older fertility rituals of Hera, alluded to in ancient art and literature but partially obscured by tales of Hera's "jealousy," a theme reiterated so strenuously and so often that it begins to look suspicious. The story of how Hera and Zeus got together says she rejected him repeatedly until he took the form of a cuckoo. The cuckoo is another polyandrous bird and a famous symbol of fertility. It is also the animal most commonly linked with Hera. The story of Zeus taking a cuckoo form is probably an allegory for an agreement that patriarchal standards of monogamy for Hera (and by extension, her people) would be relaxed somewhat in exchange for establishing Zeus in her temple. If such an agreement was made, it certainly eroded over the centuries, but this interpretation does explain why Hera insisted on marrying a philandering bird when she was supposedly so jealous.

Hera's statue in Argos depicted her holding a scepter topped by a cuckoo. In her other hand she offered a pomegranate. Also displayed in conjunction with the statue were the Seasons. Graves correctly identifies Hera as a triple goddess and goddess of the year by her link with the Seasons. (The Greeks divided the year into three seasons, not four.) As governess of the year, Hera is again a sun goddess, and her rulership of the cyclical year explains her association with weather. As early spring she comes in the form of a migrating cuckoo; at harvest she is embodied in the prolific pomegranate. And her third aspect? This is the cow, another of Hera's common associations, the animal who brings economic stability. Hera as cow feeds and nurtures the community.

Hera's multiplicity of animistic forms can be partially explained by syncretism and by the unexamined lumping together of mythical references, but even after sorting through these distortions she remains a triple deity. She is cow-cuckoo-pomegranate tree. The astrological or heavenly form of the deities is not a separate aspect, because the Greeks (along with many other Western cultures) saw the heavens as a mirror of earthly life, not an aspect of it. *As above, so below.*

Some will object to assigning Hera the pomegranate tree on the grounds that the pomegranate belongs to Persephone. The growth and systemization of the Greek pantheon resulted in functions and symbols being distributed among deities, sometimes in a territorial way, but looking to pre-patriarchal Greece, people in different locations would have worshiped the pomegranate tree under other names and with other understandings of relationships. The Hera I am describing as cow-cuckoo-pomegranate tree is Hera of Argos. Syncretism of goddesses after invasions meant that in other places some "Heras" would be different goddesses with different attributes. Another Hera might be snake-cuckoo-water lily, to make a hypothetical example.

Athena is a goddess strongly linked with the owl and the snake. The owl-snake goddess is a combination found throughout a large region of southeast Europe dating to prehistoric times. Graves surmised that as prominent a deity as Athena would be a triple goddess and speculated that her third attribute might be the goat, since her shield was made of goatskin.[69] Actually, Athena's third form is the olive tree. She is snake-owl-olive tree.

Triple goddess as land animal, flying animal, and tree or plant is not confined to Greece. Anatolian Cybele is lion-bee-pine tree. A piece of Cybele from the sky-mirror came to earth as a meteor, which formed a whole religious cult, but she is still a triple goddess. Germanic Freya is sow-falcon-fir tree. Celtic Nehalennia is dog-goose-apple tree. Baba Yaga is frog-pelican-birch tree, though this goddess is so widespread and syncretized that she has other triplicities. As near as I can tell, this animistic conception does not hold for Semitic, Egyptian, or Sumerian cultures—or if it does, it is buried too deep for me to find. Not all European goddesses are triple goddesses, of course, and some triple goddesses do not fit this earth-wings-tree pattern. I am convinced that Hecate, for example, was originally worshiped as the triple goddess of a place where two rivers joined, the original three-formed crossroads, and from there she acquired aspects associated with water, such as willow trees, dogs, and travel. As a traveling goddess, she later became associated with horses and roads.

The goddess manifested in the form of a land creature, a winged creature, and a tree corresponds to the three states of human consciousness. The earth-moving consciousness lives in the physical world of survival, social interaction, and creature comforts. The winged consciousness is experienced through dreams and meditations or shamanic journeys. In this state of consciousness we can fly. The vegetative consciousness is alive during deep sleep, a state unremembered during the waking moments except as a feeling of rested contentment. Thinking of land-moving, flying, and rooted beings as states of consciousness can give us additional information when assessing the message contained in our encounter with the natural world.

Recognizing that goddesses (and gods) often have multiple animistic forms, even beneath layers of syncretism and naïve association, can make the task of interpreting animal signs more complex. Yet by examining available information, keeping an open mind, and accepting a degree of ambiguity, animal signs can still be understood within a goddess framework without imposing a forced order through tidy systems of correspondences. Again, when signs create confusion, for whatever reason, it's certainly permissible to seek clarification through formal divination systems like cards or runes. Alternatively, you can ask for another sign. Eventually the fog will clear.

The Huluppu Tree

This story tells of the arrival of Sumerian people to what is now southern Iraq, as swamp waters receded in the region between 5000 and 4000 BCE. According to their records, the Sumerians came in boats from the south. Various Semitic and non-Semitic peoples were already settled to the north and east. The reference in the text to the respect of Inanna for the gods Enlil and An is meant to convey cooperative intentions of the settlers toward their neighbors.

This is also the story of the evolution of Inanna's cult from sacred grove to constructed ceremonial space. The events in the story represent a juncture between open air worship and the temple complex. Because the Huluppu tree is destined to support civilization, the wild creatures who live in it must be banished.

The words Huluppu, Anzu, *and* Lilith *are not Sumerian. I use these names because they appear in Wolkstein and Kramer's translation of the myth in* Inanna Queen of Heaven and Earth,[70] *which some readers will be familiar with.*

The Huluppu tree is identified by Benjamin Foster as a Euphrates Poplar.[71] This drought-tolerant tree grows well in floodplains and can survive in brackish water and high-salinity soil. It is a squat tree, which under ideal growing conditions acquires a massive trunk. It is perfect for Inanna's purpose.

The snake settled in the roots of the Huluppu tree is the bane of agricultural centers in hot arid climates. Deadly snakes are attracted by rodents who are attracted by grain. The Mesopotamians used magic to control the poisonous snake population, but for some reason the snake in this instance "knows no charm."

The Anzu-bird is a large fiercely taloned bird depicted with a lion head. Her name is sometimes translated as "heavy rain," so she could be a type of thunderbird.

There is no word in English that exactly fits the Mesopotamian Lilith. She is not a goddess, but "demon" does not fit either, despite the later demonization of the Lilith in the Bible (who may or may not be the same Lilith we're talking about here). She is an enlivened energy who does not coexist well with towns and cities. She is especially associated with the hot desert wind thought to bring sickness. Lilith usually chooses to avoid humans. The conflict comes when humans travel into her abode or for some reason she wanders into human habitations. I might have defined her as a "wild spirit," but that makes her sound like a party girl, and when Lilith shows up the party's definitely over.

Figure 85: Anzu-bird with Fallow Deer. One of the god Enki's appellations is 'Stag of the Abzu.' 2500 BCE. Photo: Capillon/Wikimedia Commons.

Our story begins, not at the very beginning, but at a beginning a long time ago. At this time, the following things have already happened: heaven and earth have separated into their separate realms; the god of the east, An, has claimed heaven for himself; the god of the north, Enlil, has claimed the firm soil for himself; and our lady Ereshkigal lays claim to the world below. In the south, our lord Enki claims the fresh water, but the south roils in frantic waves. No one lives here. To the east and north are towns and villages where people bake their bread in large ovens. They perform the correct ceremonies to glorify Enlil and An. They have everything they need to live well.

In the south the water churns with boulders and silt. No temples can be built here. The stones must settle and the water must be channeled for the south to become civilized.

To make the land habitable, Enki in his boat sets sail. Enki sets out to guide the waters to their underground passages, to guide water into caverns beneath the soil. Boulders threaten Enki as he steers his little boat. The stones bob in the water like turtles. Churning blocks of silt arise to impede his progress. Waves attack his prow like hungry wolves. Waves attack his flank like angry lions. Enki steers the abundant waves downward. He steers the abundant water into the world below.

As land emerges between the rivers, a solitary woman walks the riverbank. A solitary woman walks along the Euphrates and notices a solitary tree in the water. Its branches have been ripped by the south wind. The turbulent current has torn its roots. The woman rescues the tree from the river. She plucks the Huluppu tree from the Euphrates and plants it nearby.

The young woman is our Lady Inanna. She respects the god Enlil and the god An. She has chosen the place called Uruk, along the Euphrates, to plant her sacred garden. She places the Huluppu tree in the ground and tamps the soil with her feet. She waters the roots with her feet. Inanna tends her beloved tree in her special garden.

Inanna wonders when the tree can become a fine chair for her to sit in, a fine bed for her to lie in. She asks herself, 'When will my tree become my throne and my bed?' Inanna waits for her tree to grow. Five years pass. Inanna waits for the Huluppu wood to mature. Ten years pass. Inanna believes the tree is ready to be carved for her chair and her bed. But now the tree is not available for harvest. The trunk is heavy and thick, and the wood has not split, yet the Huluppu tree cannot be carved for a throne. Interlopers, squatters, have taken possession of Inanna's tree.

In the roots of the tree lives a snake, a snake that will listen to no one. No magical utterances will move this snake; she is entrenched and knows no charm.

In the top branches of the tree, the Anzu-bird has made her nest. The Anzu raises her young in the foliage of the tree. The Anzu-bird will not leave.

In the trunk of the tree, the fearsome Lilith, that unruly spirit, has made her home. Lilith is ensconced in the Huluppu tree and will not relocate. Inanna is distraught.

Inanna, the joyful maiden who loves to laugh, now cries. Inanna cries until dawn breaks on the horizon. As dawn breaks on the horizon Inanna says to her brother the sun god, "Oh my brother Utu, how sad am I. My throne cannot be carved; my bed cannot be assembled. My Huluppu tree has been hijacked by the fearsome Lilith, by the naughty Anzu-bird, and by the snake who knows no charm."

She tells the sun god all that has been done so far: how heaven and earth have been separated; how Enlil has taken his place in the north and An in the east; how Ereshkigal has been presented to the underworld; how Enki has risked his life in the south, his boat attacked by stones and giant waves, so that the water could be separated into rivers and solid ground; how a tree was thrust into the current and how she, Inanna, plucked it out of the Euphrates. She tells how she has tended that tree, planting it with her feet and watering it with her feet. All of these events and all of this labor has occurred over many ages so that she, Inanna, can have a nice chair. Surely Utu cannot allow intruders to live in her tree? Surely Utu cannot allow her throne to remain uncarved, her bed to remain unassembled?

Utu can allow Inanna's furniture to remain undelivered just fine. Utu can allow that Inanna has made a forceful argument, but he has not been swayed. He will not evict the denizens of the

Huluppu tree. The fearsome Lilith remains in the trunk. The defiant Anzu nests in the branches. The stubborn snake curls in the roots, knowing no charms. The beautiful heart of Inanna, usually so filled with joy, weeps in sorrow.

Inanna sobs all day and through the night. When day breaks once again, when the birds sing to the brightening sky, she spies the hero Gilgamesh and approaches him for support. Inanna addresses Gilgamesh as a brother, and he is sympathetic to her plight. Since heaven and earth have been separated; since the gods have been assigned their places; since Lord Enki has battled stones and waves; since the south has been divided into rivers and land; since the Huluppu tree has been thrust into the current and especially since she, Inanna, has tended that tree for fifteen years, of course Inanna must have her chair and her bed.

Figure 86: Grove of Euphrates Poplar, probably the fabled Huluppu Tree. Photo: BogomolovPL/Wikimedia Commons.

Gilgamesh ties a heavy belt around his waist as if it were nothing. With ease he raises his ax weighing seven talents and seven minas. With his ax Gilgamesh kills the snake who would not learn any charms. With a squawk the frightened Anzu-bird flies to the mountains with her fledglings. With a sigh the vanquished Lilith flees to the western desert.

The companions of Gilgamesh, whom he calls his sons, help the hero trim the branches and roots and bark of the tree. To Inanna, Gilgamesh presents the materials for her chair and her bed. For himself, Gilgamesh fashions a wooden rod and a wooden ball. Inanna allows him to take these things, yet they will one day be taken back from him.

Inanna now has a fine throne to sit on and a beautiful bed to lie in. Inanna is pleased.

Praise to our Lady Inanna, the joyful queen with the radiant heart.

Questioning the Unseen

1) Finish filling out the Deer Review earlier in this chapter.
2) The Anzu-bird is a composite creature, a common feature of Mesopotamian art. The head is a lion, or possibly a leopard. What kind of bird body might the Anzu-bird have?
3) Could the Huluppu tree and its wild inhabitants be seen as a single conscious entity?
4) Walking in your neighborhood you find three yellow feathers, but you cannot identify the bird species. How might you interpret this sign?
5) How would your interpretation of a deer encounter differ for the following: single fawn, two fawns, doe, doe with fawn, stag, grown hornless deer of indeterminate sex, reindeer, group of deer you see, group of deer you don't see.
6) If you have had more than one significant interaction with a deer (significant by your definition), write down the details of those meetings that stand out in your mind. Is there a meta-

message that comes through multiple encounters? If you cannot do this with the deer, do it with another animal.

7) Why did cultures throughout the Balkan region see the owl and the snake as different forms of the same goddess? What do they have in common? What is the commonality between the raven and the wolf? The dog and the goose?

8) Study and follow tracks. Learn to identify cat versus dog versus wild canine tracks. Most people are surprised to discover foxes or coyotes living in their suburban neighborhood. Cat tracks can be intriguing because cats often have agendas behind their neighborhood wanderings.

9) I despise hunters who won't follow the law, but even I have to say that the Unfortunate Hunter's punishment seems a bit harsh. Obviously, this is an example of pagan belief disguised within a storyline acceptable to Christian sensibilities. What are your ideas about the pagan practices or myths hidden in this story?

Chapter 9

Avian Wisdom

Craning Your Mind

You will disturb the lines, and the letter will not fly entire, if you destroy one single bird of Palamedes.
—Martial, *Epigrams XIII:75*

Figure 87: Juvenile Whooping Crane. Photo: Donna Dewhurst/U.S. Fish and Wildlife Service.

Whooping Cranes are large water birds with high-pitched piercing cries, a trait they share with other cranes. Adults are white with black-tipped wings and long black legs. They have long necks and red foreheads. They are exceedingly rare: in 2015 there were an estimated 442 in the wild, and when my crane was captured in 1970 there were a good deal fewer of them.

My crane was actually brown, because he was immature, and I remember him as being the same size as me—which can't be right, but that's how I remember it. The bird was running with a badly broken wing, and I was chasing him with the intention of bringing him to the animal hospital. I was hot on the trail when my father appeared on his way home from work. Uh-oh. I had been vehemently instructed by both my parents, on numerous occasions, to stop picking up injured wildlife. I was a well-behaved kid, but I was constitutionally incapable of obeying this injunction.

My father wanted to know what I was doing—not accusing yet, just wanting to know. I explained that I was trying to catch a bird.

"Why are you trying to catch a bird?" my father asked, a bit of reproach coming into his voice. I explained that the bird had a broken wing, preparing myself for the scolding to follow.

My father automatically turned to look at the bird, and to my surprise what he said was, "I've never seen a bird like that before." He caught the bird for me and together we went to the animal hospital. It was a miracle—not that my father managed to catch the bird or that the bird was too uncommon for him to identify, but that he was actually engaging in this strongly proscribed behavior.

When we got to the hospital, the vet said, "I've never seen a bird like that before." He telephoned a few days later to tell us people from the university had come and taken my bird. He was a very rare bird, a Whooping Crane, and scientists at the university needed to study him.

I think I would have forgotten the incident if the adults around me had not become so absorbed in the kind of wildlife rescue they had up until then heavily inveighed against, at least when I performed it. I pondered that mystery for weeks. An animal encounter such as this one of extreme improbability (what was a Whooping Crane doing in Ohio anyway?) has encoded in it a meaning not only for that day or that month, but also for that year or even that lifetime. Occurring at such a young age, it foretold that I was destined, if not for great things, at least for very strange ones.

But the young crane with a broken wing was not simply an animal sign, because he provoked an active response. He was captured and given medical attention, even studied by eminent biologists, thus changing the trajectory of his life and potentially that of a species perilously endangered. Life is, in the end, an active activity, and so there is a link between comprehending fate and directing it. When we encounter the crane, we move beyond the messages in our probable and improbable world as reality is revealed, reworked, and reconfigured. Animal signs teach us not only to comprehend, but also to manipulate the parameters of destiny.

Though this chapter focuses on the crane, it includes birds that look similar rather than limiting discussion to the taxonomical crane group. There are good reasons why the Common Crane, Grey Heron, and African Sacred Ibis are assigned to different biological families, but many large long-legged water birds with diverse evolutionary patterns have played similar roles in mythologies across Western cultures.

Figure 88: Common Crane. Photo (adapted): Rufus46/Wikimedia Commons.

The Common Crane is a large bird measuring a little over three feet from bill to tail. She has a white and gray body, black wings and tail feathers, and long black legs. Her neck is black with a white stripe, and she has a little red cap. She is a summer resident once common across Europe and western Asia, but she has been extirpated in much of her original range. She is an omnivore, eating mostly vegetable matter but also insects, frogs, and small fish. She breeds on the ground in marshy areas. Cranes have an elaborate meandering courtship dance. They are social birds even when not breeding.

The African Sacred Ibis plays a similar role to the Crane in mythology. She is about 2½ feet long and has black legs, neck, and head. Her rump is also black but the rest of her body is white. Her traditional range is along the Nile and in sub-Sahara Africa, as well as in southern Iraq. She is an atypical migrator, flying back and forth from breeding grounds within Africa. Like the Crane she is an omnivore. Unlike the Crane she has a short mewling voice. She nests on the ground, in cliff sides, or in trees. The male Ibis, like some human males, attracts a mate by building her a nice nest. This Ibis is a colonial nester and gregarious even when foraging.

Figure 89: African Sacred Ibis. Photo: Bernard Gagnon/Wikimedia Commons.

The Grey Heron is a common Eurasian bird who may or may not migrate. She is similar to the North American Great Blue Heron only smaller, a little under three feet in length. She has a white and gray body, a white neck with a gray stripe in front, black bands across her temples, and gray wings with black edges. She is a carnivore, mainly eating amphibians and fish. She nests colonially in trees along water. Grey Herons, like their North American cousins, have solitary habits when not breeding. They have a harsh rasping call, not often heard, which is very different from the bugling cry of the Crane.

These three species differ in voice, migratory behavior, coloring, sociability, nesting sites, and courtship rituals. The Heron differs from the other two by being totally carnivorous. The Heron also differs by bending her neck when she flies, unlike other birds who fly with their neck stretched out. What the three have in common is freshwater habitat, colonial nesting, long necks, long legs, large size (including large wingspan), large feet, and large bills (with the prize in this area going uncontested to the Ibis).

Another trait these birds share with each other and all water birds sounds obvious, but it has a less obvious implication. Water birds live in wet places where sand, mud, or clay line the shore. Tracks in these areas are evident year-round. As seen previously, trackers view tracks not simply as a means of identification but also as a form of language. Tracks in snow from mammals or even ground birds tell a fairly straightforward story, but tracks along a riverbank are more cryptic. They start and end abruptly, as the animal enters the water or the bird flies away. Understanding the story of these tracks requires experience and intuition.

During the Stone Age, water birds were tracked by hunter-gatherers seeking food and feathers. As the Neolithic Era progressed, avian-rich waterways attracted women gathering clay for pots. Many of these pots would later be decorated with

Figure 90: Grey Heron. Photo: Matthias Barby/Wikimedia Commons.

geometric water bird designs. Did the women feel a kinship with the birds who drew their own symbols in the same clay?

Water birds are highly represented in the artwork of Neolithic and Upper Paleolithic Europe, as Marija Gimbutas documented.[72] That these birds are of the water is obvious from the chevron, zigzag, and M markings on their bodies, symbols that are associated with water. Gimbutas called the symbolic markings on statuary from this period a form of proto-writing. Often these figures are anthropomorphic, with breasts or triangular vulvas. Unfortunately, it is usually not possible to identify the type of water bird. They could be geese or swans as well as cranes or herons. Some statues have unmistakable duck features. All of these birds are prominent in surviving folklore.

In southern Mesopotamia, water bird

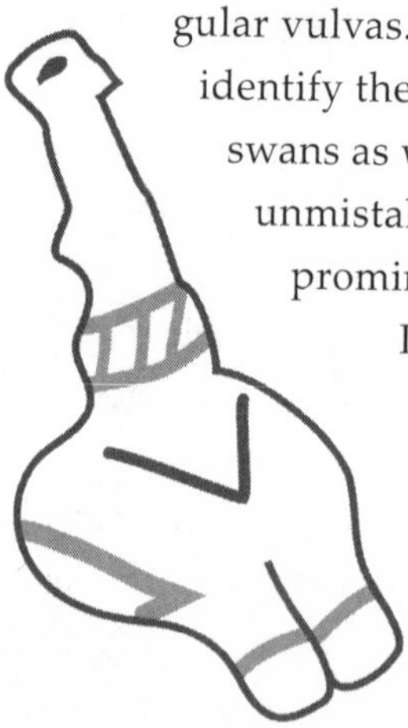

Figure 91: Goddess figures from Old Europe often feature an elongated neck and beaklike mouth. Note that the chevron functions here as symbol of the vulva. Romania, early fifth millennium.

images can again be found in art and pottery, but here there is evidence for the development of writing along a different channel. In this region we see proto-writing evolving not as religious inscription on votive images but instead as record keeping on clay tablets. Early recording devices, like sticks lodged in dirt and clay counting-pebbles, are replaced eventually by pictographs that record temple inventories. By the third millennium, true written language with grammatical structure has emerged. Signs for syllables or polysyllables are inscribed in clay with a reed stylus. The deity most closely associated with writing is Inanna, and the first Mesopotamian writing is found in the temples of her city of Uruk. Recall from the story of the Huluppu Tree in the previous chapter that this area was still partially waterlogged when first inhabited. Inanna's symbol is the reed, and she is often pictured with a lion and a backpack of reed arrows. Inanna may also have a water bird connection. She is thought to be the goddess pictured on a vase with birds, fish, and a turtle found in the city of Larsa and dated to the early

Figure 92: Mesopotamian pictogram. Late fourth millennium.

second millennium. The goddess has webbed feet like the bird pictured above her. The bird has a white belly, blue wings, a red neck and head, and a red bill. This is the famous "Ishtar Vase," which you can find on the internet or in Chapter 2 of my earlier book, *Invoking Animal Magic*.

On the Arabian Peninsula the goddess-crane connection is made explicit by the designation of the triple goddess as the Gharaniq, which translates as crane. Her manifestations are the goddesses Al-Uzza, Allat, and Menat, who fit the maiden-mother-crone archetype, something that is unusual for a Semitic goddess. The maiden-mother-crone triple goddess in general is neither usual nor highly unusual. (See the Matronae illustration in Chapter 3.) Despite assertions you may have heard to the contrary, this archetype was not "invented by Graves." That misinformation was propagated for political reasons, and unfortunately it seems to have caught fire. It is true, however, that most goddesses are not triple goddesses and most triple goddesses are not maiden-mother-crone. We can quibble about whether "maiden" is the best name for the Young Goddess or whether the Old Goddess is necessarily a "crone." We can also look at the instances where the "crone" is described as having the oldest cult and the "maiden" the most recent (which probably applies to the Gharaniq) and argue that this is an account of successively introduced goddesses, rather than, at root, a description the same goddess. The problem with these arguments is that we still must account for why these goddesses are presented as women at three different life stages if the maiden-mother-crone archetype is a modern invention.

While many dismiss maiden-mother-crone as a Graves invention by refusing to acknowledge pre-Romantic imagery that supports triple goddess archetypes, more savvy debunkers retreat into the Ice Age where records are fragmentary. This makes it easier to assert that "there is no evidence that..." The Paleolithic Era is idealized at the moment, and it is a popular contention that the "older" or "original" conception of the goddess is necessarily the correct one. I personally like to follow worship of the deity back to the basic animistic form, but my purpose is to help a clearer understanding of the deity to emerge, not to invalidate the anthropomorphic form or to equate civilization with spiritual perversion. The spiritual feminist community in the late twentieth century looked back to matriarchal times with a purpose: to get beyond the denigration of the feminine god-form in monotheistic and pre-Christian pagan religions. It was about reconnecting with traditions that helped us move forward, not about glorifying the distant past. Somehow that purpose got shifted into the concept that what is older is truer and what is newer is corrupt.

Figure 93: Kneeling supplicant with kneeling Ibis. Wood and Bronze. Egypt 330 BCE. Brooklyn Museum. Photo: luluinnyc.

If we trace Western deities to their original subjects of veneration, they become planets, weather-forms, plants, trees, and (especially) animals. Even ancestor deities take on an animal energy in conformance with the ancestor's animal clan or totem. If we go back to the really old, old, old-time religion we are back in animal land, and maybe we don't want to confine our understanding to this territory.

Returning to the Arabian crane goddesses, leaving aside the objection that there are three of them and that they are different ages and that they are linked together, we have another problem. Though the veneration of these goddesses is probably ancient, we know only a little about them, from the Islamic texts describing the destruction of their shrines and images. We don't know if these crane goddesses have any relation to writing.

In ancient Egypt we don't have to speculate about a writing and water bird connection, because here the association is explicit. The African Sacred Ibis god Thoth is the most prominent writing deity, credited with the invention of hieroglyphics. His other symbols are the marsh dwelling papyrus plant and the moon. (His association with the baboon came through syncretism and doesn't make a lot of sense.) Thoth is a physician god and a master of spells. His cult tried unsuccessfully to absorb another writing deity, the leopard-palm goddess Sheshat. This complex goddess is a calendrical goddess whose emblem is the seven-pointed star.

Also in Egypt there is a heron as first animal in one of the origin stories. As far as I can tell this bird has nothing to do with Egyptian writing, but the heron will become important when we come to Germanic writing. The origin story has the Bennu Bird, often pictured as a heron, playing a role identical to that of crocodile Neith. The Bennu Bird makes the first sound and lays the first egg. The Bennu Bird was extinct in Egypt when Greek historian Herodotus recorded a legend calling this bird the Phoenix.[73]

The Phoenicians are believed to have invented the first alphabet, or at least to have disseminated it, so exploring their alphabet mythology would be instructive. Early literature from this region is sparse, however. Destruction by Macedonian invaders plus the persecution of the older religion by Jewish, Christian, and Islamic authorities had devastating consequences for the historical record. It's unclear whether the alphabet was derived from cuneiform or hieroglyphics, although presumably Phoenician businessmen were familiar with both. It is conjectured that traders transacting business in many languages needed a more flexible recording system and so developed the phonetic script. An early Christian source quoting a late Classical source attributes the invention of Phoenician letters to a god or demi-god named Tauthos, whom he equates with Thoth.[74] Apparently Tauthos was a musician-devotee of the goddess Ba'Alat of Byblos.

Figure 94: The Bennu Bird is depicted in Egyptian art from about 1500 BCE as a heron. Illustration: Jeff Dahl.

The Greeks credit the hero Cadmus with bringing the Phoenician alphabet to Greece. Cadmus, who was born in Byblos, was an inveterate monster-slayer who conquered the Greek city of Thebes. Like Tauthos, he was a musician.

Another history of Greek writing can be traced to the crane. The hero Theseus brought veneration of the crane to mainland Greece from Crete in the form of the Crane Dance. (Minoan Crete developed the precursor to early Greek writing we call Linear A.) The Crane Dance mimicked the weaving courtship dance of cranes. Dancing pairs would hold pieces of yarn taut to maintain the proper distance as they meandered around an altar dedicated to a goddess the Greeks equated with Aphrodite.

The pattern of crane flight is supposed to have inspired the god Hermes to invent several consonants of the alphabet. The crane is considered the bird of Hermes, which almost certainly means he stole the symbol from somewhere else. Perhaps from the god Hephaestus, who is also assigned the crane due to his origin as a local river god. The cult of Hermes originated around worship of a local phallus-shaped stone. The Greeks equated Hermes with Thoth, because Hermes, like Thoth, is a scribe, healer, and magician. Hermes is a prognosticator par excellence, having learned a divination system with pebbles from the Thriae. (Remember the Thriae from the first chapter.) There seems in Greece to be a link between the development of formal systems of divination and the development of writing. In this regard it is interesting that Hermes is associated with another form of divination, that of sheep knuckles. Sheep knuckle games and oracles were popular into Greco-Roman times, and their use can be traced in Anatolia far back in pre-history. In Mesopotamia sheep knuckle impressions were used as a type of signature, predating the later cylinder seals that were used to sign documents.

The Fates, those three ladies who assign destiny, are said to have donated seven of the early letters, although those same letters are attributed to the goddess Io. You may recall Io as the cow goddess who innocently provokes Hera's wrath and is in turn provoked by Hera's gadfly. The harassed Io journeys far and wide to escape her tormentor, and one of the places she sojourns is the shrine of Dodona. This is one of the most famous oracular sites in Greece, eventually taken over by Zeus but associated with several goddesses. According to Graves these included the Graeae (Gray Ones), divinatory goddesses who share one eye and one tooth between them.[75] According to one Classical source the Graeae have heads of women and bodies of swans.[76] (Graves believes the Graeae are in fact cranes rather than swans, which would better explain their being gray.) The letters donated by Io are supposed to be calendrical in origin, which again points to divination as an impetus for the invention of writing. There was no firm line in ancient times between predicting the passage of time and predicting the future.

Eleven consonants from the Greek alphabet are attributed to Palamedes, a mythical hero from the Greek Anatolian district of Caria. Palamedes is known primarily for his significant role in the Trojan War on behalf of the Greeks, but he is also said to have created a system of weights and measures. This recalls the development of writing as accounting in Mesopotamia. Like Hermes, Palamedes fashioned angular letters based on his observations of flying cranes.

The final contributor to Greek writing is Apollo, another famous thief. Apollo appropriated the crane as one of his symbols based on his patronage of music. The Common Crane, as you may recall, has a melodic bugling cry. Apollo donated two vowel notations to add to the five others corresponding to strings on his lyre. I had always assumed that musical notation was established after writing, perhaps because like most people I learned to read music after I learned to read books, but some type of musical shorthand may have been in use prior to the development of true writing.

On the Italian Peninsula the Latin alphabet is attributed to an oracular goddess named Carmenta, who may have originated in Anatolia. The Latin alphabet is based on the older Etruscan alphabet, which was derived from the Greek. Since the Etruscan language has only been partially translated, and so much Etruscan literature was destroyed by Christians, the mythological origin of Etruscan writing is hard to trace. Etruscans were famous for their divinatory skills, particularly in the realm of augury, so a transmission of early writing in Etruria through birds and divination is plausible.

The origin of Germanic writing is complex. Late Bronze Age carvings and cave markings from Northern Italy to Sweden show some rune-like symbols, their meaning undeciphered. Readable runic script dates to the second century and was presumably derived from the Etruscan alphabet, with which it shares some symbols. The god Odin is credited with discovering the runes, eighteen of them to start, when he hung upside down from the world tree, Yggdrasil, for nine days and nine nights. It is essential to understand that runes are not and were not simply signs that could be manipulated to form language, although they certainly were used for that purpose. Runes have always been magical powers in and of themselves. They disclose hidden truths, they protect buildings, they form spells. They are the force behind what words they speak.

Since Odin found the runes while tied to the tree but did not invent them, we have to look deeper for their source. The deities who nourish Yggdrasil are the Norns Urd, Verthandi, and Skuld. They are the Norns we are usually talking about when we say "The Norns." The Norns water Yggdrasil's roots from a pool of water at the base of the tree. They are responsible for giving each person their destiny and can reveal the past, present, and future. They are usually the powers invoked when using runes for

Figure 95: Birch bark writing from Russia, thirteenth century. This is a young boy's school lesson.

divination and they are the powers petitioned for changing life circumstances. In addition to tending the tree, the Norns tend a pair of swans who are said to be the parents of all swans in the world. The Norns themselves wear cloaks of swan feathers.

Another Germanic divinatory goddess is Frigga, who knows the future but seldom speaks of it. According to some sources it is she who bestows destiny on every child. Frigga's distaff is in heaven and the stars revolve around it, which means she controls the calendar. Frigga wears a crown of heron feathers. Her sacred tree is the birch, probably the White Birch or Silver Birch. The white, supple bark of the birch has been used throughout northern Europe as a medium for writing and drawing. Natives in North America used the Paper Birch for similar purposes. Since bark is a degradable material it would be impossible to know how far back symbolic drawing on birch goes; extant pieces from Russia date to the twelfth century. Not much was recorded in Christian times about Frigga, despite her status as nominal head of the pantheon along with Odin, because clerics worked especially hard to erase all traces of her. Those who in later centuries recorded the Norse legends were men who would not have been privy to feminine traditions anyway. While Frigga is not explicitly documented as a writing goddess, information about her points in that direction.

In Ireland the link between water birds and writing again becomes clear. Swans, herons, and especially cranes play a pivotal role in mythology, and all three are associated with women. Swans are young, beautiful, and good while cranes are cross, vengeful, and jealous. Going solely on the temperament of both birds I would have chosen the swan as the more irritable one, but feminine power is viewed in these myths through a patriarchal lens. The crane in Ireland—where she is currently extinct—is a subject that could fill a book, but our focus is on the crane and writing.

The crane is the container of magic, divination, and poetry

through the body of the Irish maid Aoife (pronounced EEF-uh). Aoife gets into a spat with a rival over a lover and in the process gets turned into a crane. When two dames go toe-to-toe over a man, as they frequently do in Irish romances, the earlier legend is usually about a healer-priestess challenging an Otherworld goddess over possession of a sick or injured patient. This is easy to discern in the story of Cliodhna (CLEAN-uh) and Caitileen Og, where the fairy Cliodhna takes a man named John Fitzjames to her Otherworld isle as her lover. The woman Caitileen Og travels to Cliodhna's realm to persuade the fairy to release Fitzjames and acknowledge Caitileen Og's prior and more valid claim. (She fails.) The story about Aoife being changed into a crane and banished to the sea by her rival is probably based on another healing tale. In this case the healer (Aoife's rival) is successful in saving the man's life, and the Otherworld crane goddess is deprived of her conquest.

When Aoife dies at the ripe old age of two hundred, the god Manannan mac Lir takes her skin and makes it his famous Crane Bag. This bag holds the alphabet, which is the source of all his other treasures, such as the ability to shapeshift into various animals. Manannan's powers and abilities are legion and include prophecy, speed, and invincibility in warfare. He even has an invisibility cloak. His Crane Bag empties at the low tide and fills again at the high, pointing both to Manannan's origin as a sea god and to the infinite renewability of magical symbols.

The development of writing, archeologists tell us, evolved through religious inscriptions (Eastern Europe) or temple accounting (Mesopotamia). Mythology adds divination, calendar-keeping, music, choreography, and spellcasting to the mix. Probably any complicated task involving memory developed some primitive notation and with it a symbolic basis for record keeping and magic. Writing emerged from a number of places for a number of reasons, but it was the crane and other water birds who instructed humans on the basics of how to write.

The Habits of Highly Successful Cranes

The following questions are seldom asked these days, but the answers are still pretty incredible. This crane lore can be attested across the globe.[77]

Figure 96: Crane as sentry holding a touchstone in a thirteenth century English bestiary.

Q: How do birds like cranes, who travel to such distant places, manage to escape boredom on these long journeys?

A: Little birds sit on the cranes' backs and sing to them. This is also how tiny birds can migrate long distances.

Q: How do cranes manage the fierce changeable winds of their long journeys?

A: They swallow large stones that they use as ballasts.

Q: How do they get rid of the stones when they reach their destination, or do the stones remain in their stomachs?

A: They cough the stones up when they land even for one night's rest. A sentry holds his or her ballast stone off the ground with one foot, so if the sentry falls asleep this stone will drop and wake them up. Also, these stones can be used to locate gold.

Q: To locate gold! Where can I locate one of these stones?

A: They have all been claimed in the lands of the north, but they may still be found in the far south.

Q: Why are the stones still found there?

A: Far to the south are races of very small people, whom the cranes harass and terrorize. The little people fight off the cranes with sticks and avoid crane haunts lest they end up on a holiday platter.

Q: How do you know so much about cranes?

A: All it takes is asking the right questions.

Figure 97: A curious story found across Eurasia and the Western Hemisphere describes a race of little people who are continually at war with predatory cranes. Attic vase, fifth century BCE. Photo: Marie-Lan Nguyen/Wikimedia Commons.

Letters of the Crane

The following is adapted from a translation by Eoin Macneill.[78] No information is given on what the Crane Bag carried after Manannan mac Lir relinquished possession, so I have used my imagination. Mary Eva is a character of my own tacked onto the end of the story.

There is a tendency for interpreters of myth to read both too much and too little into the narrative. Some have found an abstract, modern, almost Jungian symbolism in this story. Others have dismissed it as unintelligible. Graves[79]points out that the contents of Manannan's Crane Bag are simply the letters of the Ogham alphabet, an insight he attained through his recognition of the role of the crane in the development of writing. Understanding the contents of the Bag as letters is deflating for some, but it is important to remember that letters grew out of religious perspective and are themselves steeped in religious symbolism.

He held the body of Aoife the Crane-woman. Never mind how he came to possess her: she had lived a long life and now she was his. He put the things inside that were hers and claimed the body for himself.

But hers was a body he could not retain. She moved rapaciously through the hands of jealous men, each claiming title for himself. And even when the Aoife skin belonged to him again, he could not keep her intact. The body emptied and filled again like retreating and expanding waves upon the shore, like the drawing in and flowing out of breath.

Manannan mac Lir placed in the body he called Manannan's Bag his own shirt and his own knife, the shoulder-strap and hook of the wizard-smith Goibne, the King of Scotland's shears, the King of Lochlainn's helmet, the bones of Asil's swine, and a Great Whale's spine. Yet the Bag was emptied twice a day when the

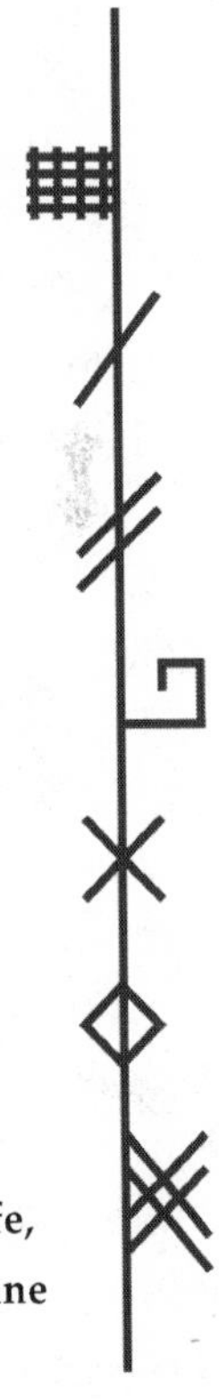

Figure 98: The letters of Manannan's Crane Bag: shirt, knife, shoulder-strap, hook, shears, helmet, swine. The vertical line holding the letters together is the whale's back.

tide ebbed.

Lugh of the Steady Arm kept the Bag a good while. He placed inside the measurement of the sun and a slingshot. Also a javelin, an anvil, his name, and three grains of barley. Finally he enclosed a promise kept.

When Lugh was slain by the Sons of Ogma, the Bag was filled with blood, along with a sword forged in the sun's own fire. Also a drop of honey containing the memory of perfect speech. A pinch of Midwinter snow fell into the mix, and a clod of Eriu's black earth. A cup of spring water lay inside, and on that floated the down from a wandering duck.

When Amairgin conquered the land, he placed inside a wind that would calm any sea. Also a piece of the Ark, and Noah's list of all the animals. A snake tooth was now inside this Bag, from the snake that was Aaron's Rod. The dangerous song of the Mermaid was confined within, along with wax from the Scythian hives. The Bag contained all the languages of Babel, jumbled together to form new speech.

The Bag passed to Manannan again, and this time he filled her with locks of his flowing hair and the flowing mane of his horse. Manannan enclosed a furious wind and three legs with no head or torso. He kept in his Bag the Cloak of Forgetfulness, a sweet apple, and a compass that always followed the scent of land.

The hero Conaire was awarded the Bag fairly, and he kept inside the speech of birds and their formations in flight. He also enclosed a stone from Tara and the hide of a bull, along with a dreaming potion. Finally he enclosed one vow that was kept and four vows broken.

Long after Conaire had been consumed in his treachery, Mary Eva scavenged the Bag from the embers. She placed inside a black kitten with a small white bib, a nautilus shell, her house keys, and a pencil that could fill a trillion pages without wearing at the nib. She included three nuggets of chocolate candy, a pinwheel that moves the stars at night, and a bolt of fabric from every pattern yet invented. She will keep the Crane Bag of Manannan until she has sewn bags for all her sisters.

And she has many.

Crane Review

Magical Qualities:
Magical Applications:
Other Associations:

Holding the Thread of Destiny

By now you have a lot of information to process when encountering an animal sign. This will make your interpretation richer and more complex. It's time to formalize a system for analyzing an animal sign.

The first thing you need to do when practicing animal divination is to examine your fears and beliefs about negative signs. Ideas about bad omens are tenacious, created in part by Christianization but also by the ease with which fear can be transmitted from mother to child. Evaluate the "bad omens" you've been given by your culture and be conscious of your reasons for perpetuating them.

When you run across an animal sign, notice the sign. This sounds obvious, but there are all kinds of ways of encountering an animal besides viewing the animal unexpectedly in the flesh. Animals cross your path through gifts, advertising, metaphors, illustrations, random conversations—the challenge is to become conscious of how full of animal imagery your life is. An animal that is a feature of your neighborhood and so would not ordinarily be considered a sign, like the lions in front of the library, might become a sign if it includes something out of the ordinary, such as a living crow is perched on the statue's head.

Another way to notice animal signs is to notice the signs of the signs, that is to be aware of tracks, browsed foliage, and scent markings. Train your ears to listen for animal sounds. Learn to distinguish bird songs and calls.

When you encounter an animal in a natural environment, pay close attention to the scene from beginning to end. How many sparrows? What were they eating? From what direction did the hawk fly, and did she fly past quickly or circle above you? In what kind of environment did your encounter occur? Along water? In a road? Was the name of the road Bobcat Way or something equally suggestive? Is there something significant about this particular day that ties in with your encounter?

If you can't identify the animal, perhaps the identification is not important. Where did the tracks lead? How many calls did the bird give? What color was he?

As you move from observation to interpretation, acknowledge your emotional state. Anxiety or preoccupation may cause you to interpret a sign in a way that might not be accurate. Aim for an attitude of openness as you listen to your intuition and assess the sign in the context of your current situation.

Your personal knowledge counts for quite a bit. This includes what you have observed and what you have learned from books or documentaries about the animal's behavior. Go next to what your culture teaches you about an animal sign. If that doesn't seem right, do some research. Learn what biologists and naturalists have to share about the animal of interest.

At this point you can move on to researching what cultures outside your own believe about the animal, if you feel inclined. By integrating this information into your own knowledge base rather than accepting it uncritically, you reaffirm your path and arrive at a more satisfying interpretation.

If you are still unsure about the meaning of a sign, that's okay. You can wait for understanding to mature. You can wait for another sign. You can pray for another sign. You can pray for yet another sign. You can discuss the encounter with another person. You can write down your reflections to see if that inspires insight. You can consult a dedicated divination system such as runes. You can decide not to interpret the experience, for now. Becoming comfortable with not understanding is part of the process.

You will probably decide eventually to interpret an animal encounter in a certain definite way, but try not to make it too definite. An important animal encounter can follow you for a long time, changing in significance as you mature. Place a significant animal interaction in the context of your other interactions with that animal, and notice any patterns. You might have to meet an animal several times to understand what she means to you.

Interpreting animal signs is an ongoing process of study. Animal divination evolved by observing animal behavior connected to things such as weather, food, predators, and astronomical events. By observing animals, reading about animals, and listening to the animal stories of other people, you will be able to interpret your next animal sign with greater ease. Try to be democratic in your studies, rather than deciding that only a few high-status animals have something to say.

Animal divination encompasses a spectrum of human experience from the material to the mystic. On one level it conforms to the hard natural sciences by yielding observable data that can be replicated by many people in controlled experiments. This data has confirmed that the behaviors of certain animals can predict earthquakes or weather changes. On another level, animal divination can reach into arcane mysteries that can only be processed through direct experience.

An encounter I had with the fox illustrates the ongoing process of interpreting signs. I was at a large family gathering back in West Virginia and went off by myself for a walk in the woods. I came across a Red Fox headed towards the party and immediately got the impression that the fox was part of the clan summit.

Shortly after this my brother moved into a house on a street that had the word "fox" in it, and I found a lovely apartment in my price range with an odd door knocker shaped like a fox. From these and other fox coincidences I realized the fox was a totem for that side of the family. The family had forgotten the fox, but the fox had not forgotten the family. I made sure from then on that I had a fox picture displayed in every place I lived. This picture was not a sign, of course, but a conscious act of magic invoking the fox as a protector.

Hanging a picture of a beaver in a workplace to promote focused activity, wearing a pair of armadillo earrings to become better armored, or incorporating dove feathers in a wand to create peaceful energy are other examples of conscious magic. Animal divination is a passive activity that involves processing external information, but it leads into active forms of magic.

Whether these "planted signs" will work in their intended manner is another thing altogether. That depends on the power of the priestess, the tractability of the obstacles, and the life lessons involved. But it's not cheating to use animal metaphors in this deliberate way—it's just a progression from divination to the fuzzy boundaries of spellcasting, something that is beyond the scope of this book.

I am on record as being critical of the "cookbook" approach to animal signs, where you see an animal, look up the "meaning" of that animal in a book, and interpret your encounter accordingly. At the same time, I don't much care for the "just go with your gut feeling" advice. What is missing from both approaches is a systematic framework combined with old-fashioned observation and study. I wish I could tell you what your animal encounter means, but I can't, not in the abstract, because there are too many variables involved. What I can tell you is that you will find the longer route more satisfying than the shortcut, and that it will lay a good foundation for further magical training.

Song of Cliodhna

Cliodhna is a Queen of the Otherworld, in Irish a bean sidh *(literally, fairy woman) or in phonetic English a banshee.*

There is in the Land of Promise a banshee who is the most beautiful of banshees. Her name is Cliodhna. She has light hair and a dark voice, like deep water or a poignant memory. You will follow her everywhere and wish never to be parted.

There is in the Land of Promise a pert wren who cannot be caged. Her name is Cliodhna. She has three bright-winged companions: one blue with a red head, one red with a green head, and one speckled with a gold head. They feast on magic apples and sing notes that will cure all woes.

There is in the Land of Promise a stone that holds the gift of speech. This stone is the stone of Cliodhna. Touch your lips to those of Cliodhna and talk persuasively forevermore.

There is in the Land of Promise a flock of tall waves, nine of them. The ninth wave belongs to Cliodhna. With it she pulls whatever she wants to her Isle in the west. She takes what she wants, goes where she wants, does what she wants, and—say what you want—she is lovely.

Questioning the Signs

1) Go back a few pages and fill out the Crane Review section for this chapter.
2) If you had a Crane Bag, what would you put in it?
3) Why would cranes be characterized as old and evil in Celtic legend?
4) You come across a heron stalking through a large pool of water known colloquially as "the old church pond." The heron does not react to your presence and even swallows a small fish while you watch. What is the heron doing in this pond? What interpretation could you place on this encounter?
5) Take an animal encounter of your own and write what happened, the logic of your interpretation, and any lingering

questions about the encounter.

6) At a lake in a park near your home, you find two lovely Mute Swans with seven cygnets swimming near the shore. While you're trying to frame your camera shot, one swan steps onto land and starts hissing and beating his wings. You take this as a sign, reasonably enough, to put down the camera and back off. What other significance, in terms of divination, might this interaction have?

7) Your ability to understand animal signs will improve if you make it a habit to continually learn more about animals. Watch an animal documentary this week, just for fun.

8) As you are driving to a swimming hole, you are forced to brake suddenly when you encounter a downed tree blocking the road. Obviously this is a sign you're not going swimming today. Your companions are mystified as you get out of the car to identify the tree and examine what caused its demise. What are the benefits to cultivating a curiosity about what is happening in your small corner of the world?

9) Have you heard another name for the stone that imparts beautiful speech? (Hint: It begins with a "B.")

Final Words

I'm trudging to my car on a day that happens to be my birthday. It's a day like any other in that I've put in a long hard long day of work. It's raining, which figures, and I'm too tired to care. I just want this day to be over. A raven calls, *raahh raahh raahh*. As I lift the handle to open the car door, the rain changes in an instant to large flakes of snow, beautiful wet snow melting on my face and my car and the pavement. This. This is the moment of power, the instant when a door opens and one thing changes into another. The raven calls again, but his call is superfluous. I get it. Things are crystallizing: this year will *not* be like the last.

Divination in the world at hand guides us into an appraisal of our lives, presenting us with answers to questions we feel but haven't yet formed. Greater powers discern at all times our struggles, our fears, our preoccupations, and our hopes. The world speaks to us, every day.

Appendix I: Deities and Heroes

Acca Larentia Ancestress and wolf goddess, possibly of Etruscan origin.

Alexander of Macedon Also called "Alexander the Great." General and empire-builder. Historical figure embellished in myth.

Allat Arabian earth fertility goddess. See Gharaniq.

Al-Uzza Arabian goddess of the morning star. See Gharaniq.

Amairgin Poet and conqueror of Ireland.

Ammut Hybrid crocodile-hippopotamus who devours the unjust.

An Mesopotamian (Sumerian) god of heaven.

Aoife Crane-woman of Ireland whose skin became the Crane Bag after she died.

Aphrodite Greek (Cyprian) goddess of love and sensuality.

Apollo Greek god of light. Overtook a number of cults along with the attributes of many deities.

Apophis Egyptian maleficent snake spirit.

Ares Thracian god assigned to warfare in the Greek pantheon.

Aristaeus Greek god of beekeeping and other cottage industries.

Artemis Greek virgin hunting goddess, mistress of animals.

Arthur British king and hero.

Asclepius Greek physician god, associated with snakes and dogs.

Asherah Hebrew mother goddess.

Athena Greek goddess of agriculture, inventions, weaving, and government.

Ba'Alat Phoenician mother goddess.

Baba Yaga Crone goddess of Russian, Ukraine and Balkan region.

Badb Catha Irish crow goddess.

Baldur Germanic god of the Underworld, son of Frigga.

Banshee See Bean Sith.

Baru Australian aboriginal crocodile ancestor.

Bast Egyptian lion and cat goddess.

Bean Sith Irish fairy woman: a Banshee.

Beiwe Saami sun goddess.

Belet-ili Mesopotamian (Semitic) mother goddess.

Bennu Bird Egyptian creator bird, identified by Greeks as the Phoenix.

Bes Egyptian dwarf god, protector of children.

Bran Welsh hero associated with crows.

Cadmus Phoenician conqueror who brought the alphabet to Greece.

Cailleach Bheur Scottish giant crone goddess and deer herder.

Caitileen Og Heroine who challenges the banshee Cliodhna.

Carmenta Roman oracular goddess.

Cat Sith Scottish fairy cat who snatches the souls of the newly dead.

Cathubodua Continental (Gaulish) raven goddess.

Cerberus Three (sometimes two) headed dog guarding the Greek underworld.

Ceryneian Hind Female reindeer belonging to Artemis.

Circe Witch-goddess of the Aegean who transforms sailors into animals.

Cliodhna Beautiful fairy woman who leaves her idyllic Land of Promise to claim earthly lovers.

Conaire Irish king and hero.

Coronis Greek crow goddess, sharing some attributes of Cronus. One of the Hydras.

Cronus Early Greek god of the harvest. Probably pre-Indo-European.

Cu Sith Giant Scottish fairy hound.

Cuchulainn Irish warrior associated with dogs who plays an important role in The Ulster Cycle.

Cybele Anatolian mother goddess.

Deborah Hebrew heroine whose name means "bee."

Demeter Greek earth and agricultural goddess. Also a goddess of bees.

Diana Roman goddess of hunting, the forest, and the moon.

Dionysus Greek god whose cult practiced ecstatic rites.

Dryades Greek female tree deities.

Dryope Greek goddess of the Black Poplar tree, whose name means "woodpecker."

Dumuzi Sumerian consort of the goddess Inanna.

Durga First female Hindu goddess who freed the world from demons.

Eikthyrnyr Horned deer who stands atop the sacred tree Laerad in the Germanic heaven Valhalla.

Eileithyia Cretan birth goddess.

El Hebrew god who rules with his wife Asherah.

Elen of the Hosts (Elen of the Ways) Historical queen reputed to have brought Christianity to Wales. Also believed to be the name of a deer goddess.

Enki Mesopotamian (Sumerian) water deity who has a helpful attitude toward humans.

Enkidu Mesopotamian wild man and friend of Gilgamesh.

Enlil Mesopotamian storm god. Identified with earth in "The Huluppu Tree."

Epona Continental Celtic horse goddess of motherhood and wealth.

Ereshkigal Mesopotamian underworld goddess of the dead.

Eris Greek goddess of discord.

Eurydice Greek heroine who is bitten by a snake while fleeing attempted rape by Aristaeus.

Fates Three sister-goddesses of prophesy. Also known as the Moirae.

Faunus Roman nature god, considered the equivalent of Pan.

Flidais Irish goddess who rides a chariot drawn by deer.

Freya Germanic goddess of wealth and love, associated with the boar.

Freyr Twin brother of Freya and also a boar deity.

Frigga Germanic goddess of the home. She wears a crown of heron feathers.

Ganga Hindu goddess of Ganges River who rides a crocodile.

Gharaniq Arabian triple crane goddess worshiped as Al-Uzza, Allat, and Menat.

Gilgamesh Early Mesopotamian king who became embedded in mythology.

Gobnait Patron saint of beekeepers.

Graeae Divinatory triple goddess.

Green Man Celtic vegetation deity. Depictions are common but name is unknown.

Gunlod Germanic giantess who held a cauldron of inspiration.

Hathor Egyptian love goddess. Usually depicted as a cow; occasionally a lion or sycamore tree.

Hecate Thracian/Greek goddess of the crossroads.

Hades Greek god of the underworld.

Hebe Greek goddess and cup-bearer who serves ambrosia to the gods.

Heidrun A nanny goat in Valhalla whose udders yield mead.

Heimdell Norse god of the far north, raised by nine mothers.

Hel Germanic goddess of the Underworld.

Hephaestus God of metal-working associated with a river in Greece.

Hera Greek marriage goddess, linked with the cow and the peacock.

Heracles (Hercules) Greek hero and shamanic deity.

Hermes Greek god of messages and thievery.

Hestia Greek goddess of the hearth.

Horus Egyptian god. Pictured as either a falcon or a human child.

Hours (Horae) Greek goddesses of the seasons.

Huginn One of the two ravens who flanks the Germanic god Odin.

Hyades Seven sisters who fostered the Greek god Dionysus as an infant. They form a constellation and bring rain.

Idunn Norse goddess of spring.

Ilia Priestess of goddess Vesta, mother of the founders of Rome.

Inanna Mesopotamian (Sumerian) goddess of fertility. Eventually syncretized with Ishtar.

Io Greek goddess turned into a cow by Hera.

Ishara Mesopotamian (Semitic) scorpion and snake goddess.

Ishtar Mesopotamian (Semitic) goddess of fertility.

Isis Egyptian healing goddess. Mother of Horus.

Iynx Nymph changed into a wryneck by Hera.

Jeremiah Hebrew prophet.

Jumala Finnish creator god who rules the ninth heaven.

Jupiter Zeus Pater. Roman equivalent of Zeus.

Khenty Khety Incarnate crocodile deity.

Laerad Sacred tree growing in Germanic heaven of Valhalla.

Lemminkainen Finnish hero who travels to the land of the dead and is rescued by his mother.

Lilith Mesopotamian spirit of desolate places.

Loki Germanic trickster god/goddess.

Lucifer Latin god of light and the morning star.

Lugh Celtic agricultural and sun god.

Maat Egyptian guardian of truth and justice.

Macha Irish horse goddess.

Mael Duin Irish hero and long distance voyager.

Manannan Mac Lir Sea god of Ireland and the Isle of Man.

Mars Roman woodpecker god and agricultural deity.

Matronae Roman name for Continental Celtic triple goddess.

Medb Irish queen whose name means "mead."

Medea Greek heroine and priestess of Hecate.

Melissae Beekeeping nymphs and priestesses of Demeter or Artemis.

Menat Arabian goddess of fate. See Gharaniq.

Moirae See Fates.

Morgan le Fey Fairy sister of King Arthur.

Morrigan Irish shapeshifting triple goddess.

Muninn One of the two ravens who flanks the Germanic God Odin.

Nehalennia Goddess of trade usually depicted with basket of apples and a little dog.

Neith Egyptian virgin creation goddess. Patron of weaving.

Neptune Roman ocean god syncretized with Poseidon.

Nina Mesopotamian (Semitic) fishing deity.

Ninhursaga Mesopotamian (Sumerian) mother goddess.

Njord Norse sea god who married Skadi.

Norns Goddesses of divination and fate.

Nun Egyptian god of the primordial waters.

Oceanus Greek ocean god.

Odin Germanic shamanic deity.

Oedipus Greek tragic hero and king.

Oisin Irish poet whose mother was a deer.

Osiris Egyptian vegetation god.

Pakhet Egyptian lion goddess.

Palamedes Greek hero who fought with the Greeks against Troy. Sometimes credited with transmission of the alphabet.

Pallas Refers to Athena or her priestess.

Pan Greek nature god most closely associated with the goat and the flute.

Penwenti Egyptian underworld crocodile deity. He swallows the sun nightly and it passes through his body.

Perchta German goddess of winter.

Persephone Greek goddess of the underworld.

Petsuchos Egyptian divine incarnate crocodile.

Picus Latin woodpecker god.

Pleiades Seven sisters pursued by the Greek hunter god Orion. Also a star system.

Poseidon Greek god of horses and the ocean.

Prometheus Greek hero who stole fire and gave it to humans.

Ra Egyptian sun god.

Ran Ocean mother goddess whose nine daughters are the waves.

Remus and **Romulus** Founders of Rome.

Rhea Greek mother goddess.

Rozhanitsa Slavic goddess of winter.

Sadb Irish woman changed into a doe by a rival.

Saturn Roman god of agriculture, especially sowing, later syncretized with the Greek Cronus.

Scorpion People Mesopotamian scorpion deities sometimes depicted with birdlike traits.

Sekhmet Egyptian lion goddess.

Selket Egyptian scorpion goddess.

Seth (Set) Egyptian god of the desert.

Shamash Mesopotamian/Akkadian sun god.

Sheshat Egyptian scribe goddess.

Shu Twin brother of Egyptian goddess Tefnut.

Skadi Norse giant goddess of the mountains who wears snowshoes.

Sleipnir Eight-legged horse who carries the Germanic god Odin.

Sobek Egyptian crocodile god.

Sothis Egyptian deity associated with the star Sirius.

Suonetar Finnish goddess associated with blood and veins. She sews Lemminkainen together when he is pulled out of the river of death.

Svadifari Germanic stallion giant.

Syrinx Greek nymph who was changed into a reed while fleeing the god Pan.

Tauthos Phoenician deity credited with invention of the alphabet.

Taygete One of the Pleiades sisters.

Tefnut Egyptian lion goddess.

Tethys Greek mother of rivers.

Theseus Greek hero who brought the Crane Dance to Greece.

Thiassi Eagle giant and father of Skadi.

Thor Germanic thunder god whose symbol is the hammer.

Thoth Egyptian god of writing, medicine and magic.

Thriae Three sister-bee-goddesses who taught the art of prophesy to Apollo.

Tiamat Mesopotamian dragon and star goddess.

Two Ladies Egyptian goddess Isis and her vulture-headed sister Nekhebet.

Ukko Finnish god of thunder.

Useret Egyptian woman who taught mothers how to heal scorpion stings.

Utnapishtim Mesopotamian hero of the flood.

Utu Mesopotamian (Sumerian) sun god.

Valkyries Norse death maidens who carry the souls of the slain on the battlefield to heaven of Valhalla.

Vassilissa Russian mythological heroine.

Venus Roman goddess of beauty, syncretized with Aphrodite.

Vesta Roman fire goddess.

Yggdrasil Germanic world tree.

Zeus Greek father sky and thunder god.

Appendix II: Ancient People and Places

Akkadian

A Semitic ethnic group of Mesopotamia. After the ruler Akkad.

Anatolia

Also known as Asia Minor, the western two-thirds of modern Turkey. Anatolia is only used to refer to the region and its cultures thousands of years ago, so you would go to Turkey to see Anatolian ruins, not vice versa.

Assyria, Assyrian

Empire in northern Mesopotamia.

Celts

Groups speaking the Celtic branch of Indo-European languages. Scholars differ on where the Celts originated and when they entered Europe, but Celtic settlements in historical times extended from Anatolia, through the Balkan region, into Central Europe, across Western Europe, and eventually to the British Isles. Though prone to war, Celts were not interested in amassing large territories or cohesive political structures and lived alongside other Indo-European and pre-Indo-European tribes. Celtic languages are spoken today only in Ireland, Britain, and northwestern France, but remnants of Celtic culture remain elsewhere. Especially when applied to the Britain and Ireland, the word "Celt" is loosely defined, including all people who settled there prior to the Roman conquest.

Cretans

See Minoans.

Egyptians

The people who farmed along the Nile River came from what is now western Egypt and Libya, relocating when increasing aridity made farming without irrigation impossible. They were dark-skinned people who were African by ethnicity as well as geography. A small number of hunter-gatherers were already living in the river valley. Nile farmers formed city-states along the river. Military conflict escalated into formation of the empire today known as Ancient Egypt.

Ephesus

Important ancient city on the coast of Anatolia.

Etruscans, Etruria

Referring to the people of a state on the northwest Italian Peninsula, which flourished from 800 BCE until the domination of Rome. Etruscans were skilled builders and engineers, and Etruscan influence extended throughout the Peninsula. Etruscans were in close contact with the ancient Greeks, whose Linear B script influenced Etruscan writing.

Gaul

A name for Celtic-dominated continental Europe during the Roman Empire. Included France and parts of Germany, Italy, Switzerland, Belgium, and the Netherlands.

Germanic

In this text referring to the culture and religion of Indo-European tribes who spoke a Germanic language and settled across Europe.

Greece

The first people living in what is now the country of Greece were from pre-Indo-European or Old European stock, and their art and religion reflect this. Subsequent Indo-European invasions influenced the culture substantially, as did contact with Mesopotamia and Egypt. Ancient Greeks were accomplished traders who established cities throughout the Aegean and eventually throughout the Mediterranean. Many Greek cites were not actually in Greece.

Hyperborea

The far north, a vaguely defined place mentioned by Greek historians.

Mesopotamia

Greek name meaning "between two rivers" for the region encompassing today's Iraq and parts of Syria, Turkey, and Iran. The culture revolved around the Tigris and Euphrates rivers. The dominant ethnic groups were Semitic and Sumerian, with Indo-Europeans arriving fairly late in Mesopotamian history.

Minoans

People who lived on the island of Crete before Indo-European invaders. Like the people who founded the first cities in Greece, Minoans probably originated in Anatolia. Indo-European conquerors invaded Crete centuries after their subjugation of peoples in the northern Mediterranean, allowing Minoan culture to flourish and grow to the point of developing a writing system called Linear A, which has not been deciphered. The geographic position of Crete allowed Minoans to incorporate ideas from Egypt and other cultures in the Eastern Mediterranean. It is assumed that most of the Minoan deities were identical to the ones in culturally similar pre-Indo-European Greece, but that has not been proven.

Mycenaeans

One of the Indo-European groups who conquered Greece and the Aegean Islands.

Norse

Referring to the pre-Christian religion of the Germanic peoples now located in Scandinavia.

Phoenicians

Traders who developed the alphabet as a way of doing business in a variety of languages. They were centered in a region of the eastern Mediterranean coinciding with parts of modern Syria, Lebanon, and Israel, but had trading colonies as far away as the Canary Islands in the Atlantic.

Romans

The Latins who founded the city of Rome and the Roman Empire. Other groups on the Italian Peninsula included Sabines, Umbrians, Etruscans, Greeks, Celts, and other Latin tribes.

Sumerians

Southern Mesopotamia is referred to as Sumer and the dominant ethnic group as Sumerian.

Thrace, Thracian

A region on the Balkan Peninsula encompassing northeastern Greece, southeastern Bulgaria, and northwestern Turkey.

Appendix III: Mathematical Terms

Equilateral triangle

A 3-sided shape with all three sides being the same length.

Factor

A whole number that can be divided out of another whole number. The factors of 8 are 1, 2, 4, and 8. ($8 \div 1 = 8$; $8 \div 4 = 2$; $8 \div 2 = 4$). The factors of 20 are 1, 2, 4, 5, 10, and 20.

Hexagon

A six-sided figure. A hexagram is a six-pointed star.

Integer

A whole number, not a fraction. Positive integers are the numbers 1, 2, 3, 4, etc.

Octagon

An eight-sided figure. An octahedron is a three-dimensional object with eight triangular faces.

Pentagon

A pentagon is a five-sided figure. A pentagram is a five-pointed star. A pentacle is a pentagram with a circle around it.

Perfect number

A number whose factors (aside from the number itself) add up to that same number. For example, the factors of 6 are 1, 2, and 3. Adding these factors gives $1 + 2 + 3 = 6$. The number 28 can be divided by itself and 1, 2, 4, 7, and 14, while adding these factors gives $1 + 2 + 4 + 7 + 14 = 28$.

Polygon

Any closed figure having three or more straight sides. For example, triangle, rectangle, pentagon.

Prime number

A whole positive number that can only be divided by itself and one. The four smallest prime numbers are 2, 3, 5, and 7. (Going by this definition, the number 1 seems like it should be a prime, but it's not.)

Right triangle

One corner is perpendicular (right angled or 90 degrees).

Square number

A number times itself. The square of 2 is 2 x 2 = 4; the square of 3 is 3 x 3 = 9. The square root is the opposite. The square root of 4 is 2; the square root of 9 is 3.

Notes

1   Andrew George, trans., *The Epic of Gilgamesh*, rev. ed. (London: Penguin Books, 2003), 70.

2   Philippe Germond and Jacques Livet, *An Egyptian Bestiary: Animals in Life and Religion in the Land of the Pharoahs*, Barbara Mellor, trans. (London: Thames and Hudson, 2001), 159.

3   Dennis C. Turner and Patrick Bateson, "Why the cat?" in *The Domestic Cat: The Biology of its Behavior*, 2nd ed., edited by Dennis C. Turner and Patrick Bateson (Cambridge: Cambridge University Press, 2000), 4. Leyhausen's now out-of-print treatise became available in English in 1979.

4   David W. MacDonald, Nobuyuki Yamaguchi and Gillian Kerby, "Group-living in the domestic cat: Its sociology and epidemiology," *The Domestic Cat: The Biology of its Behavior*, 96.

5   James A. Serpell, "Domestication and the history of the cat," *The Domestic Cat: The Biology of its Behavior*, 181.

6   Charles G. Leland, *Aradia or the Gospel of the Witches* (Custer, WA: Phoenix Publishing, 1990), 18–20.

7   William Baldwin and John Richard Stephens, "Beware the Cat," in *Mysterious Cat Stories*, edited by John Richard Stephens and Kim Smith (New York: Carroll and Graf, 1993).

8   "How Pussy Willows Got Their Name," Moggies Home of the Online Cat Guide, http://www.moggies.co.uk/html/legends.html#willows. Accessed September 7, 2014.

9   Lewis Carroll, *Alice's Adventures in Wonderland and Through the Looking Glass* (New York: MacMillan, 1926), 89.

10 Robert Graves, *The Greek Myths* (London: Penguin Books, 1992).

11 Jimmy Dunn, "The Nile Crocodile," Tour Egypt. http://www.touregypt.net/featurestories/crocodiles.htm. Accessed July 18, 2016.

12 John Steele, editor, *Mediaeval Lore from Bartholomew Anglicus*, John Trevisa, trans. http://www.gutenberg.org/ebooks/6493. Accessed through Project Gutenberg, March 6, 2015.

13 Hermes Trismegistus, "The Emerald Tablet of Hermes," Isaac Newton, trans. Sacred-Texts. http://www.sacred-texts.com/alc/emerald.htm. Accessed April 26, 2015.

14 "The Curse of the Mummy" in Tour Egypt. http://www.touregypt.net/myths/curseof.htm#ixzz3TYvRSlNV. Accessed March 22, 2015.

15 Snorri Sturluson, *The Prose Edda*, Arthur Gilchrist Brodeur, trans. (New York: The American Scandinavian Foundation, 1916), 22.

16 Lewis Spence, *Legends and Romances of Brittany* (Mineola, NY: Dover, 1997), 88–95.

17 Sylvia Plath, "Metaphors," *The Collected Poems*, edited by Ted Hughes (Cutchogue, NY: Buccaneer Books, 1981), 116.

18 Gough, Andrew. "The Bee" (Parts I, II, III) Andrew Gough. June 2008. http://andrewgough.co.uk/articles_bee1/. Accessed October 9, 2015.

19 Luis Mendez de Torres, *Tractado breve de la cultivacion y cura de las colmenas*, cited in Ethel Eva Crane, *The World History of Beekeeping and Honey Making* (New York: Routledge, 1999), 215.

20 Charles Butler, *The Feminine Monarchie*, Google Books facsimile, https://books.google.com/books/reader?id=f5tbAAAAMAAJ&printsec=frontcover&output=reader&source=gbs_atb_hover&pg=GBS.PT17. Accessed August 29, 2015.

21 Thomas D. Seeley, *Honeybee Democracy* (Princeton, NJ: Princeton University Press, 2010), 5.

22 ibid., 218.

23 Monica Sjoo and Barbara Mor, *The Great Cosmic Mother: Rediscovering the Religion of the Earth*, (New York: HaperCollins, 1991).

24 Tammy Horn, *Beeconomy: What Women and Bees Can Teach Us*

about Local Trade and the Global Market (Lexington, KY: The University Press of Kentucky, 2012), 188.

25 Hesiod, Theogeny, in *The Homeric Hymns and Homerica*, Hugh G. Evelyn-White, trans. (Cambridge, MA: Harvard University Press, 1914), lines 595-600.

26 "Bee Keeping," Ancient Egypt. http://www.reshafim. org.il/ad/egypt/timelines/topics/beekeeping.htm. Accessed October 9, 2015.

27 Deuteronomy 1:44. New English Bible.

28 Judges 4-5.

29 Diane Wolkstein and Samuel Noah Kramer, *Inanna Queen of Heaven and Earth: Her Stories and Hymns from Sumer* (New York: Harper and Row, 1983), 38.

30 Song of Songs 5:1.

31 Proverbs 24:13.

32 Proverbs 25:16.

33 Virgil, *Georgics*, H.R. Fairclough, trans., 1916, IV 219. http://www.theoi.com/Text/VirgilGeorgics2.html. Accessed October 17, 2016.

34 *Celtic Mythology* (New Lanark, Scotland: Geddes and Grosset, 1999).

35 Katrina Raphaell, *Crystal Enlightenment: The Transforming Properties of Crystals and Healing Stones* (New York: Aurora Press, 1985), 106.

36 John M. Marzluff and Tony Angell, *In the Company of Crows and Ravens* (New Haven, CT: Yale University Press, 2005), 80.

37 Bernd Heinrich, *Mind of the Raven: Investigations with Wolf-Birds* (New York: HarperCollins, 1999), 196.

38 Snorri Sturlson, *The Prose Edda of Snorri Sturlson: Tales from Norse Mythology*, Jean I. Young, trans. (Berkeley, CA: University of California Press, 2001), 64.

39 *The Elder Eddas of Seamund Sigfusson*, Benjamin Thorpe, trans. (London: Norroena Society), 143.

40 Marija Gimbutas, *The Living Goddesses* (Berkeley, CA:

University of California Press, 1999), 191.

41 Snorri Sturlson, *The Prose Edda of Snorri Sturlson*, 64.

42 Graves, *The Greek Myths*, 56.

43 Gerald Friedlander. *Jewish Fairy Tales* (Mineola, New York: Dover, 2001), 52–61.

44 Thomas R. Quackenbush, *Relearning to See: Improve Your Eyesight Naturally* (Berkeley, CA: North Atlantic Books, 1999), 108–114.

45 Josef Baudis, *The Key of Gold: 23 Czech Folk Tales* (Iowa City, IA: Penfield Press, 2001), 176.

46 Charles Godfrey Leland, *Algonquin Legends of New England* (Boston: Houghton Mifflin, 1884), Kindle edition.

47 Florence Stratton and Bessie M. Reid, *When the Storm God Rides: Tejas and Other Indian Legends* (UK: Global Grey, 2015), Kindle edition.

48 Graves, *The Greek Myths*, 593.

49 *Century Dictionary Online*, s.v. "springwort." http://triggs. djvu.org/century-dictionary.com/djvu2jpgframes.php? volno=07&page=550&query=springwort. Accessed May 7, 2016.

50 "Day 101: Ozark Animal 'Tokens,'" Mountain Man Healing website. http://mountainmanhealing.tumblr.com/post/12509 8818723/day-101-ozark-animal-tokens. Accessed May 7, 2016. Also see Randolph Vance, *Ozark Magic and Folklore* (New York: Dover Publications, 1964), 248–249.

51 L.J. Gibson, "Woodpecker pecking: how woodpeckers avoid brain injury," *Journal of Zoology* 270 (2006): 462.

52 C.W. Wu, Z.D. Zhu, and W Zhang, "How woodpecker avoids brain injury?" *Journal of Physics: Conference Series* 628 (2015): 1.

53 Charles Godfrey Leland, *Etruscan Roman Remains in Popular Tradition* (London: T. Fisher Unwin, 1892), Kindle edition.

54 North Carolina Wildlife Resources Commission, "Gray Fox," http://www.ncwildlife.org/Portals/0/Learning/docume

nts/Profiles/Gray_Fox.pdf. Accessed May 24, 2016.

55 Ylvis, "The Fox" (single), Warner Music, 2013, MP3.

56 Claude Debussy, "Syrinx," in *Katherine Bryan Plays Flute Concertos by Christopher Rouse and Jacques Ibert*, Hyperion 2013, MP3.

57 Emily L. Doolittle and others, "Overtone-based pitch selection in hermit thrush song: Unexpected convergence with scale construction in human music," *Proceedings of the National Academy of Sciences of the United States* 111, no. 46 (2014): 16616.

58 Patrick W. Gainer, *Witches, Ghosts and Signs: Folklore of the Southern Appalachians* (Morgantown, WV: Seneca Books, 1975), 159.

59 Callimachus, "Hymn 3 To Artemis," Yvonne Rathbone, trans.,   4. http://home.earthlink.net/~yvonr/pagan/classics/callhymn.p df. Accessed June 30, 2016.

60 Alexander Marshack, *The Roots of Civilization: The Cognitive Beginnings of Man's First Art, Symbol and Notation* (New York: McGraw-Hill, 1972).

61 Caroline Wise, "Elen of the Ways," andrewcollins.com, http://www.andrewcollins.com/page/articles/elen_1.htm. Accessed July 9, 2016.

62 *The Mabinogion*, Gwen Jones and Thomas Jones, trans. (New York: Alfred A. Knopf, 2001), 77.

63 John Ayto, *Dictionary of Word Origins* (New York: Arcade), 197.

64 Adrian Morgan, *Toads and Toadstools,: The Natural History, Folklore, and Cultural Oddities of a Strange Association* (Berkeley, CA: Celestial Arts, 1995), 103.

65 Andrew Letcher, "Taking the Piss: Reindeer and Fly Agaric," September 17, 2011. http://andy-letcher.blogspot.com.au /2011/09/taking-piss-reindeers-and-fly-agaric.html. Accessed July 25, 2016.

66 Monika Kropej, *Supernatural Slovenian Beings from Myth and Folktales* (Ljublijana: Zalovba, 2012), 65.

67 Willis Alan Ramsey, "Muskrat Love," Captain and Tennille, *Song of Joy*, A&M Records, 1976.

68 Graves, *The Greek Myths*, 50–55.

69 ibid., 177.

70 Diane Wolkstein and Samuel Noah Kramer, *Inanna Queen of Heaven and Earth.*

71 Benjamin R. Foster, trans., *The Epic of Gilgamesh* (New York: W.W. Norton, 2001), 130.

72 Marija Gimbutas, *The Language of the Goddess* (San Francisco: Harper and Row, 1989) 19–49.

73 R.T. Rundle Clark, *Myth and Symbol in Ancient Egypt* (London: Thames and Hudson, 1959), 245–49.

74 Eusebius of Caesarea, Praeparatio Evangelica, E.H. Gifford, trans., Chapter 9. Transcribed by Robert Pearse at https://drive.google.com/file/d/0Bw9DD8Hgvs_HNDY0OTE xM2UtZWU3Yy00MTg3LTg2NjYtNzZiNWMyMzhhNTIx/vi ew?hl=en_GB. Accessed September 4, 2016.

75 Graves, *The Greek Myths*, 142.

76 Plutarch, *Roman Questions* (59).

77 Peter Tate, *Flights of Fancy: Birds in Myth, Legend, and Superstition* (New York: Delacorte Press, 2007), 11–18.

78 Eoin Macneill, trans., *The Book of the Lays of Fionn* (London: Irish Texts Society, 1908), 118–120.

79 Robert Graves, *The Crane Bag and Other Disputed Subjects* (London: Casell and Co., 1969), 1–8.

Bibliography

Afanasev, Alexsandre. *Russian Fairy Tales*. Translated by Norbert Guterman. New York: Pantheon Books, 1976.

Bahn, Paul G. and Jean Vertut. *Journey Through the Ice Age*. London: Seven Dials, 1999.

Backman, Louise and Ake Hultkrantz, editors. *Saami Pre-Christian Religion: Studies on the Oldest Traces of Religion Among the Saamis*. Stockholm: Royal Gustavus Adolphus Academy, 1985.

Billson, Charles J. "Some Mythical Tales of the Lapps," in *A Quarterly Review of Myth, Tradition, Institution, and Custom: The Transactions of the Folk-lore Society*. London: Sedgwick and Jackson, 1918.

Black, Jeremy and Anthony Green. *Gods, Demons and Symbols of Ancient Mesopotamia: An Illustrated Dictionary*. Austin, TX: University of Texas Press, 2003.

Cooper, J.C. *An Illustrated Encyclopaedia of Traditional Symbols*. London: Thames and Hudson, 1978.

Crowder, Les and Heather Harrell. *Top-Bar Beekeeping: Organic Practices for Honeybee Health*. White River Junction, VT: Chelsea Green, 2012.

Dale, Rodney. *Louis Wain: The Man who Drew Cats*. London: Michael O'Mara, 1991.

Germond, Philippe and Jacques Livet. *An Egyptian Bestiary: Animals in Life and Religion in the Land of the Pharoahs*. Translated by Barbara Mellor. London: Thames and Hudson, 2001.

Gimbutas, Marija. *The Goddesses and Gods of Old Europe: 6500-3500 BC Myths and Cult Images*. Berkeley, CA: University of California Press, 1982.

Gimbutas, Marija. *The Language of the Goddess*. San Francisco: Harper and Row, 1989.

Gimbutas, Marija. *The Living Goddesses*. Miriam Robbins Dexter, editor. Berkeley, CA: University of California Press, 1999.

Green, Miranda. *Animals in Celtic Life and Myth*. London: Routledge, 1992.

Guerber, H.A. *The Norsemen: Myths and Legends*. London: Gresham, 1994.

Goelet, Ogden, Jr. et al, translators. *The Egyptian Book of the Dead: The Book of Going Forth by Day*. 3rd rev. ed. San Francisco: Chronicle Books, 2015.

Graves, Robert. *The Greek Myths*. London: Penguin, 1960.

Graves, Robert. *The White Goddess*. New York: Farrar, Straus and Giroux, 1948.

Hall, Manly P. *The Secret Teachings of All Ages*. San Francisco: H.S. Crocker, 1928.

Hornung, Erik. *The Egyptian Books of the Afterlife*. Translated by David Lorton. Ithaca, NY: Cornell University Press, 1999.

Houlihan, Patrick F. *The Animal World of the Pharaohs*. London: Thames and Hudson, 1996.

Johns, Andreas. *Baba Yaga: The Ambiguous Mother and Witch of the Russian Folktale*. New York: Peter Lang, 2010.

Johnson, Buffie. *Lady of the Beasts: The Goddess and Her Sacred Animals*. Rochester, VT: Inner Traditions, 1994.

Kline, Morris. *Mathematical Thought from Ancient to Modern Times*, vol. 1. New York: Oxford University Press, 1972.

Leonard, Linda Schierse. *Following the Reindeer Woman: Path of Peace and Harmony*. New Orleans: Spring Journal Books, 2004.

Lesko, Barbara S. *The Great Goddesses of Egypt*. Norman, OK: University of Oklahoma Press, 1999.

Lonnrot, Elias. *The Kalevala: Epic of the Finish People*, 2nd edition. Translated by Eino Friberg. Helsinki: Otava Publishing, 1988.

Marzluff, John M. and Tony Angell. *Gifts of the Crow: How Perception, Emotion, and Thought Allow Smart Birds to Behave Like Humans*. New York: Atria, 2012.

Matthews, John and Caitlin. *The Encyclopaedia of Celtic Myth and*

Legend: A Definitive Sourcebook of Magic, Vision, and Lore. Guilford, CT: Lyons Press, 2004.

Monaghan, Patricia. *The Book of Goddesses and Heroines.* St. Paul, MN: Llewellyn, 1990.

Monaghan, Patricia. *The Encyclopedia of Celtic Mythology and Folklore.* New York: Checkmark Books, 2008.

Nicomachus. *Introduction to Arithmetic.* Translated by Martin Luther D'ooge. New York: MacMillan, 1926.

Oliver, Merrill, editor. *Goddess and their Offspring: 19th and 20th Century Eastern European Embroideries.* Binghamton, NY: Roberson Center for the Arts and Sciences, 1986.

O'Sullivan, Patrick V. *Irish Superstitions of Animals and Birds.* Dublin: Merceir Press, 1991.

Pinch, Geraldine. *Egyptian Mythology: A Guide to the Gods, Goddesses, and Traditions of Ancient Egypt.* Oxford, UK: Oxford University Press, 2004.

Quakenbush, Thomas R. *Relearning to See: Improve Your Eyesight — Naturally!* Berkeley, CA: North Atlantic Books, 1999.

Ransome, Hilda M. *The Sacred Bee in Ancient Times and Folklore.* Mineola, NY: Dover Books, 2004.

Schwaller de Lubicz, R.A. *A Study of Numbers: A Guide to the Constant Creation of the Universe.* Rochester, VT: Inner Traditions, 1986.

Silverman, David P., editor. *Ancient Egypt.* New York: Oxford University Press, 1997.

Sinclair, Sandra. *How Animals See: Other Visions of Our World.* New York: Facts on File, 1985.

Skutch, Alexander F. *Life of the Woodpecker.* Santa Monica, CA: Ibis Publishing, 1985.

Strogatz, Steven. *The Joy of X: A Guided Tour of Math, from One to Infinity.* Boston: Mariner Books, 2013.

Taylor, Bernie. *Biological Time.* Newburgh, OR: The Ea Press, 2004.

Van Buren, E. Douglas. "The Scorpion in Mesopotamian Art and Religion." *Archiv für Orientforschung,* (1937-1939), 1-28.

Filmography

Built to Peck: How Woodpeckers Avoid Brain Injury. Lorna Gibson, Narrator. MITx Media, 2015, USA (YouTube).

Cave of Forgotten Dreams: Humanity's Lost Masterpiece. Werner Herzog, Director. 2011, USA.

Einstein Revealed. Peter Jones, Director. 1996, USA.

Elsa's Legacy: The Born Free Story. Sacha Mirzoeff, Director. 2011, USA.

Woman Shaman: The Ancients. Max Dashu, Director. 2013, USA.

Woody Woodpecker: Termites from Mars. Don Patterson, Director. 1952, USA.

Index

From the Author

Thank you for purchasing *Divining with Animal Guides*. I hope you have enjoyed this journey as much as I have. I appreciate your reviews and feedback on your favorite online sites. You can stay in touch with me by visiting my website, www.hearthmoon-rising.com.

Blessings, Hearth

MOON

BOOKS

Moon Books

PAGANISM & SHAMANISM

What is Paganism? A religion, a spirituality, an alternative belief system, nature worship? You can find support for all these definitions (and many more) in dictionaries, encyclopaedias, and text books of religion, but subscribe to any one and the truth will evade you. Above all Paganism is a creative pursuit, an encounter with reality, an exploration of meaning and an expression of the soul. Druids, Heathens, Wiccans and others, all contribute their insights and literary riches to the Pagan tradition. Moon Books invites you to begin or to deepen your own encounter, right here, right now. If you have enjoyed this book, why not tell other readers by posting a review on your preferred book site. Recent bestsellers from Moon Books are:

Journey to the Dark Goddess
How to Return to Your Soul
Jane Meredith
Discover the powerful secrets of the Dark Goddess and transform your depression, grief and pain into healing and integration.
Paperback: 978-1-84694-677-6 ebook: 978-1-78099-223-5

Shamanic Reiki
Expanded Ways of Working with Universal Life Force Energy
Llyn Roberts, Robert Levy
Shamanism and Reiki are each powerful ways of healing;
together, their power multiplies. *Shamanic Reiki* introduces
techniques to help healers and Reiki practitioners tap ancient
healing wisdom.
Paperback: 978-1-84694-037-8 ebook: 978-1-84694-650-9

Pagan Portals – The Awen Alone
Walking the Path of the Solitary Druid
Joanna van der Hoeven
An introductory guide for the solitary Druid, *The Awen Alone*
will accompany you as you explore, and seek out your own
place within the natural world.
Paperback: 978-1-78279-547-6 ebook: 978-1-78279-546-9

A Kitchen Witch's World of Magical Herbs & Plants
Rachel Patterson
A journey into the magical world of herbs and plants, filled with
magical uses, folklore, history and practical magic. By popular
writer, blogger and kitchen witch, Tansy Firedragon.
Paperback: 978-1-78279-621-3 ebook: 978-1-78279-620-6

Medicine for the Soul
The Complete Book of Shamanic Healing
Ross Heaven
All you will ever need to know about shamanic healing and
how to become your own shaman...
Paperback: 978-1-78099-419-2 ebook: 978-1-78099-420-8

Shapeshifting into Higher Consciousness
Heal and Transform Yourself and Our World with Ancient
Shamanic and Modern Methods
Llyn Roberts
Ancient and modern methods that you can use every day
to transform yourself and make a positive difference in the
world.
Paperback: 978-1-84694-843-5 ebook: 978-1-84694-844-2

Readers of ebooks can buy or view any of these
bestsellers by clicking on the live link in the title. Most
titles are published in paperback and as an ebook.
Paperbacks are available in traditional bookshops. Both
print and ebook formats are available online.

Find more titles and sign up to our readers' newsletter at
http://www.johnhuntpublishing.com/paganism
Follow us on Facebook at
https://www.facebook.com/MoonBooks
and Twitter at https://twitter.com/MoonBooksJHP